Mechanism and Mysticism

Mechanism and Mysticism

The Influence of Science on the Thought and Work of Theodore Dreiser

Louis J. Zanine

University of Pennsylvania Press

Philadelphia

Copyright © 1993 by the University of Pennsylvania
Printed in the United States of America

Library of Congress Cataloging-in-Publication Data
Zanine, Louis J.
   Mechanism and mysticism : the influence of science on the thought and work of
Theodore Dreiser / Louis J. Zanine.
      p.   cm.
   Includes bibliographical references and index.
   ISBN 0-8122-3171-6
   1. Dreiser, Theodore, 1871–1945—Knowledge—Science.   2. Literature and science—
United States—History—20th century.   3. Science in literature.   I. Title.
PS3507.R55Z88   1993
813'.52—dc20   93-16138
                                                                     CIP

To Neil Leonard

Contents

Acknowledgments

Over the long period in which this book has evolved, many people have offered their generosity and service. I am thankful for the assistance of the staffs of the Special Manuscripts Collection of the New York Public Library, the Butler Library Special Collections of Columbia University, the Marine Biological Laboratory Archives at Woods Hole, Massachusetts, the Library of Congress, the Harry Ransom Humanities Research Center of the University of Texas, and the Bayerische Staatsbibliothek in Munich, Germany. Special thanks must be given to the staff of the Theodore Dreiser Papers for their assistance during my examination of the materials in that collection. Everette Swinney of Southwest Texas State University and Sylvia Schwartz and Liz Henderson of Westbrook College were patient and generous in aiding me with their expertise in word processing technology.

Excerpts from *An American Tragedy*, *The Financier*, *The Titan*, *The "Genius"*, *The Stoic*, *Free and Other Stories*, *A Gallery of Women*, and *Twelve Men* are reprinted by permission of The Dreiser Trust. Permission to quote from *Notes on Life* and from Dreiser's unpublished essays and letters was granted by the Theodore Dreiser Papers, Special Collections, Van Pelt Library, University of Pennsylvania. Permission to use the photographs in this book was generously granted by the Theodore Dreiser Papers, the Marine Biological Laboratory Archives, and Professor Garland E. Allen.

Among those who have read a portion or the whole of my work at some stage of its development are Bethany Andreasen, Brigitte Fleischmann, Bruce Kuklick, Toby Lazarowitz, Maryanne Moffa, Murray Murphey, Berndt Ostendorf, Charles Rosenberg, William VanBuskirk, Petra Wiesmayer, and Leila Zenderland. I am grateful for their attention and suggestions. Finally, I would like to thank Neil Leonard, who first introduced me to the excitement and challenge of Dreiser's work, and to whom this book is dedicated.

Introduction

Theodore Dreiser was born in 1871, the year that Darwin published *The Descent of Man*. He died in 1945 at the dawn of the nuclear age. In the nearly three-quarters of a century that Dreiser's life spanned, the increasing precision and detail of scientific understanding and explanation revolutionized the world and our conception of it. The development of the electric light bulb, the gasoline engine, and the atomic bomb were only the tangible results of that revolution—the products of a technology that was spawned by the growing understanding of the physical world. There was, however, an additional, more intangible revolution of the mind taking place. As science gained authority with the general public as a source of enlightenment about the nature of humanity and the order of the universe, scientific explanation gradually encroached on metaphysical territory previously occupied in Western thought by religious ontology and cosmology. This assault placed the Biblical accounts of the creation of the universe, the origin of our planet, and the appearance of life on earth on the defensive. Scientific explanation redefined *Homo sapiens* as an animal evolved from lower species over a period of billions of years, rather than a special creation made in God's image. Many scientists, particularly in the Victorian era, delved into philosophy, reinterpreting traditional metaphysical and theological questions in the light of advancing scientific understanding, offering speculations about the purpose of human existence, the origin of human ethics, and even the nature of God. One result of this invasion of natural explanation into the realm of supernatural or theological explanation was to create a generation of thinkers and writers in America who struggled to reconcile the newly developing authority of science and the more traditional influence of religion that most had absorbed in their youth. Theodore Dreiser was one such writer.

This study examines Dreiser's interest in modern scientific research and the impact of scientific ideas on his thought and work. A full examination of Dreiser's lifelong fascination with science, particularly his most intensive period of study in the 1930s, has been lacking. While many scholars have noted the influence that the writings of Herbert Spencer and Jacques Loeb had on his novels, they usually refer only to the effect these men had on the development of Dreiser as a naturalist writer. The finest examination of his scientific interests has been Ellen Moers's *Two Dreisers*; her study, however, is confined mainly to the influences, both scientific and nonscientific, that went into the creation of *Sister Carrie* and *An American Tragedy*. Ronald E. Martin has devoted a chapter to Dreiser in his *American Literature and the Universe of Force*, in which he interprets the impact on Dreiser's novels of nineteenth-century theories of force or energy, particularly as they were expressed in Spencer's philosophy.[1] A fuller understanding of Dreiser's scientific interests as they related to his philosophical and spiritual concerns is the goal of my study.

Throughout this narrative, I have attempted to show that Dreiser's interest in science was primarily a religious quest to find emotionally and spiritually satisfying answers to questions about human purpose and destiny that had been traditionally addressed by orthodox religion. During Dreiser's lifetime, few evaluations of his work recognized him as a figure wrestling with essentially spiritual questions. Even today, Dreiser is frequently portrayed in college survey courses as the archetypical exponent of a bleak and hopeless materialism that characterized American naturalist thought in the late nineteenth and early twentieth centuries. As Alan Wycherley has observed in an essay on Dreiser's work, early scholars most frequently characterized Dreiser as a pessimistic naturalist based on their reading of his first six novels, his most famous and readable work.[2] Much of Dreiser's writing, however, appeared posthumously, including his final two novels, many of his difficult and, at times, poorly written essays, and his final attempted book of philosophy. The metaphysical and even spiritual subject matter of these works has caused more recent scholars to reinterpret Dreiser's earlier novels as well as to reevaluate Dreiser's place in American literature as a writer much too complex to be categorized simply as a naturalist.

Another reason that Dreiser's spiritual side was rather slow to be recognized was the emphasis placed on his hatred of traditional Christian dogma and morality, especially that of the Roman Catholic church. Dreiser's animosity toward orthodox Christianity, however, has not blinded more recent students of his work to the fact that he spent a great deal of his life trying to answer essentially religious questions about what he called "the mystery and wonder and terror of life." He was driven to know the "unknowable" about the ultimate purpose of existence in a seemingly hostile and determined universe. For many years, Dreiser's principal source of enlightenment on these questions was his personal study of scientific research.

Three studies have been helpful in identifying the spiritual motivations that underlie Dreiser's writing. The first is Robert Elias' *Theodore Dreiser: Apostle of Nature*, the best intellectual biography of Dreiser; this work was the first to unveil the brooding, questioning side of Dreiser's personality that so many critics had overlooked during his lifetime. In addition, the Dreiser essay in Charles Child Walcutt's *American Literary Naturalism: A Divided Stream* has shed light on Dreiser's thought by suggesting that his work and thought fit just as well within the transcendentalist tradition of American writers as within the naturalist school. And Marguerite Tjader's *Theodore Dreiser: A New Dimension*, an extremely valuable personal recollection of Dreiser's later years, uncovers the spiritual seeking and mystical beliefs that only his closest friends were aware of during his lifetime.[3] Each of these studies has helped to redefine Dreiser as much more than a Zola-esque materialist. They have recognized that his quest for knowledge about life and the universe was based on an intense desire to achieve some sort of spiritual peace.

*   *   *

Dreiser grew up in a household dominated by the fanatical Catholic faith of his father and influenced by the superstitious beliefs of his mother. Although as a young man Dreiser rejected much of the Catholic dogma that he had been taught as a child, his world view continued to be shaped by his belief in "Christian brotherhood" and in the individual's free will to choose between good and evil and to determine one's own fate. When he moved from rural Indiana to the sprawling chaos of urban America in the early 1890s to become a reporter, this Christian world view was challenged by his discovery of massive poverty, his perception of the lack of Christian compassion that characterized American society, and his growing suspicion of the individual's inability to determine his or her own destiny. In 1894 Dreiser underwent a significant intellectual and spiritual revolution, pre-cipitated by his discovery of evolutionary theory in the writings of Charles Darwin, Thomas Henry Huxley and Herbert Spencer. The influence of evolutionary thought, especially in the quasi-scientific speculations of Spencer, shifted his perception of the world around him from the Christian optimism of his youth to the pessimistic outlook on human nature and the universe that would characterize most of his adult life. The individual, Dreiser now recognized, was essentially helpless, possessed no free will, was compelled by "chemic" processes that determined behavior, and was locked in a struggle for existence that only the strong survived. After his exposure to evolutionary philosophy, Dreiser sensed that the great human tragedy was that the meek would not inherit the earth, but were doomed to extinction. This dramatic shift in world view from "Christian brotherhood" to "survival of the fittest" is the subject of Chapter 1.

In Chapter 2, I try to show how Dreiser's conceptualization of the evolutionary universe provided the philosophical framework in which his characters move and act in his early fiction. The tension between the individual's instinct of self-preservation and the drive for hedonistic self-fulfillment on the one hand, and the higher instinct to serve the needs of the group or the species on the other, is an important theme in both Dreiser's first published story, "The Shining Slave Makers," and his first novel, *Sister Carrie*. In his next four novels, published after a decade of personal turmoil and failure, the struggle for existence and the limitations of the individual became even more evident. In the tragedies and triumphs of Jennie Gerhardt, Frank Cowperwood, and Eugene Witla, Dreiser reworked his own dreams and fears of success and failure into fictions that are framed within a hostile universe of competition for power, prestige, and pleasure.

Between 1910 and 1925, Dreiser discovered through his reading a scientific philosophy that amplified his belief in the helplessness of the individual. Scientific mechanism revealed to Dreiser a universe that was a well-ordered machine, running according to the physical and chemical laws that science was in the process of uncovering. The "mechanistic conception of life" held that because all living beings, including humans, were composed of the same atomic particles that composed all inorganic matter, the processes of life could ultimately be reduced and understood in terms of physics and chemistry. The mechanists viewed each living being as a complex machine, a collection of chemical reactions to be studied according to precise scientific methods of experimentation and analysis; metaphysical or religious notions of "consciousness," "soul," and "life principles" had to be eliminated from the "true" understanding of human nature. Dreiser's examination of mechanistic philosophy in the writings of Jacques Loeb and others, his attraction to that philosophy, and his application of it in *The Hand of the Potter* and *An American Tragedy* are examined in Chapter 3.

The philosophy of mechanism, combined with his previous understanding of evolutionary thought, provided Dreiser with a scientific world view that gave him a satisfying system of beliefs about humanity's origin and place in the universe and the mechanistic basis of behavior and ethics. Dreiser, however, never adopted the stark materialism or atheism contained in the speculations and writings of the mechanists. He continued to have a deeply superstitious side to his personality, partly the result of his family background. A number of experiences with fortune tellers, seances, Ouija boards, and "spirit apparitions" convinced him of the existence of some controlling supernatural force in the universe. He encouraged scientists to investigate the strange supernatural phenomena that he had experienced, but was disappointed to discover that many twentieth-century scientists were dedicated exclusively to the study of natural phenomena and strictly divorced any speculation on the nature or possible existence of a universal creator or overseer from their studies. As a result, Dreiser's occult experiences and supernatural suspicions remained anomalies that he could not reconcile with the mechanistic world view. During the same years that he was attracted to mechanistic philosophy through his correspondence and conversations with Jacques Loeb, Dreiser was also drawn deeper into speculations about the supernatural through his friendship with the eccentric investigator and author Charles Fort. This growth in Dreiser's interest in the supernatural is the subject of Chapter 4.

In an effort to further his understanding of mechanistic philosophy as well as to discover some reconciliation between his faith in an unknowable, supernatural force and the facts of modern science, Dreiser began his most intensive period of scientific study in 1927. During the next ten years, he visited numerous laboratories around the United States, befriended many of America's most eminent scientists, and read numerous works on biology, chemistry, physics, and astronomy. The information he gained was to be incorporated in a book of his personal philosophy, begun in 1934 and variously called *The Mechanism Called Man*, *The Formula Called Life*, and finally *Notes on Life*. This uncompleted book was Dreiser's attempt to reconcile his increasingly intuitive perception of a supernatural entity that pervaded the cosmos with the mechanistic conception of life and the universe that he had discovered in modern science. In effect Dreiser was attempting through his studies in science in this period to find a personal religious interpretation of the meaning of life that would be free from the dogma of traditional religions and compatable with the findings of contemporary science. This period of research culminated at the Carnegie Biological Laboratory at Cold Spring Harbor in 1937, when Dreiser experienced a kind of spiritual epiphany in which he was suddenly able to intuit a "Divine

Being"'s presence in all nature. This period of Dreiser's scientific study and its climax in his mystical experience at Cold Spring Harbor are the subject of Chapter 5.

The final chapter examines Dreiser's thought in the last eight years of his life. In these years, Dreiser relied less on the testimony of modern science as a sanction for his philosophical speculations and more on the testimony of his own feelings and emotions to find the nature of God and the meaning of life. He turned to the study of mystical philosophies and religions such as transcendentalism, Quakerism, and Hinduism to enlarge his intuitive vision. He believed, nevertheless, that his increasingly mystical and pantheistic vision of God and the universe did not contradict modern science; in fact, he felt that his intuition was just as "scientific" as the empirical methods employed by laboratory scientists. Dreiser combined scientific knowledge and personal intuition into a curious, mystical interpretation of the universe that provided the answers about human destiny and purpose that he had struggled to find throughout his life.

In my conclusion I attempt to locate Dreiser's later thought in the wider context of American intellectual trends in the twentieth century and to illustrate how his final reconciliation between science and religion was actually a retreat into the romanticism of the eighteenth and nineteenth centuries.

1. The Impact of Evolutionary Thought

In 1894, while working as a reporter for the *Pittsburgh Dispatch*, Theodore Dreiser borrowed a copy of Herbert Spencer's *First Principles* from the Pittsburgh Public Library. His subsequent reading of this work was a turning point in his life, setting off an intellectual and spiritual upheaval that shattered his conception of the universe, of human nature, and of his own place in the world. "Herbert Spencer . . . ," he wrote years later, "quite blew me, intellectually, to bits." This revolution in world view was the culmination of a reading program in which Dreiser had immersed himself during the previous several months. His scientific self-education had begun with Thomas Henry Huxley's *Science and the Hebrew Tradition* and *Science and the Christian Tradition*, two books that greatly damaged Dreiser's faith in the Christian dogma upon which he had been raised. In the following months, he consumed the work of other leading contemporary scientists, including John Tyndall, Charles Darwin and Alfred Russel Wallace. But in reading Spencer's *First Principles*, followed closely by *The Data of Ethics*, Dreiser found an interpretation of the universe that seemed to combine all branches of knowledge, including much of the content of his recent scientific reading, into one brilliant, all-encompassing philosophy. "I was completely thrown down," Dreiser reported, "in my conceptions or nonconceptions of life."[1]

Dreiser's intellectual revolution, triggered by his discovery of the evolutionary writers, was typical of the experience undergone by many of the young thinkers of his generation. His close friend H. L. Mencken, while commenting on the impact of Spencer and Huxley on Dreiser's beliefs, implicitly included himself as one whose thought was remolded by these two British writers. "Who, indeed," Mencken asked, "will ever measure the effect of those two giants upon the young men of that era— Spencer with his inordinate meticulousness, his relentless pursuit of facts, his overpowering syllogisms, and Huxley with his devastating agnosticism, his insatiable questionings of the old axioms, above all, his brilliant style?" Describing Dreiser as "a youth groping about for self-understanding and self-expression," Mencken recognized the subversive influence of Spencer and Huxley on Dreiser's religious roots, sweeping him clean of "the lingering faith of his boyhood—a mediaeval, Rhenish Catholicism," as well as their constructive effect, filling him with "an intense interest in the life that lay about him, a desire to seek out its hidden workings and underlying causes." Mencken was the first Dreiserian critic to recognize the lasting impression that this discovery of Spencer in 1894 had made upon Dreiser's thought: "There is no need to go further than this single moving adventure to find the genesis of Dreiser's disdain of the current platitudes, [and] his sense of life as a complex biological phenomenon."[2]

As Mencken noted, this upheaval in Dreiser's thought was the final stage in his rejection of the Catholic heritage he had received through his father. John Paul Dreiser was a German immigrant with—according to his son—a rigid faith in Roman Catholicism. "He accepted literally the infallibility of the Pope, the Immaculate Conception, the chastity and spirituality of all priests and nuns, trans-substantiation on the altar, forgiveness of sins, communion and the like," Dreiser recalled in his autobiography. "Never have I known a man more obsessed by a religious belief. . . . I looked on him as mentally a little weak." John Paul Dreiser had attempted to instill his religious fervor in his children by having them educated in Catholic schools, in spite of the objections of his wife, who feared that the quality of such training was inferior to that of the public schools. None of the ten children, however, were able to live up to their father's strict moral expectations, and bitter family quarrels over the behavior of the Dreiser brood were frequent. "The rather indifferent religious conduct of his wife and children," Dreiser wrote, "was sufficient to convince him that they were evil to a degree and in need of driving."[3]

Dreiser's harbored bitter memories of his Catholic school years. "It was the seeds here sown," he wrote, "that definitely alienated me from the Church." He believed that his parochial education had been inadequate, teaching him "nothing of the history of the United States, nothing concerning geography, algebra, geometry, zoology, botany, nor indeed any of the sciences or arts." Except for the mastery of the three Rs, the primary function of the school, he maintained, was to indoctrinate its students in Roman Catholic dogma. Reflecting on his belief in the religious doctrines he had been taught, Dreiser claimed he had suffered from "the fear that if I did not [believe] I might die in the act of committing a mortal sin and so be consigned to eternal fire. Fear, not spiritual understanding or reverence, compelled me."[4] On one occasion, he recalled, a priest in confession had told him that he would have to abandon his reading habits, "including scientific books of all kinds," or be barred from receiving communion at the local church.[5]

During the same years, while he was growing up in the small towns of Indiana, Dreiser developed a fascination with nature that persisted throughout his life. "The earth, its surface nature, was then truly a fairyland to me," he reminisced, "and I wanted nothing better than to be alone with it." He passed many childhood hours wandering through the forests and along the rivers of his rural neighborhood, examining flowers, watching birds, searching for crayfish, or inspecting the web-spinning of spiders. "I doubt whether any child ever had a greater curiosity concerning the habitations of animals, crustacea or insects. Everything from wasps' nests to gopher holes fascinated me." Dreiser later regretted that his Catholic school education had denied him an exposure to books on natural history and biology at that impressionable age:

> For my mind was a clean slate on which many effective things could have been penciled. I was a polished crystal—accidental, it is true—reflecting all the harmonies, colors, oddities, of my little world. I was a harp on which nature idly strummed her melodies; a flower form into which she blew her endless suggestions of color; an ear attuned to indefinite delicacies of sound; an eye responsive to the faintest shadows of meaning; and yet daily, even hourly, being drilled in the wornout folderol of the Holy Roman Catholic Church.[6]

But Darwinism was "in the air" in the 1880s, and it was inevitable when young Dreiser left parochial school in 1884 and entered public education that the world of natural history would eventually be opened to him. At age fourteen, he was introduced by one of his teachers to Charles Kingsley's *Water Babies*. Kingsley, an Anglican rector whose interests in science and friendships with Darwin and Huxley made him receptive to the new evolutionary hypothesis, composed *Water Babies* as a fantasy designed to popularize Darwinian ideas to children. Dreiser "was dippy" about the book and "used to lie under our trees by the hour and read [it]":

> The mystery of the water world as portrayed in "Water Babies," the metaphysical and mystic impulses which project life and which were suggested therein, appealed to me strongly. It somehow brought back those days at Sullivan, when and where I sat beside pools and waterholes watching for crawfish and salamanders.[7]

It was even more inevitable that Dreiser would encounter evolutionary ideas during his year at Indiana University. His brief college experience in

1889–90 was subsidized by a former teacher, Mildred Fleming, whose parting words to her protege were, "The world is full of half-concealed shames and tragedies. . . . What I want you to do is to study and develop your mind. Read philosophy and history. You will see how life works and how mistaken or untrue most beliefs are. Read Spencer."[8] At the university, Dreiser met a fellow student named Russell Ratliff, who exercised a "serene and broadening influence" on him. Ratliff introduced Dreiser to "the naturalism of Spencer, Huxley, Darwin, Alfred Russel Wallace, Lecky, Draper, and others," and the two students passed many evenings discussing "philosophy and the necessary social as well as physical and other scientific data on which it rests."[9] He also came under the influence of a young assistant teacher of geology named Albrecht. Although Dreiser was unable to study geology in his freshman year, his friendship with Albrecht enabled him to accompany class expeditions into the surrounding countryside. On these trips Albrecht unearthed the fossil wonders of Indiana for his students, and Dreiser marveled at the evidence that revealed, for example, "where the sea had once been and left what traces of fish and shell life in what ancient rocks—a demonstration which was broadening as well as refreshing."[10] While there is no indication that he actually consumed any works by the evolutionary biologists and geologists during this year at the university, his conversations with Ratliff and Albrecht were enough to whet his appetite for the reading that he began in Pittsburgh four years later.

When Dreiser left Indiana University after his freshman year to pursue a career as a newspaper writer, he encountered two additional men who would influence his eventual reading. The first was John Maxwell, a copy editor at the *Chicago Daily Globe*, where Dreiser secured his first writing job. Maxwell's cynical pessimism and tragic sense of life intrigued Dreiser. "Life is a God-damned stinking, treacherous game," Maxwell declared, "and nine hundred and ninety-nine men out of every thousand are bastards." Sensing that Dreiser lacked the hardened outlook that was necessary for a good reporter, Maxwell suggested to him, "Read Schopenhauer, Spencer, Voltaire. Then you'll get a line on this scheme of things."[11] The other important formative influence was Peter McCord, a young illustrator and writer on the *St. Louis Globe-Democrat*. Like Maxwell, McCord was a pessimist who "had no faith in anything except Nature itself, and very little in that." He was exceptionally well read and encouraged Dreiser to expose himself to contemporary ideas. "Already at this age he knew many historians and scientists (their work), a most astonishing and illuminating list to me— Maspero, Froude, Huxley, Darwin, Wallace, Rawlinson, Froissart, Hallam, Taine, Avebury!" McCord embraced a bleak, materialistic philosophy which shocked Dreiser at the time, but which sounds remarkably similar to the mechanistic conception of humanity that he himself would advocate several decades later:

> He was all for meditating on the state and nature of man, his chemical components—chlorine, sulphuric acid, phosphoric acid, potassium, sodium, calcium, magnesium, oxygen. . . . He asserted boldly that man was merely a chemical formula at best, that something much wiser than he had prepared him, for some not very brilliant purpose of his or its own perhaps, and that he or it, whoever or whatever he or it was, was neither good nor bad, as we imagined such things, but both.[12]

During his Chicago and St. Louis apprenticeships, Dreiser was gradually moving further away from a belief in the Catholic dogma of his father. One incident that greatly embittered him against the Church occurred when his mother died in the autumn of 1890. A local parish priest resisted blessing her body and allowing her to be buried in consecrated ground because she had not made a final confession. The affair deeply angered Dreiser, who began to resent his father's Catholicism as a "narrow, Teutonic, bigoted religion."[13] As late as 1893, however, he had not yet rejected all the tenets of traditional Christianity. He wrote that "although largely freed of Catholic and religious dogma generally and the belief in the workability of the Christian ideals as laid down in the Sermon on the Mount, [my mind] was still swashing around among the idealistic maxims of Christ and the religionists and moralists generally." He continued believing that "God was still some kind of entity somewhere—the devil another. There were powers of good and evil," and he indicated that he "was not ready to believe as yet that Christianity and religions in general use were wholly an illusion, or that Christ never really lived." Even as late as 1893, he could still confess in a newspaper column that he found a certain spiritual comfort in his faith in God:

> The Lord didn't intend that a man should reason out everything. . . . At least there are innumerable mysteries which no person has yet been able to comprehend. . . . I may not do exactly right, but if I have faith in a greater benevolent Power, I do believe that I am happier than the man who has only his reason to depend on.[14]

When he arrived in Pittsburgh in April 1894 to work on the *Dispatch*, Dreiser came face to face with the economic inequalities of urban life that he had begun to recognize in St. Louis. His duties as a reporter would assign him one day to cover the impoverished immigrant districts, "which were crowded with the unfit, the unsuccessful, the unhappy"; the next day's assignment would carry him to interview one of "the strong men at the top, . . . so comfortable, so indifferent, so cruelly dull." This imbalance that he found in the urban, industrial society of Gilded Age America depressed and angered him. After glimpsing the luxurious surroundings of Andrew Carnegie, Henry Clay Frick, and Henry Phipps, he declared, "How I liked to flail them with the maxims of Christ." After visiting the rundown, dirty neighborhoods of destitute Eastern European laborers, he later recalled "how they haunted me and how I attempted (in my mind, of course) to indict society and comfort them with the poetic if helpless words of the Beatitudes and the Sermon on the Mount: 'Blessed are the poor,' etc."[15] As he covered various stories throughout Pittsburgh, he gradually realized that "selfish materialism" and not "Christian brotherhood" was the operating principle in the urban world. On one occasion he learned of a scandal involving the mistreatment of prisoners in a Pittsburgh jail:

> I saw how self interest, the hope of pleasure or the fear of pain caused jailers or wardens or a sheriff to graft on prisoners, feed them rotten meat, torture them into silence and submission, and then, politics interfering (the hope of pleasure again and the fear of pain on the part of some), the whole thing hushed up, no least measure of the sickening truth breaking out in the subservient papers. Life could or would do nothing for those whom it so shamefully abused.[16]

Dreiser became more dispirited as he realized that even his newspaper seemed dedicated to serving the interests of the wealthy and ignoring the problems of the poor. When he uncovered a story involving the construction of a railroad line that was inconveniencing the inhabitants of a poverty-stricken section of the city, Dreiser's editor instructed him "to write a humorous article but not to 'hurt anybody's feelings'." He later complained that "those regions of indescribable poverty and indescribable wealth . . . were always carefully kept separate by the local papers, all the favors and compliments and commercial and social aids going to those who had, all the sniffs and indifferences and slights going to those who had not."[17]

As he became more aware and more dejected about the realities of urban life, Dreiser began to recollect the pessimism of Maxwell and McCord, recalling their naturalistic philosophy, which seemed to account for the evils and tragedies that he now observed daily. Dreiser's knowledge of

the evolutionary writers who supported Maxwell's and McCord's naturalism, however, was still rather vague, only a secondhand awareness gained
through his conversations with them. "The existence of . . . Darwin,
Spencer, Wallace and Tyndall in England, and what they stood for," he
wrote, "was in part at least within the range of my intuition, if not my exact
knowledge."[18] Now, in the summer of 1894, Dreiser was ready to discover
for himself the naturalistic philosophy expressed in the writings of the
evolutionary scientists. He began with Thomas Henry Huxley.

Science and the Hebrew Tradition and *Science and the Christian Tradition*, two collections of Huxley's essays, were published in the early 1890s.
Among these essays were three of his "Lectures on Evolution" as well as
"The Rise and Progress of Paleontology," a group of introductions to and
defenses of the evolutionary hypothesis. Most of the essays, however, were
sharp analyses of the myths of the Old and New Testaments, examined
critically from Huxley's agnostic point of view. "Agnosticism," Huxley
wrote,

> is not a creed, but a method, the essence of which lies in a rigorous application
> of a single principle . . . : In matters of the intellect, follow your reason as far as
> it will take you, without regard to any other consideration . . . In matters of
> the intellect, do not pretend that conclusions are certain which are not demon-
> strated or demonstrable.

When examining a theory, Huxley explained, "The question for me is
purely one of evidence: is the evidence adequate to bear out the theory, or is
it not?"[19]

Following this principle of agnosticism, Huxley concluded that the
Bible could not be regarded as a literal account of historical events. He
declared that it was no longer possible for "men of clear intellect" to believe

> that the universe came into being in the fashion described in the first chapter of
> Genesis, or to accept as literal truth, the story of the making of woman, with
> the account of the catastrophes that followed hard upon it, in the second
> chapter; or to admit that the earth was repeopled with terrestrial inhabitants
> by migration from Armenia or Kurdistan, little more than 4000 years ago . . .
> or finally, to shape their conduct in accordance with the conviction that the
> world is haunted by innumerable demons, who take possession of men and
> may be driven out of them by the exorcistic adjurations, which pervade the
> Gospels.

Huxley drew on contemporary research in geology and paleontology to
prove that Biblical accounts of the Creation and the Deluge could not

possibly have occurred as described. The Old Testament, he maintained, was mythology, comparable to the legends of the Roman and Greek civilizations. Because the Old Testament was merely a collection of cultural myths, Huxley asked, "what about the authority and wisdom of the writers of the New Testament, who, on this theory, have not merely accepted flimsy fictions for solid truths, but have built the very foundations of Christian dogma upon legendary quicksands?" To thinkers who championed the discovery of "true" knowledge, Huxley declared, "it is clear that the Biblical idol must go the way of all idols."[20]

In addition to his Biblical criticism, these essays reveal Huxley's hostility to the dogmatic arrogance that characterized much of the history of Christian thought. He maintained that the good that Christianity had achieved in the world had been outweighed by its persecution of honest non-believers. Throughout history, Christianity had regarded skepticism as a moral offense deserving the same punishment as murder or robbery:

> If we could only see, in one view, the torrents of hypocrisy and cruelty, the lies, the slaughter, the violations of every obligation of humanity, which followed from this source along the course of the history of the human nations, our worst imagination of Hell would pale beside the vision.

But Huxley declared that religious dogmatism and unquestioning faith in the supernatural were now being challenged by "an enemy whose full strength is only just beginning to be put out." This enemy, he asserted, "is Science, in the acceptance of systematized natural knowledge, which, during the last two centuries, has extended those methods of investigation, the worth of which is confirmed by the daily appeal to Nature, to every region in which the Supernatural has hitherto been recognized."[21]

Dreiser's discovery of Huxley's Biblical criticism was a powerful experience. The books had a shattering effect on his remaining Christian faith. "Hitherto, until I had read Huxley," he wrote,

> I had some lingering filaments of Catholicism trailing about me, faith in the existence of Christ, the soundness of his moral and sociological deductions, the brotherhood of man. But on reading *Science and the Hebrew Tradition* and *Science and the Christian Tradition*, [I found] both the Old and New Testaments to be not compendiums of revealed truth but mere records of religious experiences, and very erroneous ones at that."[22]

Dreiser probably identified with Huxley when the scientist recalled that as a youth he "had been brought up in the strictest school of evangelical orthodoxy"; like Dreiser, Huxley "was told to believe, and I did believe, that doubt about any one of them [Biblical statements] was a sin, not less reprehensible than a moral delict. I suppose that, out of a thousand of my contemporaries, nine hundred, at least, had their minds systematically warped and poisoned, in the name of the God of truth by like discipline."[23]

Huxley's essays also gave Dreiser firsthand exposure to modern scientific thought. For the first time, Dreiser read a full explanation of Darwin's hypothesis and learned much of the scientific evidence on which it rested. He was so impressed by the description of paleontological studies that a few years later he wrote an article, "The Descent of the Horse," that popularized much of the material he found in Huxley's essay on the rise of paleontology.[24] The methodology of science, resting on observable facts and logical reasoning while denying the a priori conclusions of religion and metaphysics, seized Dreiser's imagination and stimulated him to read other popular scientific writers.

He next turned to the essays of Huxley's friend John Tyndall, a British physicist and geologist who, like Huxley, was a defender of Darwin's natural selection hypothesis and a champion of agnosticism. Unlike Huxley, however, Tyndall's agnosticism was tempered by an intuitive streak of mysticism. One of Tyndall's biographers has written:

> Agnostic he was, because he drew a sharp line to mark the boundary where, in his view, science ended and speculation began. But his attitude of mind was really Pantheistic, for he seemed to see beyond all the manifestations of natural phenomena, something all-pervading and all-powerful which he could not comprehend. . . . All his writings were suffused with awe at the wonders of the Universe. Awe begets reverence; reverence begets humility; and without humility there can be no worship.[25]

This description of scientific agnosticism counterbalanced by a will to believe in an immanent, universal power could also describe the tension between science and the supernatural that would characterize Dreiser's thought in the following years. Although the immediate effect of Dreiser's discovery of Huxley and Tyndall would be an undermining of his Christian faith and an awareness of the impermanency of the material world, he would never make the leap of mind to the agnostic point of view. Like Tyndall, Dreiser would continue to suspect and eventually espouse a belief in a pervasive intelligence underlying the universe.

Dreiser read the Tyndall essays collected in *Fragments of Science*.[26] Here he encountered a critique of the Mosaic account of creation similar to

Huxley's. "The Book of Genesis has no voice in scientific questions," Tyndall wrote. "To the grasp of geology, which it resisted for a time, it at length yielded like potter's clay; its authority as a system of cosmology being discredited on all hands, by the abandonment of the obvious meaning of its writer. It is a poem, not a scientific treatise." Dreiser also found in Tyndall the enthusiastic claims of many of that generation's scientists, who declared that the mission of science was to destroy the superstition and dogmatism of traditional religion:

> The impregnable position of science may be described in a few words. We claim, and we shall wrest from theology, the entire domain of cosmological theory. All schemes and systems which thus infringe upon the domain of science must, in so far as they do this, submit to its control, and relinquish all thought of controlling it. . . . The lifting of the life is the essential point; as long as dogmatism, fanaticism, and intolerance are kept out, various modes of leverage may be employed to raise life to a higher level.[27]

Tyndall proclaimed that science had uncovered many of the laws underlying the behavior of nature. In the pre-scientific age, people had assumed that supernatural entities were responsible for the fertility of crops or the operations of weather; they had offered prayers or sacrifices to these entities to please them and to receive their favors. But thanks to the rise of science, "we have ceased to propitiate the powers of nature—ceased even to pray for things in manifest contradiction to natural laws. In Protestant countries, at least, I think it is conceded that the age of miracles is past."[28]

Tyndall, like Huxley, made a powerful impression on Dreiser. A few years after reading Tyndall, when he had adopted the naturalistic philosophy that humanity was "the sport of the elements," Dreiser recalled Tyndall's realization that even the greatest mountains were subject to the destructive forces of nature. "Hacked and hurt by time," Tyndall had written of the Matterhorn, "the aspect of the mountain from its higher crags saddened me. Hitherto the impression it made was that of savage strength; here we had inexorable decay." Reflecting on this passage, Dreiser informed the readers of *Ev'ry Month* that "there is in nature a corroding breath, which causes marble and men to peel off and waste away, film by film, until nothing remains." The lesson taught to Tyndall by the famed Swiss mountain, which Dreiser in turn imparted to his readers, was that the only unchanging law of nature was that of constant universal change. "Where once it commanded his awe because of the thought that it was for all time, it now aroused his pity when he found that after all, like himself, it was for a time only."[29] The effect of Tyndall's essays on Dreiser could only have been a deepened awareness of the evolutionary world view and a broadened preparation for his next reading, Herbert Spencer's *First Principles*.

In Herbert Spencer Dreiser encountered the most popular and enthusiastic evolutionary thinker of the age, a philosopher who had been recommended by at least three of Dreiser's mentors in the previous five years. Spencer's impact on Dreiser was greater than that of his previous scientific reading because Spencer attempted to draw all the research of contemporary science into his ambitious "Synthetic Philosophy." In spite of the fact that Spencer frequently relied on his creative imagination more consistently than he relied on the results of scientific research, Dreiser was hooked by his grandiose vision of the universe and regarded it, as did many of his contemporaries, as valid, scientific cosmology. After reading *First Principles*, Dreiser was forced to reject "all I deemed substantial—man's place in nature, his importance in the universe, this too, too solid earth, man's very identity save as an infinitesimal speck of energy or a 'suspended equation' drawn or blown here and there by larger forces in which he moved quite unconsciously as an atom."[30]

The most intense impact that Spencer had on Dreiser's thought was the upheaval caused by his doctrine of "the unknowable." The opening chapter of *First Principles* ("The Unknowable") was Spencer's attempt at achieving a reconciliation between the assertions of religion and science. He began with an examination of "Ultimate Religious Ideas," a search for the one element that all religious creeds have in common after conflicting dogmas and theologies are removed. He concluded that "religions diametrically opposed in their overt dogmas, are yet perfectly at one in the tacit conviction that the existence of the world with all it contains and all which surrounds it, is a mystery ever pressing for interpretation."[31] Turning then to "Ultimate Scientific Ideas," Spencer claimed that all scientific research pointed to the conclusion that ultimate knowledge is incomprehensible to human beings. Science had progressed by grouping phenomena under laws, which were in turn grouped together into larger, more abstract laws. Scientific knowledge, Spencer declared, had therefore advanced into "causes more and more abstract."

> And causes more and more abstract, are of necessity causes less and less conceivable; since the formation of an abstract conception involves the dropping of

certain concrete elements of thought. Hence the most abstract conception, to which Science is ever slowly approaching, is one that merges into the inconceivable or unthinkable, by the dropping all concrete elements of thought.[32]

Spencer maintained, for instance, that the ultimate scientific ideas of space, time, matter, and force all possess the attribute of infinity, which could not be represented in the human mind. He concluded, therefore, that the ultimate ideas of both religion and science contained the mutual conviction that there was an "unknowable" force operating in the cosmos. "If Religion and Science are to be reconciled, the basis of the reconciliation must be this deepest, wildest, and most certain of all facts—that the Power which the Universe manifests to us is utterly inscrutable."[33]

It seems that Dreiser did not fully appreciate Spencer's purpose in writing about "The Unknowable," which had been designed as a compromise that would satisfy the claims of both religion and science. Dreiser, however, despaired after reading it, seizing on only the negative implications of the piece: human beings could ultimately know nothing about the inscrutable forces that determined their existence. "We are as nothing," Dreiser lamented, "—so small that we cannot even conjecture our position in [the world], the meaning of our life, the trend of our efforts. This is it— at once great and small, and we are born, struggle and die in it, leaving no trace, taking hence no knowledge. Surely the lever that moves the Universe is pain."[34]

Spencer's theory of "the unknowable" had several longlasting effects on Dreiser's thought. The first was that it provided him with a philosophical foundation for his lifelong brooding concern with the mystery of life. His belief that human existence was an enigma never to be explained was responsible for much of the despair, confusion, and ambiguity that characterized his later philosophical statements. Over twenty-five years after discovering Spencer, Dreiser reported to an interviewer that "the unknowable" "nearly killed me, took every shred of belief away from me":

I felt the rhythm of life, but the central fact to me was that the whole thing was unknowable—incomprehensible. I went into the depths and I am not sure that I have ever got entirely out of them. I have not much of a creed—certainly no happy or inspiring belief to this day.[35]

The assumption that life was an inexplicable illusion became one of the most frequent themes in his writing and would be reinforced several decades later by his friendship with Charles Fort, the eccentric investigator of unexplained phenomena.

Spencer's "unknowable," however, also allowed Dreiser to maintain a belief in some sort of vague, supernatural force that controlled events in the universe. After reading Huxley, Tyndall, and now Spencer, he reported that the trio had "confirmed my worst suspicions and destroyed the last remaining traces of Catholicism which I now detest as a political organization or otherwise."[36] Dreiser was unwilling or unable, however, to advocate outright atheism, for the religious and superstitious environment of his childhood in rural Indiana would always maintain a deep, unconscious hold on him. So although his readings in science and evolutionary philosophy shattered his belief in the traditional Christian God, Spencer's theory of "the unknowable" still allowed Dreiser to believe in an inscrutable power underlying the laws of nature.

From "The Unknowable," Dreiser proceeded to part two of *First Principles*, "The Knowable." The most important theme developed in this longer section was the declaration of universal evolution. Here Spencer surpassed even the most enthusiastic declarations of the evolutionary biologists in asserting that "we see at once that there are not several kinds of Evolution having certain traits in common, but one Evolution going on everywhere after the same manner." According to Spencer, evolution was a process operating not only in living species on earth but also throughout the entire universe. He declared

> that while each individual is developing, the society of which he is an insignificant unit is developing too; that while the aggregate mass forming society is integrating and becoming more definitely heterogeneous, so likewise is that total aggregate, the Earth, of which society is an inappreciable portion; that while the Earth, which in bulk is not a millionth of the Solar System, progresses toward its more concentrated and complex structure, the Solar System similarly progresses, and that even its transformations are but those of a scarcely appreciable portion of our Sidereal System, which has at the same time been going through parallel changes.[37]

Once again Dreiser saw only the negative implications of Spencer's theory. In the great process of universal evolution, he concluded now that the individual could be no more than an "insignificant unit," a "chemical atom in a whirl of unknown forces." He despaired "that man is the sport of the elements; the necessary, but worthless dust of changing conditions, and that all the fourteen hundred million beings who swarm the earth after the manner of contentious vermin, are but one form which the heat of the sun takes in its protean journey toward dissipation."[38] Trapped in a universe evolving according to the will of an "unknowable" power, humanity, as now regarded by Dreiser, was at present merely an inconsequential, partially developed speck in a progressive scheme leading to ultimate perfection.

Dreiser's emerging belief in the insignificance of the individual was supplemented by the traces of mechanistic philosophy that he encountered in *First Principles*. The mechanistic movement in science and philosophy was a crusade to eradicate metaphysical and especially vitalistic explanation from discussions and understanding of life. Mechanistic researchers and writers attempted to reduce all phenomena of life to basic physical and chemical laws. Spencer envisioned living beings as machines, constantly adapting themselves according to the law of evolution to the demands of the environment. "Life in its simplest form," he wrote, "is the correspondence of certain inner physico-chemical actions with certain outer physico-chemical actions." The fundamental processes of life could be explained according to this basic mechanistic formula of the adaptation of living needs ("internal relations") to environmental availabilities and pressures ("external relations"); digestion, for example, was simply "a set of mechanical and chemical actions responding to the mechanical and chemical actions which distinguish the food." More complex processes such as human thought were similarly explained:

> This which we call Intelligence, shows itself when the external relations to which the internal ones are adjusted, begin to be numerous, complex and remote in time or space; . . . every advance in Intelligence essentially consists in the establishment of more varied, more complete, and more involved adjustments.

Adopting certain conclusions of the mechanistic research being conducted in Europe in the nineteenth century, Spencer viewed the brain as a machine in which complex chemical reactions took place. The quality of mental activity was determined by the chemical composition of the brain, and the chemical reactions of the mind were determined by the quantity of mental activity taking place:

> [The nervous] apparatus has a particular chemical constitution on which its activity depends; and there is one element in it between the amount of which and the amount of function performed, there is an ascertained connexion: the proportion of phosphorus present in the brain being the smallest in infancy, old age, and idiotcy, and the greatest during the prime of life. . . . Yet another proof that the genesis of the mental energies is immediately dependent on chemical change, is afforded by the fact that the effete products separated from

the blood by the kidneys, vary in character with the amount of cerebral action. Excessive activity of mind is habitually accompanied by the excretion of an unusual quantity of alkaline phosphates.[39]

These passages were Dreiser's introduction to the physico-chemical interpretation of life and human nature that he would eventually so enthusiastically advocate and that he would so frequently utilize as the underlying behavioral determinants of his fictional characters. His understanding of the chemical compulsions of human behavior would be clarified and amplified in later years by his discussions with the psychologist Elmer Gates and through his exposure to the mechanistic philosophy of Jacques Loeb. At the moment of his reading of *First Principles*, however, Dreiser was most concerned about the implications of mechanistic determinism for his own hopes and ambitions. His alarm over his fate was now magnified:

> Up to this time there had been in me a blazing and unchecked desire to get on and the feeling that in doing so we did get somewhere; now in its place was the definite conviction that spiritually one got nowhere, that there was no hereafter, that one lived and had his being because one had to, and that it was of no importance. Of one's ideals, struggles, deprivations, sorrows and joys, it could only be said that they were chemic compulsions, something which for some inexplicable but unimportant reason responded to and resulted from the hope of pleasure and the fear of pain. Man was a mechanism, undevised and uncreated, and a badly and carelessly driven one at that.[40]

Spencer's mechanistic references further developed the materialistic explanation of the social inequalities of Gilded Age America that was taking shape in Dreiser's thought by intensifying his conviction that humanity was a helpless victim in a cosmic game played by inscrutable forces.

After *First Principles*, Dreiser turned to another work by Spencer, *The Data of Ethics*. The main theme of this work was that the origin of ethical conduct is materialistic, not spiritual; what is judged good and evil in human behavior is not determined according to the moral commands of a supernatural entity, but according to the laws of nature. Spencer began by asserting that all human conduct is aimed at an end and that conduct is judged as "good" if it achieves its end. In addition to employing success as a criterion in evaluating conduct, however, Spencer proposed a hierarchy of four levels of conduct that are ranked according to the nature of their ends. The simplest and most fundamental level of conduct is that which is carried out to preserve the individual's life. "Self-maintaining conduct" is simply that behavior aimed at attaining food, warmth, and the other necessities of life that allow "that increased duration of life which constitutes the supreme end."[41] On the next level is conduct that is "race-maintaining," that is, behavior motivated beyond just self-preservation toward the preservation of one's offspring. The third level of conduct includes behavior that achieves the maintenance of both the individual and its offspring without destroying the potential of others to do the same. On this level, conduct avoids aggression and antagonism within the species and seeks to respect the conduct of other individuals who are also seeking to maintain themselves and their offspring; conduct is primitively social and less competitive at this level. The highest level of conduct is behavior that actively seeks to help other members of the species to achieve their goals of self-maintenance and race-maintenance. This is the most perfect manifestation of conduct because unlike the rather passive social behavior of the third level, the welfare of the community or society is the active goal of this higher mode of conduct:

> For beyond so behaving that each achieves his ends without preventing others from achieving their ends, the members of a society may give mutual help in the achievement of ends. And if, either indirectly by industrial co-operation, or directly by volunteered aid, fellow citizens can make easier for one another the adjustment of acts to ends, then their conduct assumes a still higher phase of evolution . . . and serves to render the lives of all more complete.[42]

These four modes of conduct, when successfully achieving their ends, produce an "increase" or lengthening of life and are therefore preserved by natural selection and handed down to succeeding generations. The natural laws of evolution, not the supernatural laws of God, command the practice of ethical behavior.

Spencer addressed the seeming contradiction between the primal instinct of self-preservation and the more advanced instinct to sacrifice one's existence for the greater society. He explained that communities or societies were formed by individuals of a species when great difficulties threatened survival of those individuals. Because the greater security provided by such organization helped to promote survival of the individual members, patterns of behavior within each individual that contributed to the welfare of the group tended to survive and be selected by nature for transmission to future generations. In this way societies gained greater security, and behavior to preserve those societies evolved into instinctive compulsions just as powerful as the instinct to preserve the individual. During times of group crisis, then, especially in times of warfare, the instinct of self-preservation and the instinct of self-sacrifice came into conflict, battling within each individual to dominate behavior. In communities where the selfish instinct dominated individual actions, extinction of the group and ultimately all its members was the usual natural result. In more advanced communities, where the social instinct dominated, survival was more likely. Spencer admitted that in terms of the fate of the individual, this "compromise" was "vague, ambiguous, [and] illogical," but he insisted that when

> the welfare of society must take precedence of the welfares of its component individuals, during those stages in which the individuals have to preserve themselves by preserving their society, then such temporary compromise between the two codes of conduct as duly regards external defense, while favoring internal cooperation to the greatest extent practicable, subserves the maintenance of life in the highest degree; and thus gains the ultimate sanction.[43]

In addition to the evolutionary philosophy that shaped Spencer's explanation of ethics, his ideas on the subject were also influenced by the hedonistic doctrines that pervaded much of nineteenth-century British philosophy and psychology, such as the work of Jeremy Bentham, James and John Stuart Mill, and Alexander Vain. Spencer introduced the hedonistic dimension of his philosophy by suggesting that the pessimist for whom life is a misfortune may not regard conduct that is self-preserving as "good"; such conduct, while prolonging life, also prolongs misery. For conduct to be judged "good," Spencer concluded, it must achieve not only the goal of increased life but also the goal of providing pleasure. The pursuit of happiness is the ultimate objective of all behavior that is declared good:

> Whether perfection of nature is the assigned proper aim, or virtuousness of action, or rectitude of motive, we saw that definition of the perfection, the virtue, the rectitude, invariably brings us down to happiness experienced in some form, at any time, by some person as the fundamental idea. . . . No school can avoid taking for the ultimate moral aim a desirable state of feeling called by whatever name—gratification, enjoyment, happiness.[44]

Since, according to Spencer, pleasure is ultimately life enhancing and pain is life diminishing, conduct that contributes to the pleasure of the individual, one's progeny, or one's society not only is deemed good, but is selected for evolutionary transmission to future generations.

The Data of Ethics had a dual influence on Dreiser's thought. First, Dreiser adopted the materialistic interpretation of ethics found in Spencer's writing; ethics are not god-given and inflexible but evolutionary and relative. As Spencer pointed out, the notion of "Absolute Ethics" can apply as standards of conduct only for the individual or the society that has achieved perfection. Since *Homo sapiens* is still evolving toward its ultimate perfect state, ethics must be "relative." Spencer demonstrated to Dreiser that each society has its own ethical standards and that these frequently conflict with the ethical pronouncements of other societies. Therefore, "no specific statements of the activities universally required for personal well-being is possible"; no system of "Absolute Ethics" can even be contemplated until the evolution of the human species has reached its ultimate condition. Dreiser adopted this concept of the relativity of ethics and expressed it in his frequent criticisms of the conservative guardians of moral order who attempted to impose their rigid standards of right and wrong on American society. "Certain it is that the religionists and moralists have already been heard from sufficiently, and in vain," he complained years later in his autobiography. "It is time for science to speak."[45]

The second influence of *The Data of Ethics* was Dreiser's subsequent adoption of the hedonistic doctrine of seeking pleasure and avoiding pain. From this point in time, Dreiser would begin to define "good" and "evil" as that which causes the individual pleasure and pain. A Spencerian-like version of hedonistic ethics would eventually be exhibited in Dreiser's fiction, as well as in his personal life. Each of his novel's protagonists from Carrie Meeber and Clyde Griffiths to Eugene Witla and Frank Cowperwood would be motivated by their craving for social comfort and sexual gratification. And Dreiser's descriptions of his own innumerable love affairs and his enthusiasms over the pleasures of life would be expressed and rationalized in hedonistic terms, usually accompanied by an angry denunciation of Christian morality. Years later Dreiser's hedonism expressed itself typically in the advice he gave to one of his lady friends:

> If I could I would blow out of your mind every trace of religious & moralic cant & faith. . . . I would have you give yourself to happiness in your youth. . . .
> I could neither love nor live with anyone who was not a happy pagan. The days of social lies for me is dead. . . . Moralic cant & religious theory kill life.[46]

When Dreiser moved to New York in November 1894, he continued his reading in science and philosophy, but at a much slower pace. It was not until sometime in 1896 that he read *The Origin of Species* and *The Descent of Man*.[47] Darwin's theory of natural selection added a new element to Dreiser's developing deterministic outlook, for he was now introduced to the concepts of "the struggle for existence" and "the survival of the fittest."

Although Herbert Spencer actually originated the phrase "survival of the fittest" in his *Principles of Biology* (1864–67), there is no evidence that Dreiser ever read this book. His awareness of the phrase seems to have come from his reading of *The Origin of Species* in 1896. In the late editions of this work, Darwin adopted Spencer's phrase as an apt expression for the essence of his hypothesis that species with fortuitous variations tended to survive the "struggle for existence" in greater numbers than species without them.[48]

Reading Darwin was the final step in Dreiser's conversion to the social Darwinian philosophy that proved so popular in late nineteenth-century America. Having already received a massive dose of Spencerian philosophy, Dreiser now fell prey to the same fallacy that other social Darwinian thinkers made: he assumed that Darwin's explanation of the *biological* evolutionary development of species could be applied to the *social* evolutionary development of humankind and human society. Accepting the Darwinian concept of the biological struggle for survival among the members of a species, Dreiser, like Spencer, would assume that there was a social struggle within humankind for the attainment and use of the limited amount of power, prestige, and pleasure that was available to the human species. Taking the Darwinian observation of variation within species, Dreiser, like the other social Darwinians, would suppose that a variation of talents like intelligence, industriousness, discipline, and ambition were parceled out to individual humans at birth by some mysterious, predestinating process. And in accepting Darwin's conclusion of the survival of the fittest, Dreiser and many of his contemporaries would presume that those individuals with the most highly developed talents would succeed in rising to the highest social positions, while those who lacked the tools to survive the social competition would sink to become the dregs of society. Thus the inequalities of Gilded Age America could be interpreted as the natural result of forces and processes beyond human control. The tragedies of poverty, illness, and ignorance were necessary miseries in a huge cosmic, evolutionary process that would ultimately lead to the improvement of society as the "natural elite" took over their foreordained positions of financial, governmental, and cultural leadership.[49]

Dreiser's social Darwinian philosophy and his deterministic outlook on human nature and destiny found expression in a monthly magazine that he edited from October 1895 until September 1897. After a brief, unrewarding job as a writer for the *New York World*, Dreiser contrived a plan with his brother, the famous songwriter Paul Dresser, to create a popular magazine that would contain sheet music of the latest musical hits as well as short fiction, book reviews, and philosophical essays. The publishers of Dresser's songs, Haviland, Howley & Co., approved the idea and installed Dreiser as the editor of this new magazine, which was named *Ev'ry Month*.[50] The young writer seized the opportunity to write a monthly column called "Reflections," in which, under the pseudonym of "The Prophet," he commented at length on politics, social trends, and the state of the arts. Most importantly, however, the "Reflections" column provided Dreiser an outlet for his urge to popularize his new "scientific" point of view.

In one issue, Dreiser challenged his readers to lay aside their novels temporarily and enlighten themselves about the great advances in knowledge that had been made by the evolutionary scientists. In the typically ornate prose of the "Prophet," Dreiser called on them to discover "what Darwin, Huxley and Tyndall have to tell of their efforts in tracing the growth of all life since the time when the earth was fire and the sky a shimmering arc of bronze, studded with stars of a brighter gleam than we can now well conceive." After completing this survey of contemporary biology, Dreiser suggested, his readers would be prepared "to have the whole universe passed in review before you, as Spencer marshals it, showing you how certain beautiful laws exist, and how, by these laws, all animate and inanimate things have developed and arranged themselves." Such a tour of modern scientific thought, he suggested, would not only be enlightening but would also give the reader a new critical appreciation of fiction:

> Certainly there are a lot of beautiful and wonderful things which you do not know much about, which would interest you if you did. Why not think of them. The novels will wait, you know, and when you come to them after awhile, wise and able yourself, they will seem even better than they do now, if they are good novels, whereas, if they are bad ones, you will know too much to trouble yourself about them. Why not begin now?[51]

In a subsequent column dedicated solely to Spencer, Dreiser lavished praise on the British philosopher, referring to him as "a great father of knowledge" and "a mighty general." "His is generalship of the mind," Dreiser declared, "—the great captaincy of learning and literature, the field-marshalship of the forces of reason." Like Napoleon or Alexander, Spencer had conquered nations and "bound our minds together into one empire, and pointed the path along which progress is easiest and best." Spencer's "empire" was nature, for which he had clearly defined the laws to which every man and woman on earth were forced to submit:

They are unalterable laws, these of the empire. Rebellion neither affects them nor saves you from punishment. Familiarity proves to you how beneficent they are, how much good they will do you if submissively observed, how vast and glorious is the kingdom of life, and how admirable its philosopher and vice-regent Spencer.

In yet another metaphor, Dreiser compared Spencer to "a refreshing spring" lying "midway in a boundless life-desert" and likened himself to a mere water carrier who brought water from this oasis to "all who would be refreshed and strengthened" but who had not yet discovered the spring's existence. Dreiser here displays his sense of mission to popularize social Darwinian thought, to reveal the location of the "spring" (i.e., Spencer) to "the many [who] are still ignorant of the fact that it exists at all."[52]

In fulfilling this self-appointed mission, Dreiser wrote numerous essays for *Ev'ry Month* that demonstrated "the struggle for existence" and explained the process of "the survival of the fittest" to his public. As the most superior of all species, Dreiser wrote, *Homo sapiens* had proved to be the strongest in the competition for life; all other life forms were forced to submit to human demands. It was impossible for anyone to "progress through this world without injuring many things that lie in his path, from men to plants." In order for us to eat, "something must die, animals or plants," and to clothe ourselves, we cannot avoid "robbing the cotton plant of its bloom, or the sheep of his wool." In the mere act of walking, "grasses and flowers must be ruthlessly crushed under his feet, and the humble stones worn to thinness." In the struggle for existence, "all must die that he may live—fruits, flowers, animals and vegetables."[53]

The struggle for existence, however, was not only carried out between human beings and the other forms of life, but was also fought between humans themselves. "Everyone is trying," Dreiser wrote. "Everyone is pushing the other for place—is training that he may crowd the other out of the way, shove him back, put him below—that he may be first and free to go farther." The underlying cause for this struggle, according to Dreiser, is the hedonistic drive that Spencer had identified as the goal of all human conduct. The pleasure-seeking drive of human nature compels individuals to battle their neighbors for position:

> Why should men struggle? Well, because they want to be somebody. They want nice clothes, nice hands, their bodies kept from showing wear and painful usage. They have inherited pride, and would like people to speak well

of them. They would like to laugh, to feel merry, to have plenty to eat, a fine place to sleep, and to be healthy and admired. They would like a nice home, soft lights and shades in it, beautiful views in it, and the smiles of love.[54]

It was inevitable, Dreiser felt, that "the fittest" would be the victors in this struggle. According to the unbreakable law of nature, only those few individuals with the greatest mental and physical resourcefulness were predestined to triumph and exploit the weaker masses. "[The strong] must step in where others have failed," he wrote, "crowd out the old and feeble, override the desires and hopes of others, who also wish for success, and so on, until death. This is the law, cold, hard immutable—the law of self-preservation, and upon it all must take their stand and press forward so or die." He began to sense the tragic spectacle of the biologically and socially weak members of the human species, doomed for extinction, all around him in New York City:

> All men are not well balanced, and no wonder. How frail is man, veritably vermin upon the face of so great a globe, and in so boundless a universe. We find his race sickly and disturbed by a thousand ills. We have his weakness evidenced in the vast asylums and hospitals. . . . We see more in the weaklings who line our thoroughfares, the maimed, the halt, the blind and the deformed. . . . It is quite true that to the victor belongs the spoils, and to the strong the race, but at the same time it is sad to think that to the weak and the vanquished belong nothing. The law of preservation has been announced, and day by day we go about seeing it fulfilled in a thousand ways.[55]

Again and again Dreiser stressed a deterministic view of poverty and ignorance to his *Ev'ry Month* readers, insisting that misfortune was the result of forces of nature beyond the control of individual will. "The drudges are so numerous. . . . They have to struggle so hard for bread. They have to wear such wretched clothes. Their days are all toil, their nights weariness. . . . Who put them there? An eternal law."[56] The eternal law of Spencer's "empire" of nature was that every human being was locked in a battle to achieve some sort of success, but that few would succeed.

In the light of this social Darwinian explanation of success and failure, Dreiser encouraged his readers to feel compassion for the losers in the competitive struggle. Although he admitted that the weak were at times "disagreeable, uninteresting, [and] wearisome," his familiarity with poverty and his compassion for the impoverished drove Dreiser to encourage sympathy and charity toward the victims of the laws of nature:

The failures in this world are not to blame for their condition. They did not make the environment in which they were born; they could not regulate the early influences which prevailed over them. Poverty: it was not of their making. Ignorance: it was there to thwart their earliest aims. Good companionship: it was denied them. The pleasures of respectability in clothes, pocketmoney, home decorations—how sadly they were lacking! The help of tenderness, sympathy, advice—how remarkable were they for their absence.

The "survival of the fittest" was an unbreakable natural law, but the successful in life's struggle could nevertheless "extend a charitably regulating hand" to society's failures, especially to the unfortunate children of the poor. "Neglect the infants much longer we dare not," Dreiser warned, "else we imperil the ultimate life of the race itself."[57] Dreiser's altruistic imperative, here, reflects Spencer's fourth and highest level of human ethical conduct. The higher-evolved, civilized human must surmount the natural, beastly instinct of self-preservation and practice the ethically higher behavior conducive of species-preservation. In spite of the bleak materialism of the social Darwinian interpretation of the universe, Dreiser seized on this optimistic facet in Spencerian ethical thought and adopted an evolutionary understanding of ethics that still greatly corresponded to the commandment of Christian love that he had learned as a youth.

The tragedy of human existence, which Dreiser conveyed to his *Ev'ry Month* readers and which would appear as a constant theme in his novels, was that the innate human hungering and pursuit of pleasure and prestige were so frequently destined for failure by the inscrutable laws and forces of nature. An additional tragedy lay in the social Darwinian irony that the miseries of the masses were necessary in order to carry out the impersonal laws of nature that would ultimately bring about a more advanced society of equals. "Well, it may be but for the progress of the world that there should be such a wide gap between the very rich and the very poor, between the highly educated and the wholly uneducated; but the difference, coupled with the number of people, makes life a very fierce struggle."[58]

By the time that Dreiser had completed his tour of Spencerian philosophy, his view of human nature had been totally altered. "I was torn up root and branch by it," he reported. "Life disappeared into a strange fog."[59] The deterministic philosophy that would characterize his early novels was now well formed. His realization that nothing could be certain in a universe that was constantly changing, and his belief that the individual had little or no free will but was the slave of mysterious, powerful forces, distressed him intensely:

I fear that I cannot make you feel how these things came upon me in the course of a few weeks' reading and left me numb, my gravest fears as to the unsolvable disorder and brutality of life eternally verified. I felt as low and hopeless at times as a beggar of the streets. There was of course this other matter of necessity, internal chemical compulsion, to which I had to respond whether I would or no.[60]

*   *   *

The influence of Spencer and the other evolutionary writers in sparking Dreiser's intellectual revolution was certainly profound. Yet it must be conceded that the reshaping of Dreiser's perceptions and explanations of the world around him in those last years of the nineteenth century was brought about by more than just a few weeks' reading of a handful of books: events in his life as well as developments in the society around him had undermined the sense of order and self-confidence that young Dreiser had possessed as he set off from rural Indiana on the urban pilgrimage that would carry him from Chicago and St. Louis to Pittsburgh and ultimately New York. Personal events like the death of his mother and the continuing fragmentation of his family had increased his vulnerability and loosened his religious convictions, while his confrontation with the urban realities of the Gilded Age stripped him of his provincial naivete and substituted a growing sense of the tragic spectacle of life.

The eerie apprehension of a growing loss of control over his life that Dreiser experienced echoed the feelings of many urban Americans in the 1890s. Cities were expanding rapidly in population, territory, and shape, and millions of new immigrants were adding new visages, voices, and customs to the swelling metropolises. But more than just these very visible changes in American cities were adding to the growing mystery of urban life. As Alan Trachtenberg has suggested, much of the perplexity of urban life was due to the more subtle processes involved in the "incorporation of America" that "altered relations, defied inherited values, transformed instruments of perception and communication, even as it transformed the perceptible social world" of urban residents.[61] As the intangible hand of corporate activity reshaped the lives of millions of Americans, the cities, where corporate organization and function were concentrated, increasingly came to be perceived as enigmas of darkness, obscurity, and inexplicability by their residents.

As the city expanded into the modern metropolis, corporate needs often dictated urban plans of destruction and reconstruction. New factories, railroad terminals, or department stores, for example, were located, with the enthusiastic cooperation of city governments, to meet the demands of corporate planning, frequently resulting in the demolition of familiar community reference points or the disruption of established community activities. Transportation lines were laid out to guarantee maximum efficiency for corporate needs, to move workers to the factories or to move consumers into the shopping districts. As Dreiser discovered in Pittsburgh, railroad lines were frequently constructed with no regard for community objections, but to maximize the movement of goods.

At the same time the corporations were offering new conveniences and more leisure time and comfort to urban residents, the public was growing less self-sufficient and more dependent on "outside systems." The services of public utilities, for example, providing gas, water, plumbing and electricity often delivered through hidden, subterranean networks, undoubtedly raised the standard of living, but created a new dependency on those services that was beyond the control or comprehension of the typical city dweller. Time-consuming activities like the home preparation of food and production of clothing declined in the Gilded Age, while consumption of store-bought packaged and canned foods and purchases of ready-made clothes increased; the result was a "new life, based on the destruction of 'social artifice', [and depending] increasingly on what was marketed."[62]

Commercial institutions like advertising and the department store increasingly functioned not only in the marketing of goods but also in defining what was "normal" or "ideal" in appearance, taste, and standard of living. Advertising became a didactic force, not only educating the public in the availability and use of goods but also attaching value and status to the consumption of a particular "brand" of product. Urban department stores like Marshall Field's, Macy's, and Wanamaker's were designed as fairy tale palaces, where goods appeared magically overnight on shelves and all association with factory origins was hidden behind the spectacular facade. In all, the "incorporation" of life in America's cities in the late nineteenth century led to a new sense of dislocation, a rising passivity of the public, a decreasing intelligibility in human relations, and a growing uneasiness that lives were being manipulated by "forces" beyond individual control.

Trachtenberg suggests that changes taking place in American newspapers, a field of corporate enterprise where Dreiser began his writing career, were partly responsible for the growing inexplicability of cities. With the development of a new type of journalism in the 1880s and 1890s, newspapers attempted to increase circulation by concentrating on the unique and shocking and by presenting news as a spectacle of sensation and adventure. To expand readership, it was deemed essential to supplement national and international news, which was increasingly provided in packaged form by telegraphic news agencies and which tended to make all newspapers look and read alike, with some sort of vicarious adventure, a surrogate experience that would go beyond ordinary everyday reality. Led by Joseph Pulitzer's *New York World*, with which Dreiser found brief employment in 1895, the urban newspaper audience more frequently were addressed "as passive spectators than as active participants, consumers of images and sensations produced by others."[63] One such means of exciting readership was to publish journalistic excursions into the menacing, impoverished districts of the city. Reporters like Jacob Riis and Stephen Crane led readers through "the other half" and the New York Bowery, and Dreiser received similar assignments in Pittsburgh and New York to uncover stories of wretchedness in ghetto society. This journalism of spectacle only tended to increase the city's social mystery, to heighten artificial experience of the unusual and the appalling while reducing real experience to the level of the ordinary and the banal, and to draw attention to hideous social conditions that could be explained only in terms of forces that were beyond control or reform.

In the presence of the invisible and intangible socio-economic transformations resulting from the organization and functioning of such supra-personal institutions as corporations, therefore, it was only natural that Dreiser and many of his contemporaries should have imagined the existence of other supra-personal agencies, processes, or laws manipulating their lives. In an age when individuals felt a growing loss of control over their lives, it should not be surprising that they began to conceive of themselves as insignificant atoms "in a whirl of unknown forces" beyond their command. In a society where a feeling of mystery and a sense of personal dislocation were on the rise, it should not be unexpected that a newly elaborated conception of cosmic unknowableness gained popularity. And in an era when the span between wealth and poverty was stretching to distances never before known in that society's history, it was only natural that a new conception of society, seemingly based on scientific authority and explaining those inequalities in terms of natural law, should gain credence. Herbert Spencer's philosophy offered much to Dreiser and his generation in providing answers and explanations for the growing social, intellectual, and personal questions and crises of Gilded Age America.

A remaining question is why Spencer's rather bleak, materialistic conception of humanity, society, and the universe should have had such power in overthrowing the more comfortable, paternalistic Christian ideals that Dreiser had learned as a youth. The answer may lie in the similarities that in fact existed between the Christian and social Darwinian world views. Both cosmologies provided a rationalization for the existence of suffering as well as a hopeful vision of the ultimate destiny of humankind. Roman Catholicism viewed misery and pain as temporary ordeals of the material world, the endurance of which would be rewarded in the spiritual world of heaven. Social Darwinism regarded poverty and misery as unfortunate but necessary evils to be endured by individuals in order that the society might progress toward an ultimate heaven on earth through the evolution of a perfect social order. While Roman Catholicism, therefore, viewed moral behavior in terms of its value for individual salvation, evolutionary philosophy regarded ethics in terms of its survival value for the larger community, either for the society or for the species.

An important difference, however, between Roman Catholicism and evolutionary thought concerned the matter of free will. While the Church insisted that individuals had the freedom to choose between good and evil acts, the naturalistic view of humanity that arose in the second half of the nineteenth century tended to eliminate individual responsibility for behavior by reducing each person to a puppet prisoner of natural laws that governed behavior. While such a deterministic view contradicted the Catholic theology in which Dreiser was formally raised, it was not necessarily so far removed from the more general theological conception of humanity that had dominated America since the time of the Puritans. For the new naturalistic conception of humanity, as Henry Steele Commager has pointed out, was ironically nothing more than "a new Calvinism" that "shifted the responsibility for the sorry mess into which mankind had drifted from society itself to the cosmos. . . . Denying free will to men, it placed responsibility for what seemed evil not on an omnipotent and inscrutable God but on an omnipotent and inexorable Nature."[64] Just as Calvinism explained the possibility of salvation or damnation by means of the predestination of souls randomly determined at birth by an almighty God, evolution accounted for the survival or success of a portion of humankind and the extinction or failure of the remainder in terms of a random distribution of endowments, skills, or flaws inherited or not inherited by chance. Instead of the Puritan dichotomy of saint and sinners, or the elect and the damned, social Darwinism divided humanity into the strong and the weak. Such similarities between Calvinist and social Darwinian thought may have lessened Dreiser's resistance or even promoted his acceptance of the determinism of evolutionary philosophy. For although Calvinism was intellectually in decline during the Gilded Age, it seems likely that in the conservative environment of rural Indiana Dreiser would have been exposed to such vestigial remnants of Calvinist theology as still persisted in the American mind.

Dreiser's movement from a primarily religious ordering of his identity and experience to a secular world view heavily influenced by the scientific theories and pseudo-scientific philosophies of his day was not unusual but rather exemplified the growing prestige of science among the public. Historians of science have noted that by the end of the nineteenth century, science had advanced in value and stature in American society to the point where it had replaced traditional religious cosmology as a source of authority in providing explanations of human nature and of the individual's relationship to the world and the universe. Charles Rosenberg has emphasized that the shift from religious to secular interpretation "should be seen, not as a struggle between conflicting ideologies, but as a constantly shifting equilibrium between secular and religious imperatives. The similarity between scientific and religious values made it natural for most Americans to move fluidly from one intellectual and emotional realm to another."[65] With his discovery of Huxley, Tyndall, Spencer, and Darwin, Dreiser underwent just such a mental transition in beliefs and attitudes in the mid-1890s.

The border between scientific and religious explanation, however, would never become a clearly defined line for Dreiser. Although he strongly rejected the conventional dogmas of both his personal Roman Catholic heritage and the more general Protestant tradition that dominated American morals and religious thought at the turn of the twentieth century, he did not surrender an intense desire to seek answers to what were essentially spiritual questions about human purpose and destiny. "There are thousands and perhaps hundreds of thousands of victims of strange forces walking about, whose raison de être [sic] may never be appreciated by men . . . ," he later wrote. "Who shall plumb the deeps below deeps, the highs above highs?"[66] Dreiser's answer for nearly forty years following his discovery of evolutionary thought would be science. Dreiser's interest in science would become a quest for spiritual enlightenment, because in the work of the evolutionary writers and in the philosophy of scientific mechanism that he would soon discover, he found an unfolding interpretation of humanity and its place in the universe that addressed many questions that were previously the concern of Christian dogma. "Isn't seeking knowledge (scientific) a form of prayer?" he argued with Mencken in 1909. "Aren't scientists and philosophers at bottom truly reverential and don't they wish (pray) ardently for more knowledge?"[67] In their attempts to solve "the eternal mystery" of human origin and nature, scientists appeared to Dreiser to be preaching a new "gospel" that rested on an experimental method, observable facts, and logical reasoning, rather than on the unquestioning faith and mythologies of traditional religion.

2. The Evolutionary Universe in Fiction

In September 1897, Dreiser left *Ev'ry Month* and began free-lancing with a number of popular magazines. Many of his articles during this period were devoted to popularizing the ideas that he was accumulating through his continued self-education in science. Promoting the latest scientific work in popular magazines was a natural activity for a young writer attempting to sell pieces to the mass market in the late nineteenth century. Scientific knowledge had grown increasingly esoteric during the previous century, passing beyond the understanding of the general public. The benefits of these advances of knowledge, however, were everywhere apparent in transportation, industry, and agriculture. The growing vogue of "popular science" literature was therefore encouraged by publishers, who detected the widespread curiosity of the public about the mysterious principles behind the rapid changes occurring in everyday life. Dreiser's growing journalistic skills, his continuing interest in scientific subjects, and his didactic urge to educate the public about the benefits of science brought him modest success in this new field.

Among the articles that he sold during this period were two pieces on the life and achievements of John Burroughs, a well-known American naturalist whose work Dreiser had read. In another piece he led his readers on a tour of the New York Museum of Natural History, describing the museum's fossils and paleontological work that exposed the evolutionary past of all life. He wrote a series of articles about plant life and the cultivation of crops, in which he marveled at "the subtleties of chemistry and physics" that were revealed in the growth of plants. He also published several articles about advances in technology that were revolutionizing industrial production and transportation.[1]

During this period Dreiser was also developing his talents as a writer of fiction. It is in his fiction from this period, rather than in the factual scientific articles that he was writing for magazines, that the cosmic Spencerian outlook that he had recently absorbed was most fully displayed. From the pages

of Huxley, Tyndall, Darwin, and Spencer, Dreiser had assimilated a materialistic interpretation of the universe and humanity that made emotional
and intellectual sense of the swirling changes, the human suffering, and the
great mysteries that Dreiser had confronted in recent years, more sense than
the dogmatic Christianity or genteel idealism that he had, at least consciously, rejected as useless relics. It was an interpretation that explained
human behavior in the context of the evolutionary universe, whose cosmic
processes of change dictated struggle and competition as the nature of all life
and survival and self-gratification as the goal of all conduct. It was not,
however, an entirely bleak interpretation of human existence and nature,
since, as Spencer had suggested, there was still the possibility for altruistic
behavior—for living beings to cooperate with one another in order to
triumph over the struggle inherent in life. Finally, it was an interpretation
that Dreiser passionately wanted to share with others, as was evidenced in
his *Ev'ry Month* essays. Dreiser's urge as an author to explain experience and
behavior in the light of the revolutionary ideas he had absorbed is certainly
one of the main factors that gives his fiction its artistic depth and establishes
him as an innovator in the American literary tradition.

Of the first four short stories that he wrote and sold during his early
career as a writer of fiction, the most revealing in terms of this evolutionary
orientation was his Spencerian allegory, "The Shining Slave Makers."[2] In
this fantasy the protagonist, McEwen, takes a seat in the shade of a large
tree in a city park on a hot summer afternoon. After thoughtlessly flicking
an ant from his trousers and stepping on it, he notices an entire community
of ants scurrying about on a path in front of him. Moments later, McEwen
finds himself transformed into a dream world of ants, himself a tiny black
ant in a jungle of grass. His behavior is immediately determined by an
instinctive, animal struggle to survive. Facing the threat of starvation, he
realizes quickly that each ant's quest for sustenance is solitary and even
selfish; in the famine-struck universe of the black ants, food is not shared
but is greedily guarded from others. A second threat, however, evokes the
ants' higher, more social instincts; when the colony is attacked by a horde
of red ants, McEwen experiences the communal self-sacrifice and friendship
of his black comrades at war. After suffering mortal wounds in the battle,
McEwen awakens from his dream, amazed and enlightened by his other-
worldly experience. As he crouches over the lawn for a final inspection of
the jungle he has just inhabited, he finds the battle still raging between the
two armies of ants:

> What a strange world! he thought. What worlds within worlds, all apparently
> full of necessity, contention, binding emotions and unities—and all with
> sorrow, their sorrow—a vague, sad something out of far-off things which had
> been there, and was here in this strong bright city day, had been there and
> would be here until this odd, strange thing called *life* had ended. (115)

McEwen is overcome by the realization that life at all levels is driven by
competition, both individual and group struggle, as well as by cooperation.

The Spencerian dimension of this allegory is partially obvious: survival
is the paramount instinct that drives life. Dreiser portrayed the actions of
McEwen and his fellow ants as compulsions arising from the instinct for
self-preservation, lacking contemplation or understanding. McEwen's desperate search for food is described as "a sense of duty, necessity, and a kind
of tribal obligation which he more felt than understood" (100). When he
encounters a fellow ant who has found the fortune of a huge crumb of food,
his plea for a share of the nourishment is menacingly rejected. The Spencerian lesson illustrated so clearly at the beginning of McEwen's dream is
that in the predatory world of the jungle, where survival of the fittest is the
primary, operative natural law, the primal determinant of behavior for the
beast is survival of the self.

Spencer, however, had also written about several more advanced levels
of behavior in *The Data of Ethics*. In the hierarchy of ethical conduct, he had
insisted, the highest grade of conduct was that which promoted the survival
of the larger society of which the individual was a member. In "The Shining
Slave Makers," Dreiser first presented a qualified example of this higher
level of conduct when McEwen reencounters the ant with the large crumb
of food. The ant now lies mortally wounded, crushed by a boulder. The
dying ant gives up its formerly precious possession to McEwen with the
words, "I am done for. . . . You may as well have this food now, since you
are one of us. The tribe can use what you do not eat" (102). Like the tycoon
who bequeaths his riches for the welfare of society, the dying ant passes his
fortune on to the tribe. But although the larger community benefits from
this action, both Spencer and Dreiser believed that this sort of conduct,
which did not really entail any great sacrifice, was not the highest possible
grade of ethical conduct, was not truly altruistic in nature. To hoard the
means of survival from others until the moment of death was exemplary
only of the primal instinct of self-maintenance; higher conduct entailed
sacrificing the means of individual survival for the welfare of the group.

In the latter part of the story, when McEwen's tribe is attacked by the
army of red ants, Dreiser constructed several incidents that illustrate this

loftier Spencerian conception of ethical behavior. When McEwen rescues another ant called Ermi from a vicious attack by four red ants, his behavior is still instinctive, "a feeling of tribal relationship which was overwhelming coming over him" (106), but the primal instinct to survive, "a horror of death," has now been overpowered by a social instinct to save his comrade. Later, driven by "an insane lust for battle" that is similarly instinctive and unthinking, McEwen participates in a raid by his colony on a group of red ants. It is in this battle that McEwen is mortally wounded, despite a heroic effort of self-sacrifice by Ermi to rescue his tribesman. Such actions by McEwen and Ermi, endangering their own survival in order to ensure the survival of a comrade, exemplified the pure sacrifice that both Dreiser and Spencer envisioned as the ultimate in cooperative or altruistic behavior.

"The Shining Slave Makers," then, is much more than a portrait of the brute patterns of "the struggle for existence" and "the survival of the fittest." It is an illustration of the cooperative behavior that Dreiser believed was a possible and even necessary component of conduct to overcome the struggle faced by all levels of existence. The element of sacrifice and cooperation for the benefit of the larger community in this story recalls the altruistic compassion for the weaker members of humanity that Dreiser had so often advocated in his *Ev'ry Month* meditations. In several "Reflections" columns devoted to the subject of the struggle for existence and "the law, cold, hard immutable—the law of self-preservation," Dreiser's pessimistic portrayal of the universe had been tempered by a call for charity and compassion for the weak: "all honor to him who fights bravest but with as much charity and as many tears as the dread of failure will permit." At times his rhetoric betrayed a still lingering element of Christian duty. He insisted, for example, that the "well balanced man, strong in body, sturdy in brain and of an equable temperament, is alive to the obligation so effectively implied in the Golden Rule."[3] This is the lesson that McEwen derives from his experience in the ant world; although natural law has fixed "contention" as the primary condition of existence, a higher law or "golden rule" also allows "binding emotions and unities."

The materialistic interpretation of ethical behavior that *The Data of Ethics* revealed to Dreiser, therefore, was importantly an interpretation that still gave sanction to "Christian brotherhood." This was significant because Dreiser's ethical outlook was still very much shaped by his Catholic up-bringing as well as by the call for Christian cooperation that he had more recently encountered and so much admired in the writing of Tolstoy.[4] In Spencer's evolutionary universe, God and the Ten Commandments were simply replaced with a more secularized imperative to love one's neighbor. The tension and drama inherent in each individual's attempt to act with charity and compassion toward others while functioning in a hostile universe that demanded self-preservation fascinated Dreiser at this stage of the development of his thought. The conflict of humanity's attempt to overcome the "beast" instinct of self-preservation and to evolve the higher "human" nature of social cooperation—in Spencerian terms, the conflict between egoism and altruism—is a theme that provides much of the intensity and depth to Dreiser's first novel, *Sister Carrie*.

*   *   *

It is well known that Carrie's story is partially based on the experience of Dreiser's sister, Emma, who in 1885 was seduced by L. A. Hopkins, a married man and cashier of Chapin and Gore's, a fashionable tavern in downtown Chicago. After the affair was discovered by his wife a year later, Hopkins stole $3,500 from his employers and fled with Emma briefly to Montreal and then to New York City, where Dreiser reestablished contact with his sister in 1894. Emma's seduction and Hopkins's theft, however, provided only a skeletal framework, around which Dreiser constructed a novel that bore little resemblance to his sister's adventures. Ellen Moers and Donald Pizer have identified many of the personal experiences as well as the fears and desires that Dreiser incorporated into his novel to deepen his characters, to devise a more dramatic narrative, and to give his characters feelings and thoughts that corresponded in many instances to his own.[5] A train ride on which he met his future wife, his initial awe of New York City, his envy of the conspicuous wealth he saw displayed on the city's streets and in the restaurants, his delight with the musical comedy of the Broadway stage, his journalistic experience in covering poverty, and his own fears of deteriorating into a Bowery bum were among the moments and moods that Dreiser molded into his novel.

The facet of *Sister Carrie* that I wish to consider in the following discussion is the Spencerian interpretation of human nature that Dreiser presents in the novel. The evolutionary view of humankind is most clearly presented in several passages in which Dreiser's narrative voice shifts into an omniscient point of view. This expository voice, similar to the all-knowing voice of the "Prophet" essays in *Ev'ry Month*, is didactic in tone, instructing readers about their evolutionary nature and the deterministic limitations of their species. Because the behavior and motivations of his characters are so often covert expressions of his cosmic outlook, these passages are extremely enlightening for the analyst of Dreiser's fiction in explaining the hidden forces driving his characters as well as Dreiser's overall philosophical outlook at the time that he wrote his fiction.

Dreiser's most explicit references to human evolution come rather early in the novel and at an important point in the narrative. Carrie has come to Chicago seeking a more adventurous and fulfilling life than the sedate, restricted existence she has lived with her parents in rural Wisconsin. For a brief time she boards with her sister Minnie and her husband Hanson, while she seeks and eventually begins employment as a factory girl. Shortly, however, the dreary atmosphere of the Hanson household and the physical and mental strain of her job lead her to accept the advances of Charles Drouet, a salesman whom she had met on her train ride to Chicago. Carrie disappears from the Hanson flat and is established by Drouet as his mistress, complete with a comfortably furnished apartment and many of the fashionable clothes she had craved while working in the factory. Presenting such shocking behavior by his heroine required great delicacy if Dreiser was not to offend the genteel, Victorian sensibilities of his audience. He struggled laboriously to maintain his readers' sympathy for Carrie, even stalling in his composition for two months after completing chapter 9 out of fear that his work thus far "was rotten."[6] His efforts resulted in a prolonged explanation of Carrie's instinctual compulsions that extends through three chapters. This portrait of Carrie's motivations displays the conception of the evolutionary nature of humanity that Dreiser had absorbed from his readings, and it corresponds completely with the hedonistic view of human behavior that he had found in Spencer.

At the beginning of chapter 8, at the very narrative moment when Carrie has just left the Hansons to become Drouet's mistress, the passage most revealing of Dreiser's evolutionary point of view appears:

> Among the forces which sweep and play throughout the universe, untutored man is but a wisp in the wind. Our civilization is still in a middle stage—scarcely beast, in that it is no longer wholly guided by instinct; scarcely human, in that it is not yet wholly guided by reason. On the tiger no responsibility rests. We see him aligned by nature with the forces of life—he is born into their keeping and without thought he is protected. We see man far removed out of the lairs of the jungles, his innate instincts dulled by too near an approach to free will, his free will scarcely sufficiently developed to replace his instincts and afford him perfect guidance. He is becoming too wise to hearken always to instincts and desires; he is still too weak to always prevail against them. As a beast, the forces of life aligned him with them; as a man, he

> has not yet learned to align himself with the forces. In this intermediate stage he wavers—neither drawn in harmony with nature by his instincts nor yet wisely putting himself into harmony by his own free will. He is even as a wisp in the wind, moved by every breath of passion, acting now by his will and now by his instincts, erring with one only to retrieve by the other, falling by one only to rise by the other—a creature of incalculable variability. We have the consolation of knowing that evolution is ever in action, that the ideal is a light that cannot fail. He will not forever balance thus between good and evil. When this jangle of free will and instinct shall have been adjusted, when perfect understanding has given the former the power to replace the latter entirely, man will no longer vary. The needle of understanding will yet point steadfast and unwavering to the distant pole of truth. (73)

This particular passage divides human evolution into a trinity of stages corresponding to the past, present and future natures of humankind. In the past, "man" was in the beast stage, driven by "instincts and desires" which compelled certain actions (just as in the tiger). Inherent behavioral commandments "guided," "protected," and "aligned" the beast with the "forces of life." In the future, "man" will achieve the human stage, an ideal, Spencerian summit of evolution in which "perfect understanding" will completely replace instinctual knowledge as the guide to behavior. Human reason will evolve new commandments that will guide, protect, and realign "man" in harmony with nature. In the present, *Homo sapiens* is in a beast-human stage, at times compelled by the animal commands of its past nature, at times free to follow the moral commands that reason has evolved. The warring elements of instinct and free will in the beast-human have made the individual a confused, wavering "wisp in the wind."

Within this lecture on evolution, Dreiser also introduces a somewhat covert discussion of ethics whose ultimate purpose is to sustain the reader's sympathy for Carrie at the narrative moment when she surrenders her virtue to Drouet. The ethical dimension of the passage is curiously introduced when Dreiser asserts that the beast-human of the present stage is balanced "between good and evil." Dreiser implicitly associates evil with the actions of the beast, although the beast itself is free of responsibility since all behavior follows the commandments of the instincts. That instinctual behavior, however, is aligned with "the forces of life," a vague phrase that Dreiser leaves undefined and that seems to have a dual meaning. The "forces of life" with which the beast finds itself aligned would seem to be interchangeable with the phrase "natural law," and, as Dreiser had learned from his reading of Darwin and Spencer, the fundamental law of biological evolution was "survival of the fittest." Self-preservation was the law of the jungle, and the ultimate commandment of the beast's instincts was "thou shalt do whatever is necessary to survive." The behavior of the beast, therefore, was selfish, at times brutal, and, as seen from the more highly evolved commandments of human reason, "evil." Dreiser associates "good" with behavior guided by reason, a still evolving faculty in the beast-human of the present. In the ideal human stage of the distant future, reason will fully replace instinct in guiding, protecting, and aligning humans with "the forces of life." Once again the vagueness of the term "forces of life" is problematic, because the passage seems to imply that the "forces of life" by which civilization is regulated are different from those of the jungle. Although it is left unstated at this point in the novel, later developments and discussion in *Sister Carrie* indicate that Dreiser believed that those "forces of life" that guide the civilized human are the higher instincts that evoke altruistic conduct. The higher commandment evolved by human reason is "thou shalt do unto others as you would have them do unto you." In Dreiser's ideal vision of the ultimate moral evolution, as in Spencer's, self-gratification will be replaced by selflessness; altruism will replace egoism.

In addition to the obvious evolutionary material and the more covert lecture on Spencerian ethics, there is a third subject introduced into the passage that is more troublesome to analyze: the subject of free will. Dreiser discusses free will as a steadily increasing human faculty as evolution proceeds beyond the beast, stating that "perfect understanding" will give "the former [free will] the power to replace the latter [instinct]." Although Dreiser asserts that the development of free will is progressing at the present stage of evolution, his description of human behavior in the future is very deterministic in tone. The compass "needle of understanding" can point in only one direction, although Dreiser seems to take comfort that it points toward the magnetic "pole of truth." Nevertheless, when "[man] wisely [puts] himself into harmony with nature by free will," when "man will no longer vary," he will, in effect, surrender free will and submit to the forces of life. The primal instinct of self-preservation will merely give way to a higher instinct of altruistic self-sacrifice. By giving up choice in order to pursue the ideal moral truth that will eventually be recognized, the human will simply return to the same controlled state of being as the beast; the jungle may blossom into civilization, but it will still be the same determined universe of forces. This fuzzy, here-today-gone-tomorrow conception of free will that Dreiser ascribes to the beast-human in the present stage of evolution suggests that the author himself was uncertain and perhaps altering his thoughts on the subject. Certainly his later fiction and philosophical writing reveal an intense rejection of the notion of free choice. The present passage could simply be an indication that a vestige of the Roman Catholic belief in the doctrine of free will was still trying to maintain itself amid Dreiser's newly acquired deterministic point of view.

While the passage discussed above reveals several dimensions of Dreiser's philosophical thought, it is also important to recall why the author inserted this lesson on human biological and moral development into the novel at this point, just when Carrie has submitted to Drouet's advances and allowed herself to become his mistress. In Dreiser's next paragraph, he narrows the focus of his philosophical lecture on evolution to his protagonist:

> In Carrie, as in how many of our worldlings do they not, instinct and reason, desire and understanding warred for the mastery. In Carrie, as in how many of our worldlings are they not, instinct and desire were yet in part the victors. She followed whither her craving led. She was as yet more drawn than she drew. (73–74)

The author has here given the reader insight into Carrie's behavior thus far in the novel, while at the same time issuing a plea for sympathy for his heroine. By describing Carrie as "yet more drawn than she drew," Dreiser warns that in the battle between instinct and reason, between self-gratification and selflessness, between egoism and altruism, the reader must expect Carrie to be dominated by the beast side of her personality. Carrie's behavior, like that of the tiger, is regrettable, but she herself should not be judged as evil. By admitting that a higher code of behavior exists, Dreiser attempted to placate the moral sensibilities of his genteel turn-of-the century readers, while at the same time struggling to maintain an affinity between his audience and his heroine, who "as in how many of our worldlings" is compelled to follow her cravings.

These paragraphs provide a pseudo-psychological explanation of the rather selfish yearnings for self-gratification that Carrie exhibits on nearly every page of the previous seven chapters. As we first meet Carrie parting from her parents, the author informs us, "Self-interest with her was high, but not strong. It was nevertheless her guiding characteristic" (4). The mere mention by Drouet of several merchant stores during his encounter with Carrie on the train arouses "memories of longings the displays in the latter's establishment had cost her" (7). During Carrie's first visit to a Chicago department store, she is overwhelmed by desires for material possessions:

Each separate counter was a show place of dazzling interest and attraction. She could not help feeling the claim of each trinket and valuable upon her personally and yet she did not stop. There was nothing there which she could not have used—nothing which she did not long to own. The dainty slippers and stockings, the delicately frilled skirts and petticoats, the laces, ribbons, haircombs, purses, all touched her with individual desire. (22)

Before she has worked a single day, she has mentally spent many times over her first weekly four-fifty in earnings:

Portions of its fullness were passed over every counter and broken in small change a thousand times, and yet it did not fail. Silks, woolens, lingerie and fine feathers—the necessities and frivolities of fashion as she understood it—all strained its marketing power, but it did not break. . . . The lights, the tinkle of car bells, the late murmur of the city, bespoke its power to her. "I will have a fine time," she thought to herself over and over and over. (30)

In one of his Prophet-like philosophical speculations, Dreiser paradoxically bemoans the baseness of Carrie's consumer desires while explaining the high emotional value of the objects for one at Carrie's instinctual stage of evolution:

Your bright-eyed, rosy-cheeked maiden . . . may reasonably be dead to every evidence of the artistic and poetic in the unrelated evidences of life, and yet not lack in material appreciation. Never, it might be said, does she fail in this. With her the bloom of a rose may pass unappreciated, but the bloom of a fold of silk, never. If nothing in the heavens, or the earth, or the waters, could elicit her fancy or delight her from its spiritual or artistic side, think not that the material would be lost. The glint of a buckle, the hue of a precious stone, the faintest tints of the watered silk, these she would devine [sic] and qualify as readily as your poet if not more so . . . if not because of some fashionable or hearsay quality, then on account of their true beauty, their innate fitness in any order of harmony, their place in the magical order and sequence of dress. (23)

Carrie's self-centered acquisitiveness, like her fall from virtue, is indeed regrettable, but Dreiser urges his readers to understand that it is inevitable in a primitively developed personality dominated by the selfish instincts of the beast rather than the altruistic intellect of the human.

Dreiser provides further rationalization for Carrie's fall in the crucial chapter 8 by explaining that her conscience is underdeveloped. "There was no household law to govern her now," he explains. "Carrie had no excellent home principles fixed upon her. If she had she would have been more consciously distressed" (77–78). Dreiser suggests here that for the instinctual beast-human, not possessed of the higher moral enlightenment that flows from reason, an ethical code of conduct may still be learned; the conscience, as he defines it here, is a matrix of learned behavioral compulsions, as opposed to the innate compulsions of instinct:

> Habits are peculiar things. They will drive the really non-religious mind out of bed to say prayers that are only a custom and not a devotion. The victim of habit, when he has neglected the thing which was customary with him to do, feels a little scratching in the brain, a little irritating something which comes of being out of the rut, and imagines it to be the prick of conscience, the still, small voice that is urging him ever to righteousness. If the digression is unusual enough, the drag of habit will be heavy enough and the unreasoning victim will return and perform the perfunctory thing. "Now, bless me," says such a mind, "I have done my duty," when as a matter of fact it has merely done its old unbreakable trick once again. (77–78)

This passage is interesting not only because it reflects Dreiser's anti-spiritual, materialistic conception of conscience but also because once again he is deflecting responsibility away from his heroine. Through no fault of her own, through some oversight in her ethical upbringing, Carrie has not gained the moral strength to resist Drouet's advances. Because the learned, habitual compulsions of conscience are lacking, the innate compulsions of instinct dominate. As Carrie comes under the spell of "the fine invisible passion that was emanating from Drouet, the food, [and] the still unusual luxury" at their after-theater, pre-seduction dinner, her instinctual desires for comfort, fashion, and security are heightened by the inscrutable forces of her environment:

> She was again the victim of the city's hypnotic influence, the subject of the mesmeric operations of super-intelligible forces. We have heard of the strange power of Niagara, the contemplation of whose rushing flood leads to thoughts of dissolution. We have heard of the influence of the hypnotic ball, a scientific fact. Man is too intimate with the drag of unexplainable, invisible forces to doubt longer that the human mind is colored, moved, swept on by things which neither resound nor speak. The waters of the sea are not the only things which the moon sways. All that the individual imagines in contemplating a dazzling, alluring, or disturbing spectacle is created more by the spectacle than the mind observing it. These strange, insensible inflowings which alternate, reform, dissolve, are, we are beginning to see, foreshadowing the solution of Shakespeare's mystic line, "There are more things in heaven and earth, Horatio, than are dreamt of in your philosophy." We are, after all, more passive than active, more mirrors than engines, and the origin of human action has neither yet been measured nor calculated. (78)

At the crucial moment when the habitual force of conscience could still save her virtue ("If any habits had ever had time to fix upon her, they would have operated here"), the meager resistance of her conscience cannot overcome the inertia of her inner instinctive forces and the mysterious attractive forces of her outer environment.

Carrie's seducer, Drouet, is similarly portrayed as at the mercy of determining forces: instinct still predominates over reason in him as well. Drouet possesses "a mind free of any consideration of the problems or forces of the world and actuated not by greed but an insatiable love of variable pleasure—woman—pleasure" (6). Dreiser deflects responsibility from Drouet, thereby hoping to maintain the reader's sympathy, by portraying him in much the same mold as Carrie. Drouet's instinctual desire for women parallels Carrie's instinctual desire for fashion and comfort. "He loved to make advances to women, to have them succumb to his charms, not because he was a cold-blooded, dark, scheming villain, but because his inborn desire urged him to that as a chief delight" (63). And like Carrie, he is capable of "no speculation, no philosophizing" that would inform or guide the action of a man of reason. "He had no mental process in him worthy the dignity of either of those terms. In his good clothes and fine health he was a merry, unthinking moth of the lamp" (63). Like Carrie, Drouet possesses an underdeveloped conscience, and so there are no habitual moral compulsions to interfere with his pleasure-seeking nature:

> That worthy had his future fixed for him beyond a peradventure. He could not help what he was going to do. He could not see clearly enough to wish to do differently. He was drawn by his innate desire to act the old pursuing part. He would need to delight himself with Carrie as surely as he would need to eat his heavy breakfast. He might suffer the least rudimentary twinge of conscience in whatever he did, and in just so far he was evil and sinning. But whatever twinges of conscience he might have *would be* rudimentary, you may be sure. (75)

Dreiser's most straightforward comparison of Drouet and Carrie's identical natures is that "deprived of his position and struck by a few of the involved and baffling forces which sometimes play upon man, he would have been as helpless as Carrie—as helpless, as non-understanding, as pitiable, if you will, as she" (63).

When Dreiser resumed writing his novel after his two-month pause, he picked up at chapter 10. He must have felt that his explanation of Carrie's behavior thus far needed further amplification, because half of that chapter is devoted to a further examination of the ethical dilemma arising from Carrie's submission to Drouet:

> In the light of the world's attitude toward woman and her duties, the nature of Carrie's mental state deserves consideration. Actions such as hers are measured by an arbitrary scale. Society possesses a conventional standard whereby it judges all things. All men should be good, all women virtuous. Wherefore, villain, hast thou failed! (87)

Dreiser suggests here that a mere condemnation of Carrie based on the conventional or arbitrary scale of morality would be an inadequate response to her behavior. In considering Carrie's actions and the motives behind them, conventional religious ethics are simply lacking. In the immediately following passage, however, Dreiser also belittles the "liberal," evolutionary conception of morals that would judge behavior only in terms of its survival value: "For all the liberal analysis of Spencer and our modern naturalistic philosophers we have but an infantile perception of morals. There is more in it than mere conformity to a law of evolution. It is yet deeper than conformity to things of earth alone" (87–88).

Dreiser's perception of the "unknowable" creeps into this passage. He implies that the determinants of human behavior emanate from inscrutable, immaterial forces beyond the understanding of scientific analysis. Carrie's actions are driven by a more subtle, inexplicable goal than mere survival:

> It is more involved than we as yet perceive. Answer first why the heart thrills, explain wherefore some plaintive note goes wandering about the world undying, make clear the rose's subtle alchemy, evolving its ruddy lamp in light and rain. In the essence of these facts lie the first principles of morals. . . . Before this world-old proposition we stand, serious, interested, confused; endeavoring to evolve the true theory of morals—the true answer to what is right. (88)

Dreiser suggests cryptically here and more directly in the following paragraphs that Carrie's surrender to Drouet is motivated not so much by survival as by the desire for beauty, pleasure, and comfort. And yet Herbert Spencer's interpretation of human behavior was precisely this same interpretation that Dreiser was now developing for Carrie. Spencer had declared pleasure as the ultimate goal of all human conduct and had built an evolutionary rationale for pronouncing pleasure seeking morally good. Rather than rejecting Spencerian ethics, Dreiser was merely shifting emphasis here from the scientific and evolutionary foundations of Spencer's theories to the mysterious, hedonistic aspect of his philosophy.

In her new environment Carrie becomes "comfortably established—in the eyes of the starveling beaten by every wind and gusty sheet of rain, she was safe in a halcyon harbor." Dreiser paints Carrie's apartment in words that project comfort, beauty, and warmth. Her apartment faces Union Park, "a little, green-carpeted breathing spot" that is "a vista pleasant to contemplate." The rooms are "comfortably enough furnished," and the flat is "cozy in that it was lighted by gas and heated by furnace registers . . . a method of cheerful warming." When she looks into her mirror, the reflection now reveals "a prettier Carrie there than she had seen before." All in all, Carrie has been established in her Ogden Place flat "in a pleasant fashion, free of certain difficulties which most ominously confronted her" (88–89). The more complex goal of human behavior, which Dreiser cryptically suggested several paragraphs earlier, now becomes more visible. Beyond mere survival, human behavior is motivated to achieve comfort, beauty, and warmth. Life is the fundamental goal of the beast, but the good life is the higher goal of the human being. Only at this higher level of existence can one appreciate the finer experiences of life, the thrill of a "plaintive note" of music or the beauty of a rose.

In the immediately following debate between Carrie and her under-developed conscience ("only an average little conscience, a thing which represented the world, her past environment, habit, convention, in a confused, reflected way" [89]), Dreiser explores this conception of behavior further. Carrie's conscience chastises her in the voice of convention: "Look at those who are good. How would they scorn to do what you have done. Look at the good girls, how will they draw away from such as you, when they know you have been weak. You had not tried before you failed" (89–90). Her conscience, however, is "never wholly convincing" because

> there was always an answer. Always the December days threatened. She was alone; she was desireful; she was fearful of the whistling wind. The voice of want made answer for her.
>
> We do not make sufficient allowance for the natural elements in our philosophy. Our logic is bare of the voice of the wind. How potent is the answer a pang of hunger makes to the cry, "Be good." How subtle is the influence of a dreary atmosphere. (90)

Interrupting this debate between the voice of Carrie's conscience and the voice of Carrie's want, Dreiser juxtaposes a description of the passing of summer's warmth and the arrival of the cold, windy, cheerless days of winter. The subtle influence of winter's "dreary atmosphere," Dreiser asserts, is a compulsion to seek even greater comfort, beauty, and warmth as substitutes for the diminished light and warmth of the sun:

> If it were not for the artificial fires of merriment, the rush of profit-seeking trade and pleasure-selling amusements; if the various merchants failed to make the customary displays within and without their establishments; if our streets were not strung with signs of gorgeous hues and thronged with hurrying purchasers, we would quickly discover how firmly the chill hand of winter lays upon the heart;—how dispiriting are the days during which the sun withholds a portion of our allowance of light and warmth. We are more dependent upon these things than is often thought for. We are insects produced by heat and wither and pass without it. (90–91)

When the voice of Carrie's conscience then condemns her as a "dawdler" and "lingerer in the lap of ease," Carrie retorts, "No. . . . What else could I do? I was so bad off. Where could I have gone? Not home again—oh, I did not want to go there. I was in danger of being hungry. I had no clothes. Didn't I try?" (91). Carrie's conscience would have her either return home to her parents or return to the life of a factory girl. Both options would allow her to survive, but only marginally. Carrie evaluates and balances the good and bad resulting from the life lived along the natural, instinctive lines of the pursuit of pleasure (a life sometimes condemned by conventional morals) and the life led along lines of an artificial, conventional morality (a life sometimes leading to an ascetic-like poverty). Which life was truly ethical, and which life was truly evil?

> Thus would she sway, thus would all men, similarly equipped, between this truth and that evil—between this right and that wrong. It is all a weighing of advantage. And whoso is it so noble as to ever avoid evil, and who so wise that he moves ever in the direction of truth? (91)

Just as Dreiser had earlier rejected survival as the sole criterion in evaluating behavior, at the end of her inner debate Carrie rejects those options that would allow mere survival.

Dreiser introduces yet another discussion of Carrie's motivations in chapter 11. He explains that Carrie's desires are not merely longings for material possessions in themselves, but longings for the more immaterial status or prestige that are suggested by the objects. "We are most wholly controlled by desire," he reasserts, but "the things that appeal to desire are not always visible objects." The more subtle ideals of style, refinement and elegance enter Carrie's awareness as she begins for the first time to recognize the "strikingly different way of living" implied in "fine clothes, rich foods, superior residences" (97). Once she has become aware of the invisible associations of superior status that are contained in material possessions, it is no longer the acquisitions themselves or even the fear of poverty that are the primary motivations of her conduct; it is rather her compulsion to appear superior, or, in the more converse terms suggested by Dreiser's description, it is her repulsion from the appearance of poverty that drives her:

> Once these things were in her hand, on her person, she might dream of giving them up. . . . She could possibly have conquered the fear of hunger and gone back; the thought of hard work and a narrow round of suffering would, under the last pressure of conscience, have yielded—but spoil her appearance—be old-clothed and poor-appearing—never. (98–99)

Immediately following Dreiser's reflections on Carrie's status drive, her attraction to George Hurstwood begins to develop. Carrie's longing for the refinement and elegance of higher position are clearly what attracts her to the manager and host of Hannah and Hogg's saloon (Fitzgerald and Moy's in the printed edition). Hurstwood's occupation has given him an air of refinement and superiority that allows him to converse with the more well-to-do patrons of the saloon, and when Carrie first meets him, she is attracted to all the trappings of success that he possesses: "his fine clothes, his clean linen, his jewels, and, above all, his own sense of his importance" (43). She quickly senses higher, ideal qualities in Hurstwood that Drouet lacks:

> It was driven into Carrie's mind that here was the superior man. She instinctively felt that he was stronger and higher and yet withal so simple. . . . She was sure that Drouet was only a kindly soul but otherwise defective. He sank every moment in her estimation by the strong comparison. (110)

Dreiser contrasts the material fulfillment offered by Drouet and the superior, ideal fulfillment offered by Hurstwood in the two moments when each man first touches Carrie's hand. When Drouet takes Carrie's hand at the conclusion of their first dinner, he presses two ten-dollar bills into it, symbolic of the very material relationship they will soon develop. When Hurstwood shakes Carrie's hand at the conclusion of an evening at the opera, the mere touch of this man whom she has idealized as the embodiment of refinement and superiority causes Carrie to sense "some feelable current [sweeping] from one to the other" (110). Dreiser also symbolically suggests the contrast between the material and the ideal in the men's very occupations: Drouet, a "drummer," sells material objects for a living, while

Hurstwood sells his charm and sociability. Drawn uncontrollably to Hurstwood's appearance of superior social position, Carrie soon switches her affection to the embodiment of her rising status dreams.

By the end of this chapter, Dreiser has completed his three-chapter explanation of the motivations that underlie his heroine's behavior. In chapter 8, where his primary concern was to explain and excuse Carrie's seduction, Dreiser relies heavily on an interpretation of evolutionary theory to portray Carrie as a less developed specimen on the scale of human evolution, unguided by reason but compelled to follow the instinct to do whatever is necessary to survive. In chapter 10 where he describes Carrie's life as Drouet's mistress, his explanation shifts into a more hedonistic direction; admitting that Carrie's survival was never really in danger, he now explains her behavior as a pursuit for material comfort. In chapter 11 where Dreiser prepares the narrative turning point of Carrie's stronger attraction to Hurstwood, her behavior is explained as a less material, more ideal quest for position and status. In these three chapters, Dreiser has constructed a triple-leveled hierarchy of human motivation, positing survival, comfort, and status as the three ends that drive human behavior. Each of the three levels of motivation are variants of the egoistic self-gratification that Spencer maintained was the fundamental goal of all conduct.

Dreiser's own desires for comfort, position, and success in both career and sexual matters, as already mentioned in Chapter 1, were very strong throughout his life. Carrie's personality was at least partially drawn from those hedonistic tendencies in her creator. The Spencerian diagnosis of her character, therefore, reveals more than Dreiser's philosophical and quasi-psychological attempt to limit responsibility and lift guilt from his heroine. In explaining the egoistic instincts and hedonistic drives behind Carrie's behavior, Dreiser was examining his own impulses toward self-gratification and interpreting his own existence within the evolutionary universe of Herbert Spencer. This is not to assert that Dreiser portrayed Carrie as a mirror of his own personality or that he fully endorsed her rather unthinking, selfish behavior. For, as we saw earlier, his Catholic upbringing, his reading of Tolstoy, and his awareness of Spencer's ennobling of altruistic behavior had led him to conclude that although egoism was the primal determinant of all conduct, more highly developed humans were guided by reason and acted to serve the greater community as well as themselves. Dreiser's advocacy of higher ethical behavior, whether it be termed "Christian brotherhood" or the "evolutionary triumph of cooperation over competition," caused him to take a more critical attitude toward Carrie in the closing chapters of the novel.

In the second half of the novel, after Hurstwood's theft forces him and Carrie to flee to New York, Dreiser introduces the character Bob Ames. Ames is clearly superior in intellect to any man who has affected Carrie's life thus far. The conversations between Carrie and Ames touch on literature, the theater, philosophy, and ethics. Ames's occupation as an electrical inventor or engineer suggests that the latest scientific theories and knowledge are also within his mental grasp.[7] Ames is the embodiment of the third level of "man's" evolution, the human stage, which Dreiser had described in his earlier lecture on evolutionary development. He is the man guided by reason, whose conversations with Carrie bring the self-centered behavior and shallow existence of Dreiser's heroine into clear contrast.

Ames appears twice in the second half of the novel. His first appearance comes in chapter 35, when Carrie accompanies her well-to-do neighbors, the Vances, and their western "Cousin Bob" to dinner at Sherry's, a lavish restaurant whose extravagant show of wealth impresses and attracts Carrie at first. Ames, however, is critical of the wasteful display surrounding them. "I sometimes think it's a shame for people to spend so much money this way," he declares. "They pay so much more than these things are worth. They put on so much show" (333–34). Carrie is surprised by this dismissal of all that she admires, but she begins to develop a fond respect for the opinions of this superior but modest man. Her curiosity grows when Ames spurns *The Opening of a Chestnut Burr* and *Dora Thorne*, two popular genteel novels high in Carrie's estimation. She begins to sense that "this man was far ahead of her. He seemed wiser than Hurstwood, saner and wiser than Drouet" (335). She recognizes Ames's inner strength and happiness after he declares, "I shouldn't care to be rich, . . . not rich enough to spend my money this way. . . . A man doesn't need this sort of thing to be happy" (335–36). Ames has a profound effect in upsetting Carrie's desires for status and wealth. She begins to detect a "new attitude forcing itself distinctly upon her for the first time" (335). She senses that Ames's life is one of complete fulfillment, and that his fulfillment is far removed from the material possessions and status that have been her primary motivation. She is troubled when she returns home to Hurstwood that evening and reviews Ames's conversation in her rocking chair. "Through a fog of longing and conflicting desires, she was beginning to see. Oh, ye legions of hope and pity—of sorrow and pain. She was rocking and beginning to see" (337). What Carrie begins to understand is that there is a possibility of fulfillment higher than the self-fulfillment that she has pursued throughout her life.

The nature of that fulfillment becomes clearer in Carrie's second encounter with Ames, years later, after she has achieved success, wealth, and status on the Broadway and London musical stage. At yet another dinner with the Vances, Carrie proudly announces to Ames that she has been reading Hardy and Balzac, authors whom Ames had recommended to her at their previous meeting. In the pursuant discussion of Balzac, Ames expounds his own ideas on the nature of true fulfillment:

> "If a man doesn't make knowledge his object, he's very likely to fail. . . . It's the man who fails in his mind who fails completely. Some people get the idea that their happiness lies in wealth and position. Balzac thought so, I believe. Many people do. They look about and wring their hands over every passing vision of joy. They forget that if they had that, they couldn't have something else. . . . Your happiness is within yourself wholly if you will only believe it," he went on. "When I was quite young I felt as if I were ill-used because other boys were dressed better than I was, were more sprightly with the girls than I, and I grieved and grieved, but now I'm over that. I have found out that everyone is more or less dissatisfied. No one has exactly what his heart wishes. . . . It comes down to this," he went on. "If you have powers, cultivate them. The work of doing it will bring you as much satisfaction as you will ever get. The huzzas of the public don't mean anything. That's the aftermath—you've been paid and satisfied if you are not selfish and greedy long before that reaches you." (482–83)

Carrie is deeply disturbed by Ames's assertions, for she recognizes herself in his description of the unfulfilled life. She has sought true happiness through wealth and position and has pursued her career in the musical theater to attain the "huzzas of the public," and yet Ames seems to be dismissing both the status and the acclaim that she has achieved. Ames suggests to Carrie that she could still find higher fulfillment and deeper happiness by using her gifts to pursue success in the more serious theatrical world of comedy-drama. The true artist, he declares, does not seek acclaim from the masses, but strives to serve the masses:

> "The world is always struggling to express itself—to make clear its hopes and sorrows and give them voice. It is always seeking the means, and it will delight in the individual who can express these things for it. That is why we have great musicians, great painters, great writers and actors. They have the ability to express the world's sorrows and longings, and the world gets up and shouts their names. . . . You and I are but mediums, through which something is expressing itself. Now, our duty is to make ourselves ready mediums. . . . You must help the world express itself. Use will make your powers endure. I should say turn to the dramatic field. You have so much sympathy and such a melodious voice—make them valuable to others. You will have them so long as they express something in you. You can preserve and increase them longer by using them for others. The moment you forget their value to the world, and

they cease to represent your own aspirations, they will begin to fade. . . . You can't become self-interested, selfish and luxurious, without having these sympathies and longings disappear, and then you will sit there and wonder what has become of them. You can't remain tender and sympathetic, and desire to serve the world, without having it show in your face and your art. If you want to do most, do good. Serve the many. Be kind and humanitarian. Then you can't help but be great." (485–86)

Ames's description of the role of the artist reveals once again Dreiser's vision of the conflict between egoism and altruism, and it displays the Spencerian ethical notion that the highest form of conduct, attainable only by the more highly evolved person of reason, transcends primitive, self-serving conduct. The description by Ames is Dreiser's own declaration of artistic purpose; it is a statement of self-definition. Like Carrie, Dreiser had followed his hedonistic tendencies and had pursued wealth and fame. Now, however, using Ames as his spokesman, Dreiser declares his higher goal of serving the masses, of allowing himself to become the "ready medium" of expression for the longing, the frustration, and the tragedy of humanity, of cultivating his powers as an artist through the novel that he would present to the world. The inner conflict between egoism and altruism, between the beast and the human of his own personality, would continue in his private life, but at his writing table, Dreiser defined himself as the man of reason who had overcome his instincts of self-gratification, the artist who dedicated himself and struggled to serve his audience of confused and frustrated readers.

Dreiser leaves Carrie's future path in ambiguity. Certainly she gives great consideration to Ames's suggestion that she become a serious actress and cultivate more altruistic goals. She ponders this "solution being offered her. Not money. . . . Not clothes. . . . Not applause—not even that—but goodness—labor for others" (486). Even Ames perceives that his advice has awakened a more "perfect Carrie in mind and body, because now her mind was aroused" (485), indicating that, for the moment at least, reason is challenging instinct. As he makes his final farewell to Carrie, Ames now senses in her "something which craved neither money nor praise" (487). In the famous conclusion, however, where the omniscient narrator describes the newly awakened frustration and longing in Carrie's soul after her parting from Ames, Dreiser suggests that Carrie is destined never to find true happiness or fulfillment:

She felt very much alone, very much as if she were struggling hopelessly and unaided, as if such a man as he would never care to draw nearer. All her nature was stirred to unrest now. She was already the old, mournful Carrie—the desireful Carrie,—unsatisfied.

Oh, blind strivings of the human heart. Onward, onward it saith, and where beauty leads, there it follows. Whether it be the tinkle of a lone sheep bell o'er some quiet landscape, or the glimmer of beauty in sylvan places, or the show of soul in some passing eyes, the heart knows and makes answer, following. It is when the feet weary in pursuit and hope is vain that the heartaches and longings rise.

Carrie! Oh Carrie! ever whole in that thou art ever hopeful, know that the light is but now in these his eyes. Tomorrow it shall be melted and dissolved. Tomorrow it shall be on and further on, still leading, still alluring, until thought is not with you and heartaches are no more. (487)

The final paragraph in this ornate burst of romantic melancholy suggests that Carrie's desire to attain the fulfillment of a true artist is temporary. The "light" that Ames has given Carrie will fade in time "until thought is not with you." Carrie's momentary inspiration to serve will dissolve, and her "guiding characteristic" of self-interest will continue to rule. The instincts of the beast-human will predominate in her.

The tragedy of Carrie's character, then, is not in the loss of her virtue to Drouet or in her willingness to be seduced by the married Hurstwood. Dreiser did not punish his heroine with a horrible death, crippling disability, or tragic failure as the genteel formulas of the day demanded. Carrie's willing seductions were merely the fulfillment of the instincts of her lower evolutionary nature. Her tragedy lies rather in the limitations of her nature. Carrie is advanced enough both to recognize the higher fulfillment of Ames's altruistic ideals and to find them appealing, but because self-interest is the paramount compulsion of the beast, she is incapable of surmounting those limitations of her lower nature. Dreiser's heroine is a prisoner of biological determinism.

Carrie's misery at the end of the novel is subtle and abstruse. Those genteel readers who focused on Carrie's theatrical achievements and material success and who were unaffected by the more subtle tragedy of her unfulfilled longings in the final pages were bound to be outraged at Dreiser's failure to construct a more calamitous downfall for his immoral heroine.[8] The fate of her married seducer Hurstwood, however, has all the cathartic satisfaction necessary for the reader who demanded doom for violators of the moral code. Hurstwood's slide from respectable, middle class host to saloon keeper to strikebreaker to penniless beggar to Bowery suicide inversely parallels the path of Carrie's rise from factory girl to successful musical comedy actress. Like Carrie's, his fate is determined by his biological nature, but unlike Carrie, Hurstwood is never clearly defined in evolutionary terms. While his fall is, like Carrie's limitations, portrayed at least partially as the result of biological determinism, the fatal flaw is not evolutionary in nature, but chemical. In order to cloak Hurstwood's disintegration in the guise of scientific realism, Dreiser relied not on his great master, Herbert Spencer, but on quite another source.

Dreiser had briefly encountered the physico-chemical interpretation of life and behavior that characterized late-19th-century mechanistic science in Spencer's *First Principles*. His first in-depth exposure to mechanistic thought, however, as well as the origin of the peculiar chemical explanation of Hurstwood's downfall, was derived from a timely meeting with a researcher of the chemical nature of the mind, Elmer Gates. Dreiser first met Gates at his suburban Washington "Laboratory of Psychology and Psychurgy" in February 1900, to interview "our foremost American investigator" for an article for *Pearson's*. Gates made a great impression on Dreiser, not only because of his research on the chemical nature of the mind but because he was the first scientist whom the writer met with whom he could observe and discuss the practice of science. Gates would come to be regarded by Dreiser as one of "the great mental leaders upon whose periodic appearance the advancement of thought depends."[9]

Gates's laboratory, "an institution devoted to the science of mind and its practical application," had been constructed in Chevy Chase, Maryland from the money that he had raised from a number of unusual and suspicious inventions. Among Gates's contrivances was an electrical device that allegedly could extract perfume from flowers, enabling the user to "turn a pint of water into rose water in 6 seconds." He also supposedly developed a new advance in microscopy, with which he claimed "the power of the eye is increased 3,000,000 times instead of 10,000 times, as hitherto." In yet another project, Gates was striving to extract all current scientific knowledge from books and journals to be assembled eventually in "a scientific Bible"; such a collection would be regarded as holy, he claimed, for "what is more sacred than truth, and what more satanic than falsehood."[10] These inventions and projects, however, were merely the means by which Gates secured the funding for his more important scientific research on the mind.

Gates's study of mental processes was carried out with the conviction that the mind "is not a spiritual, but a physical mechanism." "Every conscious mental experience," he asserted, "causes, by its functional activity in some definite part of the brain a series of distinct structural and chemical changes." He claimed that every sensory experience caused the deposit of chemicals in certain brain cells, and that the repetition of a sensory stimulus eventually caused "a sense-memory structure" to develop from these deposits. The resulting structures tended to cause the brain cells in the surrounding area to multiply. Gates based his claims on experiments in which he taught dogs to distinguish among a number of colors. In subsequent autopsies of these dogs, he contended that in "the occipital areas of the brain I found a far greater number of brain cells than any animal of like breed ever possessed." Gates' seeming ignorance that dogs are color blind was a crucial oversight in his method, but he, nevertheless, claimed that his experiments served "to demonstrate the fact that more brains can be given to an animal, or a human being, in consequence of a better use of mental faculties." In further experiments, Gates trained several generations of guinea pigs "in the use of the visual faculty" and discovered that "the children of the fourth generation were born with a greater number of brain cells in the seeing areas than other guinea pigs that had not been thus trained." From this experiment he concluded that "mental activity creates in organisms certain structures transmissible to their offspring." Ignoring the growing scientific consensus that "acquired characteristics" such as his "sense-memory structures" were not inherited by succeeding generations, Gates declared that his experiments had immense implications for the future of humanity:

> The demonstration that mental activity creates structure places the matter of evolution largely in our hands to direct and augment it. . . . Henceforward man can take the Archimedian lever of progress in his own hands (or brains) by directly augmenting the fundamental cause of evolution and progress,— getting more mind, and learning how to utilize it. Mind is at once the cause and the end of progress—the method and the goal.[11]

Dreiser was particularly interested in Gates's conclusions regarding the chemical effects of emotions on the mind. Gates claimed that negative emotions produced harmful chemicals that could damage the brain's "sense-memory structures." "The evil emotions produce *cacastates*, and the good and agreeable emotions produce *eunastates*,—the former are life-destroying and the latter are life-augmenting. Right and wrong has a chemical basis and criterion."[12] In the process of "brain-building" it was therefore necessary for one to avoid all situations that caused "irascible, malevolent, and depressing emotions" and to pursue a tranquil, trouble-free life of happiness and moral behavior. When his wife became pregnant, Gates applied his theories about the transmitting "sense-memory structures" to his own future offspring. He instructed his wife to avoid "all evil passions, anger, envy, etc., and [to cultivate] good emotions, social and altruistic instincts, art, literature, dramas, the sublime in nature, heavens, the spirit of the cosmos, etc." As a result of this prenatal regimen, Gates claimed that his son was born with a greater than normal mental capacity; the child "at the age of 21 months, he says, knew 11,000 words."[13]

Dreiser was impressed by Gates's research, and the two became close friends, corresponding for the next ten years and discussing matters of science and literature that touched on their mutual interests. When Dreiser informed Gates that he wanted to write an article about his research, Gates cooperated by sending him the manuscript of his forthcoming book, *The Relations and Development of the Mind and Brain*, and by reducing the principles behind his studies on the mind to a list of pithy maxims that emphasized the cosmic significance of his quest. "Through mind Truth becomes regnant in the Universe," he informed Dreiser; "even in its very chemical nature the Universe is moral," and "happiness is more of a means than an end." In addition, Gates often clarified important aspects of his research for Dreiser's use in writing about him. In one letter, for instance, he reviewed his conclusions about the chemical effects of good and truth and evil and falsehood on the mental powers:

> An evil emotion engenders the poisonous katastates which slowly destroy the structure in which memory is engendered, whilst a good emotion augments the nutritive processes which tend to perpetuate it; the same is true of intellections: a false image, concept or idea is a structural embodiment which prevents normal and sane judgments and consequently prevents successful adaption to environment and therefore tends to destroy or limit the life of the organism in which it is embodied; whilst true ideas by creating sane judgments tend to complete the life of the organism and thus it is that evil and falsehood are evanescent while truth and good are self perpetuating.[14]

Dreiser eventually wrote an article titled "The Training of the Senses," which described Gates's research and his enthusiastic conclusions that "the senses can be educated to a much higher degree." The article reveals that Dreiser had absorbed Gates's opinions about the negative effects of "katastates" on human behavior. "Feeling can be misled by false knowledge," Dreiser wrote. "Abnormal emotions will mislead all our feeling." The article, however, also reveals Dreiser's growing absorption with the activities and conclusions of science. He praised "the religious mission" of Gates and his associates, who were discovering "the processes by which knowledge is achieved and by which it is applied to the betterment of human affairs."[15] It is perhaps ironic that Dreiser's first significant encounter with a man of science, an encounter that intensified his faith in the "gospel" of science, should come with such an undisciplined speculator and likely charlatan as Elmer Gates. But because of the spiritual and cosmic quest that lay behind his interest in science, because he was impatient to discover a key that would unlock the mysteries of the "unknowable," and frankly, because he was an untrained layman whose scientific knowledge was primarily based on self-education, Dreiser would frequently confuse pseudo-science with science throughout his life.

Dreiser never published "The Training of the Senses," but the influences of Gates's research were fully displayed in *Sister Carrie*. When Dreiser met Gates in early 1900, he was already well into the writing of the novel. The scientist took an interest in the work, becoming "so enthusiastic over the plot as I explained it to him, that he asked me to allow him to arrange for me to deliver a lecture on the purpose of the novel before the Players Club in New York, this fall."[16] Dreiser had been troubled in constructing Hurstwood's deterioration and had temporarily laid his work aside at the time he met Gates. But the scientist's theories on the chemical power of the emotions on the behavior of humans now stimulated Dreiser to finish the novel. When he described the depressing effect of New York City on Hurstwood's mind, the Gatesian influence was now apparent:

> So long . . . will the atmosphere of this realm work its desperate results in the soul of man. It is like a chemical reagent. One day of it, like one drop of the other, will so affect and discolor the views, the aims, the desires of the mind, that it will thereafter remain forever dyed. A day of it to the untried mind is like opium to the untried body. A craving is set up which, if gratified, shall eternally result in dreams and death. Aye, dreams unfilled—gnawing, luring, idle phantoms which beckon and lead, beckon and lead, until death and dissolution dissolve their power and restore us blind to nature's heart. (305)

As Hurstwood's degeneration continued, Dreiser even adopted the use of Gates's jargon in his descriptions:

> Now it has been shown experimentally that a constantly subdued frame of mind produces certain poisons in the blood, called katastates, just as virtuous feelings of pleasure and delight produce helpful chemicals, called anastates. The poisons, generated by remorse, inveigh against the system and eventually produce marked physical deterioration. To this Hurstwood was subject. (339)

Although he was unaware of the faulty experimental methods and unsound conclusions of Gates's speculations, Dreiser obviously believed that his use of this pseudo-scientific theory and jargon gave his novel the aura of scientific realism that he hoped to achieve.

＊   ＊   ＊

After the publication of *Sister Carrie* in August 1900, another Dreiser novel did not appear until 1911. In the decade that passed between the publication of his first two novels, Dreiser suffered a nervous collapse, due partly to the failure of *Sister Carrie* to find a receptive audience, and in the years following his recovery, he returned to his former editorial career, managing several popular magazines. In 1910, after losing his final editorial position because of a scandal involving his romantic attachment with a seventeen-year-old girl, Dreiser began to write again. In the next five years, he published four novels: *Jennie Gerhardt* (1911), *The Financier* (1912), *The Titan* (1914), and *The "Genius"* (1915).[17] The remainder of this chapter will study Dreiser's continued use of the evolutionary universe as a context into which he placed his characters, and will identify and analyze certain continuities and shifts in the Spencerian outlook of his thought in these novels.

The social Darwinian "struggle for existence" lay at the heart of each of these novels. In the Gerhardt family's desperate efforts to eke out a living in the face of their hardships, in Frank Cowperwood's Herculean battles for financial domination and sexual conquest, and in Eugene Witla's struggles to capture beauty in his paintings and in his bedroom, Dreiser once again portrayed his vision of the human competition for self-preservation: "Malevolence, life living on death, plain violence—these were the chief characteristics of existence. If one failed in strength in any way, if life were not kind in its bestowal of gifts, if one were not born to fortune's pampering care—the rest was misery" (*The "Genius"*, 242).

Occasionally, Dreiser employed metaphors from nature (usually involving ocean life) to portray human struggle as merely a more highly evolved manifestation of the instinct of self-preservation that drives the behavior of every living creature. The most famous example is Dreiser's fish tank battle at the opening of *The Financier*. As young Cowperwood watches a lobster and a squid struggle against one another in a shop window aquarium at a Philadelphia fish market, he realizes that the slow, unprotected squid is doomed by the weakness of its nature. As the victorious lobster slowly devours its foe, the larger lessons of life begin to become apparent to the boy:

> The incident made a great impression on him. It answered in a rough way that riddle which had been annoying him so much in the past: "How is life organized?" Things lived on each other—that was it. Lobsters lived on squids and other things. What lived on lobsters? Men, of course! Sure, that was it. And what lived on men? he asked himself. Was it other men? . . . That was it! Sure, men lived on men. (8–9)

In *The "Genius"*, Dreiser's autobiographical protagonist, Eugene Witla, reaches a similar insight, recognizing "how the big fish fed upon the little ones, the strong were constantly using the weak as pawns" (348). Unlike Cowperwood, Witla is initially disturbed by the realization that this grim law of nature applies even to human social relations, but he gradually recognizes a certain order or efficiency resulting from the arrangement:

> Formerly the hierarchies of power in the universe and on earth were inexplicable to him—all out of order; but here, where he saw by degrees ignorant, almost animal intelligence, being directed by greater, shrewder, and at times it seemed to him possibly malicious intelligences . . . , he began to imagine that in a rough way life might possibly be ordered to the best advantage even under this system. (313)

In spite of his doubts about his own strength and ability to prevail, Witla acknowledges that "the survival of the fittest was the best" (348).

Both of the examples cited above implicitly reveal the same conception of the human "struggle for existence" that Dreiser had displayed in *Sister Carrie*; unlike the lower beasts that struggled merely to maintain their lives, humans competed to gain and maintain power, prestige, and pleasure. "Life is a battle," Jennie is warned. "If you gain anything you will have to fight for it" (*Jennie Gerhardt*, 109). Cowperwood's financial struggle to acquire a fortune is more than the mere pursuit of money; "the financier wants it for what it will control—for what it will represent in the way of dignity, force, power" (*The Financier*, 182). And as Witla rises from failure and mental breakdown to temporary success and status, he comes to appreciate the order, beauty, and fitness that characterizes the life-style of the victors in the social "struggle for existence":

> Here was no sickness, no weariness apparently, no ill health or untoward circumstances. All the troubles, disorders and imperfections of existence were here carefully swept aside and one saw only the niceness, the health and

strength of being. He was more and more impressed as he came farther and farther along in the scale of comfort, with the force and eagerness with which life seems to minister to the luxury-love of the human mind. He learned of so many, to him, lovely things, large, wellkept, magnificent country places, scenes of exquisite beauty where country clubs, hotels, seaside resorts of all descriptions had been placed. He found sport, amusement, exercise, to be tremendously well organized and that there were thousands of people who were practically devoting their lives to this. . . . He was beginning to see clearly how the world was organized, how far were its reaches of wealth, its depths of poverty. From the lowest beggar to the topmost scene—what a distance. (*The "Genius"*, 472–73)

Dreiser here fused the Darwinian concept of the fit with the socio-economic concept of the leisure class to create a striking social Darwinian vision of the rewards of struggling successfully.

Throughout the novels Dreiser made plain that in his opinion one could triumph in the human struggle for life—the individual could attain the social rewards of comfort, status, and dominance—only by challenging the limitations of conventional morality. Self-preservation by definition required selfish, at times deceitful behavior. At the conclusion of *The Financier*, Dreiser commented on the treachery that Cowperwood employs to defeat his enemies—and on the disparity between the Christian code of conduct and the code of conduct demanded by nature—in yet another metaphor drawn from ocean life. Dreiser compared Cowperwood to the black grouper, or *Mycteroperca bonaci*, a fish whose ability to camouflage itself by altering its color to match the surrounding environment allows it to deceive and capture its prey. The creative force that endowed this fish with such nasty and devious powers was certainly not a providential God whose universe is built on ideals of virtue, honesty, and justice:

> Would you say, in the face of this, that a beatific, beneficent creative, overruling power never wills that which is either tricky or deceptive? Or would you say that this material seeming in which we dwell is itself an illusion? If not, whence then the Ten Commandments and the illusion of justice? Why were the Beatitudes dreamed of and how do they avail? (447)

Clearly the universe was not moral, and nature did not demand moral behavior of its residents. Both the fish and the financier destroyed their prey through employment of the ruthless abilities of their natures, and if the fish was judged free from moral responsibility, so too must the financier.

What determined one's success in the "struggle for existence" was one's ability to surmount the pious ideals of humankind's erroneous moral-

ity and to bring oneself to act in accordance with the cold demands of a
hostile universe. Certainly this is what determines the success or failure of
Dreiser's protagonists. Cowperwood, Dreiser's most successful protagonist, lives by the motto, "I satisfy myself" (*The Titan*, 16, 407). His hardened code of behavior excludes "the age-old notions of chivalry, self-
sacrifice, duty to higher impulses. . . . Cowperwood saw things in no such
moralistic or altruistic light" (*The Titan*, 406–7). He dismisses the Christian code of ethics and has no regard for those idealists and moralists who
condemn him:

> That thing *conscience*, which obsesses and rides some people to destruction, did
> not trouble him at all. He had no consciousness of what is currently known as
> sin. There were just two faces to the shield of life from the point of view of his
> peculiar mind—strength and weakness. Right and wrong? He did not know
> about those. They were bound up in metaphysical abstrusities about which he
> did not care to bother. Good and evil? Those were toys of clerics, by which
> they made money. And as for social favor or ostracism . . . , well, what was
> social ostracism? . . . Morality and immorality? He never considered them. But
> strength and weakness—oh yes! If you had strength you could protect your-
> self always and be something. If you were weak—pass quickly to the rear and
> get out of the range of the guns. He was strong and he knew it, and somehow
> he always believed in his star. (*The Financier*, 240)

The slaves of conventional morality, Cowperwood believes, are blind to the
means to victory embodied in the law of survival; they are doomed to
mediocrity:

> There are some people who believed in some esoteric standard of right—some
> ideal of conduct absolutely and very far removed from practical life; but he had
> never seen them practice it save to their own financial (not moral—he would
> not say that) destruction. They were never significant, practical men who
> clung to these fatuous ideals. They were always poor, nondescript, negligible
> dreamers. (*The Financier*, 200)

Contrasted with the amoral outlook and material success of Cowperwood is the selfless generosity and sad fate of Jennie Gerhardt, perhaps the
most tragic of Dreiser's many portraits of failure. "[Jennie's] affections were
not based in any way upon material considerations. Her love of life and of
personality were free from the taint of selfishness" (*Jennie Gerhardt*, 364).
In spite of her loving, noble nature, Jennie is buffeted by one misfortune
after another. "She was never a master of her fate. Others invariably controlled" (413). A victim in a universe of struggle, Jennie has never cultivated
the talents necessary for survival. "Love was not enough in this world—
that was so plain. One needed education, wealth, training, the ability to

fight and scheme. She did not want to do that. She could not" (366). In the final pages of the novel, Dreiser even employs the Darwinian terminology of failure to describe once again the tragic flaw of Jennie's nature: "Was not her life a patchwork of conditions made and affected by these things which she saw—wealth and force—which had found her *unfit*? She had evidently been born to yield, not seek" (416—emphasis mine).

In these novels, then, Dreiser adopted what can only be called a Machiavellian attitude toward ethics. His "tooth and claw" formula for success reveals a change, but also an element of continuity, regarding the influence of Spencerian theory contained in his first important short story, "The Shining Slave Makers," and his first novel, *Sister Carrie*. The continuity lies in Dreiser's persistent rejection of orthodox morality and in the closely related celebration of hedonism. "The world is dosed with too much religion," he wrote in the conclusion of *The Titan*. "Life is to be learned from life, and the professional moralist is at best but a manufacturer of shoddy wares" (499). The attack here is on what Dreiser perceived to be an artificial, human-made morality that was based not on the true, amoral nature of the universe but on the false assumptions of convention. The preachers, or religionists as Dreiser most frequently referred to the guardians of moral order, were merely "poor windblown sticks of unreason who saw only what the current palaver seemed to indicate" (*The Titan*, 471). One of Dreiser's most impassioned assaults on the artificial and erroneous morality of orthodox religion appears in his chapter describing the birth of Jennie's child. The creation of life, the most beautiful process in nature, is in the case of Jennie and her child an occasion of humiliation and gossip, guilt and censure—only because the mother is unwed:

> "Conceived in iniquity and born in sin," is the unnatural interpretation put upon the process by the extreme religionist, and the world, by its silence, gives assent to a judgment so marvelously warped.
>
> Surely there is something radically wrong in this attitude. The teachings of philosophy and the deductions of biology should find more practical application in the daily reasoning of man. No process is vile, no condition is unnatural. The accidental variation from a given social practice does not necessarily entail sin. . . . No poor little earthling, caught in the enormous grip of chance, and so swerved from the established customs of men, could possibly be guilty of that depth of vileness which the attitude of the world would seem to predicate so inevitably. (*Jennie Gerhardt*, 92–93)

Dreiser's refusal to condemn Jennie as a sinner bears similarity to the moral impartiality with which he deals with Cowperwood's numerous love affairs. Cowperwood is "a superman, a half-god or demi-Gorgon" in his financial as well as sexual conquests; if the conventional rules of morality do not apply to such a titan in business affairs, neither can they apply in affairs of love. "How could the ordinary rules of life or accustomed paths of men be expected to control him? They could not and did not" (*The Titan*, 478). As the lover of sixteen women over the course of *The Financier* and *The Titan*, Cowperwood is clearly incapable of following the "accustomed path" of monogamy.[18] He finds no value or relevance in "this one-life, one-love idea," disregarding even the evolutionary significance of the monogamous relationship to social development, of which he has some awareness:

> How had it come about that so many people agreed on this single point, that it was good and necessary to marry one woman and cleave to her until death? He did not know. It was not for him to bother about the subtleties of evolution, which even then was being noised abroad, or to ferret out the curiosities of history in connection with this matter. He had no time. Suffice it that the vagaries of temperament and conditions with which he came into immediate contact proved to him that there was great dissatisfaction with that idea. (*The Financier*, 120)

Cowperwood's relationships with women are impermanent—"people outgrew each other"—and with no moral guilt—"he saw nothing wrong in the sex relationship. Between those who were mutually compatible it was innocent and delicious" (*The Financier*, 268). While corresponding to the real-life affairs of Charles Yerkes, the Gilded Age entrepreneur on whom the character was based, Cowperwood's varietism concerning sexual affairs was also shared by Dreiser. His unstable marriage to Sara White Dreiser was in its final stage as Dreiser was writing these novels, and he increasingly surrendered to the "veritable paroxysms of emotion and desire" that attractive women aroused in him. His need to explain Cowperwood's numerous betrayals of his wife in terms of a rejection of conventional mores and an embrace of an amoral pursuit of hedonistic pleasures was no doubt a part of Dreiser's deeper need to rationalize his own behavior to his acquaintants, his wife, and himself. In building a rationalization for both himself and Cowperwood, Dreiser reached back to the hedonistic doctrine he had found in Spencer's *The Data of Ethics*. The sanction for sexual varietism that he sought lay in Spencer's maxim that "gratification, enjoyment, [or] happiness" were life enhancing, self-preserving, and, therefore, in the moral judgment of nature's evolutionary universe, "good."[19]

While these novels reveal a continuing presence or even strengthening of the hedonistic outlook which Dreiser found certified in *The Data of Ethics*, the concern for altruism that Spencer had endorsed in that same work and that Dreiser had incorporated as the ethical point of view in his early fiction was now lacking. Service to one's fellow beings, the high ethical ideal for which Bob Ames had been Dreiser's eloquent spokesman in *Sister Carrie*, was regarded in these later novels with cynicism. "Virtue" Dreiser now defined as "that quality of generosity which offers itself willingly for service to others, and, being this, it is held by society to be nearly worthless" (*Jennie Gerhardt*, 87). The altruistic Jennie is pummeled again and again by fate and society, while the egoistic Cowperwood, despite his financial ups and downs, ultimately triumphs and prospers. While it is true that Dreiser's sympathies were with the victims of the struggle like Jennie, his respect seemed increasingly drawn to the victors.

The battles that Dreiser had undergone in the decade following the writing of *Sister Carrie* had no doubt given him a more self-concerned perspective on survival and a greater appreciation of the value of strength. The conflict over *Sister Carrie*'s publication, his emotional breakdown and near-suicide, his growing dissatisfaction with his marriage, and his passionate and self-destructive affair with seventeen-year-old Thelma Cudlipp had given Dreiser personal exposure to "the struggle for existence." His decade of struggle had forced his earlier concern for the higher ethical goal of self-sacrifice to become secondary to his more immediate concern for personal self-preservation. His autobiographical novel, *The "Genius"*, then, reveals how Dreiser envisioned himself as an artist and as a human being struggling within a conceptual universe that he had absorbed from his evolutionary readings and within his everyday reality of controversy, emotional conflict, and disappointed dreams. While the novel is correctly regarded as one of his worst, it is most interesting as a critical self-evaluation of how Dreiser had fared thus far in the evolutionary universe of struggle.

Like Dreiser, Eugene Witla encounters Herbert Spencer and evolutionary theory as a young adult. In describing Witla's reaction, Dreiser recounts his own unsettling discovery of *First Principles*; the book "had literally torn him up by the roots and set him adrift." Witla is numbed by the Spencerian triple shock of the unknowable, the impermanence of life, and the insignificance of humankind:

> He had walked the streets for a long time after reading some of these things, speculating on the play of forces, the decay of matter, the fact that thought-forms had no more stability than cloud forms. Philosophies came and went, governments came and went, races arose and disappeared. . . . He came to the conclusion that he was nothing, a mere shell, a sound, a leaf which had no general significance, and for the time being it almost broke his heart. (150)

In a reversal of Dreiser's order of reading, Witla next reads Darwin, Huxley, and Tyndall, who "showed him a beauty, a formality, a lavishness of form and idea in nature's methods." The evolutionary scientists, however, cannot overcome the trauma Witla has sustained from his prior reading of Spencer. "He was still gloomy. Life was nothing save dark forces moving aimlessly" (150). And yet having learned the nature of the evolutionary universe, Witla does not apply the lessons of strength and self-preservation in his actions. He has received an intellectual awakening and an emotional jolt from Spencer, but does not translate this understanding into conduct geared toward personal progress.

Witla's artistic career undergoes two collapses that parallel the two low points of Dreiser's career. His first collapse is a complete mental, physical, and emotional breakdown caused by the "overindulgence physically" of his relations with his wife, as well as by the emotional strain of their quarrels after her discoveries of his former lovers. Draining him of his energy and depriving him of his freedom, marriage temporarily destroys Witla's art and nearly devours him. The first collapse, then, is the result of Witla's disastrous decision to marry Angela Blue after seducing her at the home of her parents. Witla surrenders to conscience and convention, although he is very wary of the effect that marriage may have on his art. His decision is an indication of his lack of strength; it is a moment of weakness that he, like Dreiser, would come to regret.

As he recovers from his illness, Witla begins to toughen his attitude toward life and to cultivate an inner strength. "He was no longer, or at least not going to be, he thought, the ambling, cowardly, dreaming Witla he had been. He was going to stand up, and he did begin to" (416). He does not return to his painting, but develops a career as a commercial art director for New York magazine publishing houses. There, the new Witla continues to toughen as

> his self-reliance, coolness under fire, ability to work long and ardently even when his heart was scarcely in it, were all strengthened and developed. . . . He had lost that fear of very little things, for he had been sailing through stormy seas. Little storms did not—could never again—really frighten him. He had learned to fight. (426–27)

Witla's rise to power, prestige, and pleasure, however, is temporary. His second collapse is precipitated not by an error in judgment made from the pressure of convention, but by an error made from the pressure of his inner nature.

Early in the novel, Dreiser indirectly indulges in self-criticism of his own uncontrollable sexual desires and conquests as he describes the flaw in Witla's personality that will ultimately cause his second collapse. "The weakness of Eugene," Dreiser writes, "was that he was prone in each of these new conquests to see for the time being the sum and substance of bliss, to rise rapidly in the scale of uncontrollable, exaggerated affection, until he felt that here and nowhere else, now and in this particular form was ideal happiness" (274). In rationalizing his autobiographical counterpart's self-destructive sexual urges, Dreiser resorted to the sanction of science once again. His explanation is a precursor of the mechanistic determinism that would increasingly enter his thought in the following years:

> It is a question whether the human will, of itself alone, ever has cured or ever can cure any human weakness. Tendencies are subtle things. They are involved in the chemistry of one's being, and those who delve in the mysteries of biology frequently find that curious anomaly, a form of minute animal life born to be the prey of another form of animal life—chemically and physically attracted to its own disaster. (275)

Dreiser then resorted directly to the authority of science, quoting a half page from a *Century Magazine* article on "Protozoa and Disease" by Gary Nathan Calkins.[20] This Columbia University zoologist's discussion of the feeding habits of paramecium, vorticella, and actinobolus is interjected into Dreiser's discussion of Witla's sexual habits, thereby associating human sexual desire with the most basic, primitive level of instinctive behavior of the most basic, primitive form of life. Witla's eventual seduction of eighteen-year-old Suzanne Dale, like all the other affairs in which he becomes involved, is analogous to the self-destructive actions of the biologist's unicellular animals, which are determined—to quote Dreiser's quote of Calkins—by "definite chemical and physical laws which the individual organism can no more change than it can change the course of gravitation" (275). Both the zoologist and the author saw their subjects as determined by their natures, forced to act by impulses beyond volition. "Eugene did not know of these curious biologic experiments at this time, but he suspected that these attractions were deeper than human will."

Witla's rise to power, prestige, and pleasure, then, is halted by the uncontrollable force of his passion for the teenage Suzanne. After another bout with depression and a long quest for philosophic meaning, he returns to his art to portray both the beauty and the brutality of existence. Witla finally settles down somewhere between Frank Cowperwood and Jennie

Gerhardt on Dreiser's scale of success and failure. Like Jennie, he is a victim of his own weaknesses and of social convention, but his errors never destroy him completely. Like Cowperwood, when he can summon his internal strength, he achieves much status and success in the struggles of the commercial world. In the end, however, Witla recognizes his strengths and weaknesses and adapts to the realities of his nature by returning to his true calling. Recognizing that his character would never allow him to triumph in the struggle for existence, Witla chooses the more modest goal of survival by making use of his artistic talents and insight to portray to others the beauty and tragedy of life in this universe of mystery and struggle.

Witla's ups and downs and the final state of rest that he achieves illustrate the much discussed concept of "equation" that Dreiser had developed from his understanding of Herbert Spencer's theories. Ronald Martin has suggested that Dreiser's "equation" concept was in origin "a clumsy approximation of Spencer's concept of equilibrium," and Donald Pizer has stated that Dreiser "was really drawing upon the idea that Spencer more commonly called 'rhythm'."[21] The Spencerian notions of "equilibrium" and "rhythm," however, are more relevant to the larger universal concept of "equation inevitable" that was to become an important philosophical idea in Dreiser's later thought. (See Chapter 6.) The idea of "equation" that appears in these novels is a simpler precursor to "equation inevitable"; it is Dreiser's theory of the limitations of individual achievement. The strength or ability of the individual to gain power, prestige, and pleasure is in constant opposition to the strength or ability of forces surrounding the individual. The opposing forces may be other individuals, the society at large, or simple fate. The inner pressures acting on the individual and the outer pressures of the environment, both social and natural, constantly act on and adapt to one another. Dreiser's "equation" concept, then, seems likely to be derived from Spencer's definition of life as "the correspondence of certain inner physico-chemical actions with certain outer physico-chemical actions."

In *Jennie Gerhardt* Dreiser expounds on the limits that the environment places on life. A fish "may not pass out of the circle of the seas without courting annihilation," while a bird "may not enter the domain of the fishes without paying for it dearly." Animals are clearly limited by the environment to which they are adapted, or, in Dreiser's words, "from the parasites of the flowers to the monsters of the jungle and the deep, we see clearly the circumscribed nature of their gyrations—the emphatic manner in which life has limited them to a sphere." In a classic social Darwinian projection, Dreiser then applies this obvious law of nature to the human social environment. The "opinions, pleas, arguments, and quarrels of society" place more intangible limits on the actions and movements of individuals. In the case of animals, to violate the boundaries of nature results in death; in the case of humans, to disregard the boundaries of society results in social destruction: "so conditional is the well-defined sphere of social activity that he who departs from it is doomed. After having been accustomed to this environment, the individual is practically unfitted for any other state" (*Jennie Gerhardt*, 235–36). All Dreiser's protagonists, then, are portrayed as individuals with powerful, innate forces compelling them to act in ways that, at times, transgress the powerful, exterior forces of social convention. And because Dreiser believed that it was inevitable that the seeker of power, prestige, and pleasure subvert the restrictions of social opinion, at times society must exert its force to undermine the challenger's advance. Witla's individual strength, then, is overpowered by the combined strength of his lover's mother, Mrs. Dale, his employer, Mr. Colfax, his rival colleague, White, and his wife, Angela. He overestimates his newly acquired strength, and in following the uncontrollable power of his interior instincts to have Suzanne Dale as his lover, a counterbalancing exterior power is summoned up to destroy both the relationship and Witla's rise to status and success. Even Cowperwood is temporarily undone at the finale of both *The Financier* and *The Titan* by a combination of forces (enemies, business rivals, reformers, accidents of fate), which the individual force of his great strength cannot overcome. In the conclusion of the latter novel, Dreiser gives his most direct explanation of this idea of "equation":

> At the ultimate remove, God or the life-force, if anything, is an equation, and at its nearest expression for man—the social contract—it is that also. Its method of expression appears to be that of generating the individual, in all his glittering variety and scope, and through him progressing to the mass with its problems. In the end a balance is invariably struck wherein the mass subdues the individual or the individual the mass—for the time being. For, behold, the sea is ever dancing or raging.
>
> In the meantime there have sprung up social words and phrases expressing a need of balance—of equation. These are right, justice, truth, morality, an honest mind, a pure heart—all words meaning: a balance must be struck. The strong must not be too strong; the weak not too weak. But without variation how could the balance be maintained? Nirvana! Nirvana! The ultimate, still equation. (*The Titan*, 501)

"Equation" is characterized here as an amoral process inherent in the law of evolution. By shifting power back and forth between the individual and the masses, nature compels constant readjustment in society, thus achieving the essential change or "variation" that is central to evolution or social progress. With each pendulum swing of power, society advances into a higher state, culminating eventually when the pendulum's motion will dissipate in the "ultimate still equation" of "Nirvana!" This process, to repeat, is amoral, free of any purpose in establishing "right, justice, truth [or] morality." These ideals are merely "social words" invented in the past to describe the incorrect human perception of the purpose of this process. Dreiser is once again distinguishing the artificial morality of humankind from the real, impartial nature of the universe.

In spite of the insights that Dreiser believed he had achieved in understanding the evolutionary universe, these four novels continue to display what was ultimately Spencer's most profound effect on Dreiser's thought: the unknowable nature of the universe. Existence is described in *Jennie Gerhardt* as "a kaleidoscopic glitter, a dazzling and confusing showpiece which is much more apt to weary and undo than to enlighten and strengthen the observing mind" (125). To Cowperwood, "life . . . , as to every other man of large practical knowledge and insight, was an inexplicable tangle" (*The Financier*, 200), while a minor character in *The "Genius"*, reflecting Dreiser's own thoughts on the inscrutability of life, meditates "upon the inexplicable tangle, chemical and physical, of life—the blowing hither and thither of diseases, affections, emotions and hates of all kinds" (606). Closely allied to this human blindness in comprehending the ultimate meaning of existence is Dreiser's continuing conviction that the individual was of no importance to the vast cosmic processes that took place in the universe: "It isn't me that's important in this transaction apparently—it's the general situation. The individual doesn't count much in the situation. I don't know whether you see what I'm driving at, but all of us are more or less pawns. We're moved about like chess men by circumstances over which we have no control" (*Jennie Gerhardt*, 392). As he contemplates the vast constellations of space, even Cowperwood has a humbling moment of self-doubt about his own significance. "His own life appeared very trivial in view of these things, and he found himself asking whether it was all really of any significance or importance" (*The Financier*, 417–18).

It is appropriately Dreiser's autobiographical counterpart, Eugene Witla, who undergoes the greatest struggle with the overpowering realities of the unknowable and the insignificance of the individual. The long philosophical conclusion of *The "Genius"* following Witla's second collapse is unsatisfying as a resolution to the novel, but it reveals much about

Dreiser's thought during this period. As Witla struggles to overcome his sorrow and despair following the breakup of his affair with Suzanne, he first considers Christian Science as a possible cure for his pain. His initial reaction to Mary Baker Eddy's religion is one of scorn, for he discovers in her textbook, *Science and Health*, such traditional Christian beliefs as the Old Testament flood, the immaculate conception of the Virgin Mary, and the existence of contemporary miracles. In spite of these irritating elements of orthodoxy, Witla continues his studies because "any straw was worth grasping at which promised relief from sorrow, despair, and defeat" (*The "Genius"*, 674). He is soon attracted by the metaphysical core at the heart of Christian Science:

> Its main tenet is that God is a principle, not a personality understandable or conceivable from the mortal or sensory side of life (which latter is an illusion), and that man (spiritually speaking) in His image and likeness. Man is not God or any part of Him. He is an idea in God, and as such, as perfect and indestructible and undisturbably harmonious as an idea in God or principle must be. To those not metaphysically inclined, this is usually dark and without significance, but to those spiritually or metaphysically minded it comes as a great light. Matter becomes a built-up set or combination of illusions, which may have evolved or not as one chooses, but which unquestionably have been built up from nothing or an invisible, intangible idea, and have no significance beyond the faith or credence, which those who are at base spiritual give them. (669)

Within this explanation of the nucleus of Christian Science belief lie many of the philosophic ideas that Dreiser would eventually espouse. All reality, including the existence of life, was only a thought in the mind of some creative being or force. The physical universe ("Matter"), whether one accepted or scorned evolution as a basic law of the universe, was merely an unknowable illusion.

Through Witla's winding search for philosophical meaning, Dreiser presents his own continuing conviction that some sort of creative force or being was responsible for the existence of the universe. As Witla rereads Huxley's *Science and the Hebrew Tradition* and *Science and the Christian Tradition* and other works of science in the "great light" of Christian Science doctrine, he becomes fascinated "to find that the evolutionary hypothesis did not after all shut out a conception of a ruling, ordaining Divinity" (676). Dreiser goes to great lengths to convince the reader that the notion of a creator is not incompatible with the findings of modern science, calling on the direct testimony of three men of science. He quotes first from George M. Gould, whose studies on cellular mechanics led him to conclude that "Life, or God, is in the cell. . . . The cell is God's instrument and mediator in materiality; it is the mechanism of incarnation, the word made flesh and dwelling among us" (677).[22] Next comes the testimony of Edgar Lucien Larkin, whose microscopic observations of particle movements had revealed to him a controlling order that implied the omnipresent power of a creative mind:

> I cannot look into these minute moving and living deeps without instantly believing that they are mental—every motion is controlled by mind. The longer I look at the amazing things, the deeper is the conviction. This micro-universe is rooted and grounded in a mental base. Positively and without hope of overthrow, this assertion is made—the flying particles know where to go. (677–78)[23]

As his final scientific authority on the spiritual foundation of the universe, Dreiser quotes for nearly two pages from Alfred Russel Wallace's *The World of Life: A Manifestation of Creative Powers, Directive Mind and Ultimate Purpose*. Wallace was, of course, the biologist who had developed the evolutionary hypothesis almost simultaneously with Charles Darwin in the 1850s. In his later life, Wallace had grown fascinated by occult phenomena, especially spiritualism and seances. Although his colleagues in evolutionary science criticized his interest in spiritualism (Tyndall found it "unworthy of notice" and Huxley dismissed it as "disembodied gossip"[24]), Wallace publicly moved toward mysticism in his final books. In *The World of Life* (1910), Wallace stated that his lifelong career of researching the processes of life had brought him to a firm conviction of the existence of

> a Mind far higher, greater, more powerful than any fragmentary mind we see around us—a Mind not only adequate to direct and regulate all the forces at work in living organisms, but which is itself the source of all those forces and energies, as well as of the more fundamental forces of the whole material universe.[25]

The long quotation from this book that Dreiser incorporates into his novel displays Wallace's belief not only in a creative mind but also in a host of creative spirits carrying out the instructions of the "Infinite Being" in overseeing and guiding the creation of the universe. Successive groups of "angels," Wallace suggests, created "the primal universe of ether," fashioned "those vast systems of nebulae and suns which constitute our stellar universe," and established the conditions on our planet "required for the full development of a life world from amoeba to man." Wallace then suggests that human evolution will eventually progress beyond the material stage into a spiritual stage, at which time the human race will take its place in this hierarchy of angels to participate in the next phase of the Deity's plan:

> This speculative suggestion, I venture to hope, will appeal to some of my readers as the very best approximation we are now able to formulate as to the deeper, the most fundamental causes of matter and force of life and consciousness, and of man himself, at his best, already a little lower than the angels, and, like them, destined to a permanent progressive existence in a world of spirit. (*The "Genius"*, 679–80)

The fact that Dreiser interrupts his novel for over three pages to present the reader with these seeming scientific documentations of the existence of a creative force suggests that he was attempting to accomplish more than merely chart the winding path of Witla's philosophic quest. The tone of the novel slips in these pages from narrative to didactic, and Dreiser's description of Witla's conclusions drawn from these readings is a confession of his own conviction in a creative power:

> God was a principle like a rule in mathematics—two times two is four, for instance—and was manifest daily and hourly and momentarily in a hall bedroom as in the circling motions of suns and systems. God was a principle. He grasped that now. A principle could be and was of course anywhere and everywhere at one and the same time. One could not imagine a place for instance where two times two would not be four, or where that rule would not be. So, likewise with the omnipotent, omniscient, omnipresent mind of God. (680)

Dreiser immediately clarifies that this belief in God was independent of conversion to any particular religious organization: "Fortunately the theology he was now interesting himself in was not a narrow dogmatic one in any sense, but religion in its large aspects, a comprehensive resume and spiritual co-ordination of the metaphysical speculation of the time, which was worthy of anyone's intelligent inquiry" (680–81). The spiritual belief that Dreiser had adopted was stripped of all the conflicting theological dogma of organized religions. It was a barebones theology, a "comprehensive" religion divested of all detail except for the existence of a universal creator of some sort. This "religion in its large aspects" corresponds to Spencer's assertion in *First Principles* that all religious creeds, while contradictory in their specific theological details, have the shared "tacit conviction" that the universe is a "mystery calling for interpretation." The interpretation that Dreiser had chosen was that the universe was the embodiment of a thought or plan in the mind of God.

Both Dreiser and his autobiographical creation Witla ultimately rejected Christian Science, and the reasons for that rejection are most revealing of Dreiser's opinions on organized religion. Witla finally rejects Christian Science, not for the Christian trappings of dogma that he finds so ridiculous, but because he cannot reconcile his own belief in the amoral, at times cruel nature of the universe with the religion's conception of the creator as a providential, loving God. While his Christian Science counselor tries to instruct him that all evil and suffering are the products of the human mind, Witla cannot overcome the conviction that they are an immanent part of the fabric of the creation. "The universe," he is sure, "the spirit of it that is, was subtle, cruel, crafty, and malicious" (675). In light of the suffering that he has undergone and the suffering that he has caused his wife (Angela dies in childbirth at the novel's conclusion), Witla cannot convert to Christian Science. Instead his religious meditations last only as long as his depression. In explaining Witla's temporary attraction to Christian Science, Dreiser's omniscient, didactic narrator reappears to present the author's personal evaluation of organized religion: "If I were personally to define religion, I would say that it is a bandage that man has invented to protect a soul made bloody by circumstances; an envelope to pocket him from the inescapable and unstable illimitable." As Witla recovers, the relevance of religion in his life disappears: "the need for religion is impermanent, like all else in life. As the soul regains its health, it becomes prone to the old illusions" (714).

These belittling comments describe Dreiser's opinion not only of Christian Science but of all organized religion. Traditional faiths were burdened by erroneous dogmas that were fabricated by theologians and that conflicted with the laws of nature as revealed by scientists. Even the very untraditional faith of Christian Science proposed the existence of a benevolent creator of a harmonious universe, in contradiction to the scientific revelation of an evolutionary universe of struggle. Dreiser's personal faith was dogma-free, positing only the existence of an unknowable, impersonal creator. In order to fill in details in his personal theology, Dreiser would increasingly turn to the observations of science rather than the speculations of theologians, for in studying the nature of the universe, scientists were uncovering the mechanistic, clockwork laws that the mysterious creator had established to govern its creation. He was even willing to grab onto the theories of any scientist, from the eminent Alfred Russel Wallace to the relatively obscure George Milbry Gould, who was willing to confess a faith in a creator's existence. Dreiser overlooked that these scientists' religious convictions rested just as much on faith and speculation as any theologian's convictions. This oversight only underlines Dreiser's greater faith in the authority of science to explain to his satisfaction the mysteries of the creator's universe. In his view, theologians only created illusions; scientists discovered facts.

The problem that would ultimately confront Dreiser in using science to discover the spiritual meaning of the universe was that science confined itself to the study of the physical universe only. Dreiser's creative force or being existed in a greater unknowable realm of spirit that lay somewhere beyond the domain of matter and substance. In the essay on "Ultimate Questions" that Dreiser quotes at the end of The "Genius" Herbert Spencer contemplates the inscrutability of infinity and eternity and concludes that even science will ultimately be restricted in its sphere of understanding:

> Theist and Agnostic must agree in recognizing the properties of Space as inherent, eternal, uncreated—as anteceding all creation, if creation has taken place. Hence, could we penetrate the mysteries of existence, there would remain still more transcendent mysteries. That which can be thought of as neither made nor evolved presents us with facts the origin of which is even more remote from conceivability than is the origin of the facts presented by visible and tangible things. (715)[26]

Eugene Witla, upon reading this passage in his copy of Spencer's Facts and Comments, concludes that it "is certainly the sanest interpretation of the limitations of human thought I have ever read." That Dreiser chose to end his autobiographical novel with this assertion of the cosmic inscrutability of existence illustrates the continuing dominance of Spencer's original impact on his thought. Both his and Witla's search for the true meaning of existence had ended thus far in the realization that these ultimate questions were beyond the abilities of human perception and understanding. In the later years of his life as the limitations of Spencer's doctrine of the unknowable became more emotionally disturbing to him—as his frustration in finding a satisfactory explanation for existence increased—Dreiser would eventually lose confidence in the observation and reason of the scientific method and ultimately embrace the extrasensory modes of perception of faith and intuition.

3. The Lure of Mechanistic Science

In January 1915 Theodore Dreiser applied to the New York Public Library for a study room to pursue "investigations . . . in the line of chemistry and physics."[1] In this study room, he began his readings in "mechanistic science," a philosophy proposing that all life could be understood in terms of the same chemical and physical laws that governed inorganic material, and that human behavior could be interpreted entirely by the chemical processes taking place within the body. Dreiser had first encountered this physico-chemical interpretation of life over twenty years earlier in Herbert Spencer's chemical determinism, and his awareness had been deepened through his exposure at the turn of the century to Elmer Gates's peculiar theories of psychology and through his reading several years later of Carl Snyder's *The World Machine*. After a fifteen year period of relatively little reading in science, in 1915 Dreiser plunged back into his program of scientific self-instruction, spending much of the next ten years studying and discussing mechanistic science and reading such mechanistic explorations as George W. Crile's *Man—An Adaptive Mechanism* and Jacques Loeb's *The Mechanistic Conception of Life*. In 1921 Dreiser told his friend Edward H. Smith that

> not unlike yourself perhaps, I am fairly well convinced that man did not make himself, and I am keenly interested in the work of all those who are trying in a legitimate scientific way to find out who or what did, and how,—Loeb, for instance, with whom I am in occasional correspondence, Crile, Fischer, Carrel, Ballou and a score of others. Many of these are interested solely in the chemical foundation, which is the next floor, apparently, below us. Loeb, Crile, Carrel, and a number of others have certainly made some very curious and illuminating experiments, as you know.[2]

Jacques Loeb was undoubtedly the most important philosophical mechanist whom Dreiser read during this period. Loeb zealously preached his philosophy to the public and to his fellow scientists in order to combat what he saw as the millennia of religious and philosophical superstition that had falsely interpreted humanity's place in the universe. He wrote a series of books that popularized his mechanistic philosophy and outlined his experiments in language comprehensible to most educated general readers. His research was well publicized and critically commented upon in newspaper articles and editorials, and he wrote articles about his work for popular magazines and journals.[3] His research home in New York City at the Rockefeller Institute of Medical Research allowed Dreiser the opportunity to meet him and to witness his experiments at first hand. These visits with Loeb deeply affected Dreiser's ideas and eventually influenced his portrayal of Clyde Griffiths in *An American Tragedy*.[4]

Born to an Alsatian Jewish family in 1859, Loeb developed an early interest in philosophy through his reading of Spinoza, Kant, and Schopenhauer. His original intention to study metaphysics was abandoned when he realized that philosophy was inadequate as a means to study the questions of human motivation and the problem of free will that intrigued him intellectually. "The mistake made by metaphysicians," he wrote years later, "is not that they devote themselves to fundamental problems, but that they employ the wrong means of explanation and substitute a play on words for explanations by means of facts." Rejecting the useless words of philosophy, Loeb turned to science to "convince by realities hidden from the eye."[5] He began the study of medicine at Berlin in 1880 and received his degree in physiology from Strasbourg in 1886.

While an assistant in physiology at Würzburg, Loeb was introduced to the physico-chemical foundation of mechanistic science by his colleague Julius Sachs, a botanist whose work had been greatly influenced by the "Mechanistic Quadrumvirate" of Hermann von Helmholtz, Emil duBois-Reymond, Carl Ludwig, and Ernst Brücke, the pioneers of mechanistic research in Germany. Sachs's studies in plant physiology had greatly developed knowledge about plant tropisms (that is, the forced attractions or repulsions of plants to such stimuli as light or gravity). From Sachs, Loeb gained the insights he had sought concerning the problem of free will. If he could show that lower animals behaved according to physical and chemical laws, just as Sachs had successfully accomplished for plant development and movement, he hoped eventually to reveal that human behavior was subject to the same physical and chemical laws on a more complex level, and thus prove that the notion of free will was an illusion.[6]

In 1891 Loeb emigrated from Germany to the United States, where he accepted positions at Bryn Mawr in that year, at the University of Chicago in 1892, and at Berkeley in 1903. In 1910 he became the director of the Rockefeller Institute of Medical Research in New York, where he remained until his death in 1924.

Loeb's research fell into four main areas, in each of which, he felt, mechanistic science could remove from biology such philosophical and theological concepts as free will, consciousness, and the existence of the soul. These four areas were the nature of fertilization and artificial parthenogenesis (artificial fertilization of an egg by chemical means), the physico-chemical nature of death, the study of the brain and the central nervous system, and the study of animal tropisms and instincts. Loeb's studies in fertilization and artificial parthenogenesis captured greater publicity than any of his other work. He felt that his contributions to the precise scientific investigation of fertilization would remove traditional mysticism from discussions on the beginning of life. In 1912 he wrote that his experiments had succeeded in proving "that the process of the activation of the egg by the spermatozoon, which twelve years ago was shrouded in complete darkness, is today practically completely reduced to a physico-chemical explanation." His work in artificial parthenogenesis began with his well-publicized success in fertilizing the eggs of sea urchins by treating the eggs in sea water with a slightly higher concentration of salt. He eventually showed that artificial parthenogenesis could be performed on the eggs of many species of animals "from the echinoderms [the biological phylum containing sea urchins and starfish] up to the frog; and it may possibly one day be accomplished also in warm-blooded animals."[7]

In addition to studying the physico-chemical nature of the beginnings of life, Loeb's mechanistic research was aimed at removing superstitious beliefs about the nature of death. He believed that the answers given to questions about life and death in the period before mechanistic science had "assumed the anthropomorphic form characteristic of all explanations of nature in the pre-scientific period. Life was assumed to begin with the entrance of a 'life principle' into the body. . . . Death was assumed to be due to the departure of this 'life principle' from the body." Loeb maintained that life began with the acceleration of the rate of oxidation in the egg and ended with the cessation of oxidation in the matured organism. His experiments in subjecting fruit flies to various levels of temperature from the moment of fertilization until their death confirmed to him that life was a matter of chemical and physical processes. He discovered in these experiments that the lower the temperature of the environment that he provided for the fruit flies, the more slowly the chemical processes of life proceeded and the longer the flies lived. Loeb concluded that the "duration of life is the time required for the completion of a chemical reaction or a series of chemical reactions."[8]

Loeb hoped that his research on the brain and central nervous system of animals would similarly eliminate "superstition" from the study of life. "The physiology of the brain has been rendered unnecessarily difficult," he complained, "through the fact that metaphysicians have at all times concerned themselves with the interpretation of brain functions and have introduced such metaphysical conceptions as soul, consciousness, will, etc." He conducted numerous experiments in comparative physiology of the nervous systems of lower animals and concluded that the processes of the brain were the result of the chemical activity that occurred in individual cells. He also recognized, however, that because mechanistic science had not yet achieved a complete understanding of cellular chemistry, any insights into such a process as associative memory, which he felt was central to unraveling the illusion of consciousness, was a matter of further physico-chemical study:

> We have to remember that all life phenomena are ultimately due to motions or changes occurring in colloidal substances. The question is, Which peculiarities of the colloidal substances can make the phenomena of associative memory possible? For the solution of this problem the experience of physical chemistry and the physiology of the protoplasm must be combined. From the same sources we must expect the solution of the other fundamental problems of brain physiology, namely, the process of the conduction of stimuli.[9]

Finally, Loeb's most important research was done in the field of animal tropisms, work for which he was frequently nominated for the Nobel prize, although he never received the prize itself.[10] He experimented on and developed theories of heliotropism (the attraction and repulsion of animals to light), thermotropism (heat), geotropism (gravity), galvanotropism (electricity), and chemotropism (chemicals) in an effort to show that animals did not move randomly or possess free will, but were compelled to move and act according to physico-chemical processes stimulated by sources outside their bodies.

One of Loeb's most publicized experiments in animal tropisms was designed to show that a certain species of caterpillar behaved in a characteristic manner, not because they were guided by some inherited, instinctual survival knowledge as many Darwinian biologists asserted, but because they were chemically compelled to act. Biologists had long observed that these caterpillars, upon hatching from their nests, immediately crawled to the top of their trees to feed on the springtime buds. If they did not climb to the top, they starved. Yet Loeb successfully showed that these caterpillars journeyed upward not because they possessed some innate "knowledge" of the food at the top but because they were compelled to climb by the attraction of light. He proved this by placing the creatures into a glass tube with a light at one end and their favorite food at the other. The caterpillars invariably crawled to the end of the tube with the light and remained there until they starved, although a source of food was inches away in the darker end.[11] Loeb concluded from this experiment that the caterpillars were helplessly compelled by a chemical reaction taking place within them to produce behavior that was detrimental to their survival. He extended the same conclusion to moths that helplessly fly into a flame and destroy themselves. Concerning such fatal attractions, he deduced, "The animals are slaves of the light."[12]

Although he worked almost exclusively with lower animals in his investigations, throughout his books and articles Loeb hinted that his "mechanistic conception of life" must also apply to humans. "But how about the higher animals and human beings?" he asked rhetorically. "Are there laws for lower forms of life but no laws for the higher ones?" Loeb was convinced that human beings are driven by the same physico-chemical compulsions to which all life is subject, except that in humanity's case the processes are more complicated and more difficult to understand:

> Our wishes and hopes, disappointments and sufferings have their source in instincts which are comparable to the light instinct of the heliotropic animals. The need of and struggle for food, the sexual instinct with its poetry and its chain of consequences, the maternal instincts with the felicity and the suffering caused by them, the instinct of workmanship, and some other instincts are the roots from which our inner life develops. For some of these instincts the chemical basis is at least sufficiently indicated to arouse the hope that their analysis, from the mechanistic point of view, is only a question of time.[13]

Dreiser, who first read Loeb in the mid-1910s, was immediately attracted to this physico-chemical conception of life and humanity. In 1945 he described his discovery of Loeb to James T. Farrell:

> In New York when I was living in Tenth Street, around 1910 or 12, I came across some magazine articles by him, which I read with great interest. (Also one of his books). I then wrote him telling him of my interest in his work. I also told him of some chemical and physical observations of my own. He answered my letter inviting me to come and see him at the Rockefeller Institute. I went. And from then on until the time of his death he either wrote me occasionally or sent me some pamphlets or printed deductions of his own.[14]

Dreiser's recollections of his relationship with Loeb require some scholarly readjustment. Dreiser probably did not read any of Loeb's work until 1914 or 1915, when he applied for his study room at the New York Public Library. He did not move to West 10th Street until July 1914, and Loeb had published no magazine articles in non-scientific journals until November 1914, when "Freedom of Will and War" appeared in the *New Review*.[15] Since Dreiser's discovery of "some magazine articles" by Loeb most likely occurred around 1914 or 1915, his first reading of Loeb's work was probably either "Freedom of Will and War" or another article called "Mechanistic Science and Metaphysical Romance," which the *Yale Review* printed in July 1915. Both of these articles contain key elements of Loeb's mechanistic outlook, and it is easy to understand why Dreiser, after reading them, was immediately drawn to Loeb's writing.

In "Freedom of Will and War," Loeb (a pacifist and a Socialist) speculated on why the masses ("even the Socialists") had so uniformly become the willing pawns of "the military caste and their friends to whom war means economic and social advances" and those 'rulers', adventurous statesmen, and diplomats to whom war means 'glory', 'power', and a place in 'history'." Loeb offered a biological analogy to explain popular support for the Great War in Europe. He pointed out that a certain species of small water crustaceans, under normal conditions, swims "incalculably free" in a container of water. But if just a drop of carbonated water is added to the container, the crustaceans, as one mass, swim in the direction of the strongest light. Loeb proposed that the carbonated water chemically destroys their freedom of will by reducing "the number of their degrees of freedom" available to them and by compelling them to swim toward the light. Loeb argued that humans also possess a certain "number of degrees of freedom" that are reduced by certain internal chemical reactions activated by external stimuli:

> We are still accustomed to speak of "the blinding effect of passion in humans." What happens in the case of the "passion" or supreme "emotion" of a human seems to be the setting free of definite chemical substances by some agency— e.g., those which cause the complex reactions of fear. Such substances often annihilate all degrees of freedom of action in the individual except in one direction or way.[16]

Loeb concluded that certain words or phrases could stimulate the secretion of these substances in a reader or listener, thereby arousing passion in that individual, reducing freedom of will, and making it impossible to resist those who would urge certain actions. Enthusiasm for the Great War, therefore, was the result of cunning political and economic leaders, adept at manipulating the collective physico-chemical emotions and passions of the masses by their words of jingoistic nationalism.

The second essay, "Mechanistic Science and Metaphysical Romance," was Loeb's attack on those philosophers and vitalists in science who denied his "mechanistic conception of life." He opened by pointing to the contemporary advances in chemistry and physics that had proven the existence of the atom. He argued that because all matter, organic or inorganic, was composed of atoms and molecules, biology must also become grounded in the basic principles of chemistry and physics. "According to mechanistic science," he wrote, "it should in the distant future be possible to reduce these specific life phenomena to the ultimate elements of all phenomena in nature, that is, motion of electrons, atoms, or molecules."[17] Loeb next revealed some of his own mechanistic experiments and conclusions in the field of animal tropisms, emphasizing how the laws of physics and chemistry determined the behavior of lower animals and declaring that someday these same laws would aid in the understanding of human behavior. He closed the article with an attack on those who preached an interpretation of the nature of life based on mere speculation. Metaphysicians, he argued, tried "to get at truth 'instinctively' or by 'intuition.'" Unfortunately, most intellectuals usually followed the "romantic" concepts of metaphysics rather than the precise deductions of mechanistic science, because the scientific method was slow and tedious, while metaphysics was capable of producing instant answers based on ideas and fantasies that were incapable of being tested. Yet

> romanticists have for several thousand years tried their luck at solving the "riddle of the universe." The result has been one metaphysical system after another, each doomed in turn to collapse, derision, and oblivion, as soon as mechanistic science was able to test its contentions. . . . What progress humanity has made, not only in physical welfare but also in the conquest of superstition and hatred, and in the formulation of a correct view of life, it owes directly or indirectly to mechanistic science.[18]

Dreiser indicated that in addition to "some magazine articles" by Loeb, he read "one of his books" at that time. This was Loeb's most famous book, *The Mechanistic Conception of Life*.[19] Through this work, Dreiser discovered all the elements of Loeb's mechanistic philosophy: the rejection of free will, the denial of the metaphysical "life principle" in the human being, and the prescription of physico-chemical experimentation and analysis as the only method that would lead to a true understanding of human nature. Loeb wrote in this work that

> the contents of life from the cradle to the bier are wishes and hopes, efforts and struggles, and unfortunately also disappointments and suffering. And this inner life should be amenable to a physico-chemical analysis? In spite of the gulf which separates us today from such an aim I believe that it is attainable. As long as a life phenomenon has not yet found a physico-chemical explanation it usually appears inexplicable. If the veil is once lifted we are always surprised that we did not guess from the first what was behind it.[20]

Perhaps Dreiser was most fascinated by the questions concerning the nature of ethics that mechanistic philosophy posed. For if all life was to be understood from a physico-chemical point of view, free from religious or metaphysical explanations of the origin of ethics, "our social and ethical life [would] have to be put on a scientific basis and our rules of conduct [would have to] be brought into harmony with the results of scientific biology." Loeb believed that human ethics are rooted in instincts and that the ethical instincts are inherited just as the form of our bodies is inherited. "We seek and enjoy the fellowship of human beings because hereditary conditions compel us to do so. We struggle for justice and truth since we are instinctively compelled to see our fellow human beings happy." At one point, however, Loeb described how certain individuals, human mutations seemingly lacking in ethical instincts, could evolve from a flawed social environment. It is an explanation that closely resembles Dreiser's thematic purpose in *An American Tragedy*, which he wrote a decade after first reading *The Mechanistic Conception of Life*. Loeb wrote:

> Economic, social, and political conditions or ignorance and superstition may warp and inhibit the inherited instincts and thus create a civilization with a faulty or low development of ethics. Individual mutants may arise in which one or the other desirable instinct is lost, just as individual mutants without pigment may arise in animals.[21]

Like Herbert Spencer, then, Loeb envisioned ethics as inherent rather than acquired, and progressing as the race evolved. On the question of lower or brute behavior, however, Loeb offered a slight variation on Spencer's hierarchical conception of ethical behavior. While Spencer regarded the most advanced humans as those who overcame the brute, egoistic tendencies of self-fulfillment and served the advancement of their society, Loeb warned that negative social conditions could pervert the higher ethical disposition of humanity and breed atavistic behavior of a primitive sort. As a leftist in "economic, social and political" matters, Loeb had fashioned an interpretation of ethics that could nicely embrace his reformist interests, a mechanistic construction of ethical conduct that still provided a home for the social critic. This conception of ethics, with its corollary that a corrupt environment could corrupt the natural human ethical inclinations, was one that Dreiser would find an attractive alternative to Spencerian ethics as he also became more active in championing reform causes. Spencerian thought, after all, had classical economic theory at its heart and was essentially anti-reform.

When Dreiser had read Spencer in the 1890s, he had been shocked and depressed at the tragic social Darwinian implications of the doctrine of "the survival of the fittest." Poverty, suffering, ignorance, and disease seemed the inevitable fate of those who were not born strong enough to compete in the social struggle for existence. In the last few decades of his life, however, Dreiser grew increasingly critical of the socio-economic system of the United States. While he did not abandon the social Darwinian outlook that the strong and talented were predestined by nature to triumph over the weak and ignorant, he found within the American capitalistic system little of the altruistic concern for the underdog that Spencer had prescribed:

> The deep trouble with America to-day is that the gifted and strong individual, however self-centered and selfish and wholly unsocial, is supposed nevertheless, to remain uncurbed because he is part of a presumably wholly social state which was organized to guarantee the right of equal opportunity for all. But equal opportunity for all cannot possibly and by the very same phrase mean unlimited license for the cunning and the greedy who take advantage of that equal opportunity to establish special or, in other words, unlimited individual privileges, and the power that goes with the same, while the remaining ninety to ninety-five per cent of the citizens of this land trudge in comparative want. And yet, that is exactly what has happened. The cunning and the strong have made great use of the land of real opportunity.

American capitalism had aggravated the natural tension between the strong and the weak into a precarious imbalance between wealth and poverty, and Dreiser was increasingly drawn in his later years to socialist ideology and alternatives:

> we must have either a real competitive system which would make it impossible for minority groups to establish monopolies and crush competition—or, if this cannot be done, then the people must take a hand in the running of the monopolies. Either a competitive system that is truly competitive, with the

advantages to national progress which competition has in the past shown itself to possess—or a co-operative system of monopolies, with the power over them—their social control—coming from the bottom, not from the top, and with all the social advantages which are inherent in true co-operation flowing downward to the many.

As Dreiser abandoned the hopeless determinism of Spencerian thought and embraced the possibility of reforming the socioeconomic environment around him, Loeb's ideas may have eased this transition from social Darwinism to Socialism.[22]

Dreiser was probably also very interested in Loeb's experiments in tropisms, especially heliotropisms. Dreiser's constant use of light imagery and the attractions of his characters to light in *Sister Carrie* had approached a form of literary heliotropism. When Carrie looks for a job early in the novel in the workshops of Chicago, she feels uncomfortable applying at a shop that is "dingily lighted" (25), and at another that is "miserably lighted" (27), but finally takes a job at "a goodly institution. Its windows were of huge plate glass. She could probably do well there" (29). Carrie loves to walk in the sunlit morning streets because "in the sunshine of the morning beneath the wide blue heavens, with a fresh wind astir, what fears, except the most desperate, can find a harborage in the human breast? In the night or the gloomy chambers of day, fears and misgivings wax strong, but out in the sunlight there is for a time cessation even of the terror of death" (35). Similarly, Fitzgerald and Moy's is "a strange glittering night-flower, odour-yielding, insect-drawing" (47), whose bar is "a blaze of lights" (43), and whose patrons "craved . . . the glow" (47); "here come the moths in endless procession to bask in the light of the flame" (46). In New York, the restaurants that attract Carrie are "aglow" with "shining tables" and "incandescent lights, the reflection of their glow in polished glasses" (331), while the flat where she and Hurstwood begin to deteriorate is "rather dark . . . shut in as it was" (358) with "only a light in the kitchen" (349). The growing gloominess of Hurstwood's and Carrie's declining situation occasionally lifts temporarily by the mere arrival of sunshine in their flat. Hurstwood's dark mood brightens for a moment one afternoon as he contemplates "the glory of the day. Out came the sun by noon . . . and poured a golden flood through their open windows. . . . Hurstwood could not keep his eyes from Carrie. She seemed the one ray of sunshine in all his trouble" (300). Carrie's doubts and depression over abandoning Hurstwood are overcome by a similar emotional boost provided by the sunshine at her window. "The blue heavens, holding their one golden orb, poured down a crystal wash of warm light. It was plain, from the voice of the sparrows, that all was halcyon outside. Carrie raised the front windows and felt the south wind blowing. 'It's lovely out today,' she remarked" (437–38). Carrie leaves Hurstwood to pursue her career under the bright lights of the Broadway stage; she moves into a set of "nice, light, outside rooms" (451) in a "great hotel [that] showed a hundred gleaming windows" (465), while Hurstwood, in a room with only a small gas jet for light, extinguishes that light in order to commit suicide.[23] Such heliotropic attractions are so common throughout *Sister Carrie* that one must conclude that this light imagery was a conscious motif created by Dreiser in 1900. He must have been delighted fifteen years later to discover the physico-chemical basis of heliotropism in Loeb's writing.

Loeb's use of lower animals to discover laws of nature and behavior that might also be applied to humans must have also struck a familiar note with Dreiser. He had also occasionally pondered in his writing the similarities that existed between animal and human behavior. "Bless us," he had written in 1906, "how closely these lesser creatures do imitate us in action—or how curiously we copy them!" Fascinated by sea creatures, Dreiser mused about the lessons taught by the hermit crab's efforts to secure a roomier shell. "[Who], prowling about and viewing another's comfortable home, or his excellent business, or the beauty of his wife, if the desire seized him, would not seize upon one or all of these, and by a process of mental gymnastics, or physical force, not unlike that of the hermit crab, endeavor to secure for himself the desirable shell?" He similarly noted the resemblance of certain human conduct to the habits of the parasitic shark sucker. "What weakling, seeing the world was against him, and that he was not fitted to cope with it, would not attach himself, sucker-wise, to any magnate, trust, political or social (we will not call them sharks), and content himself with what fell from his table?" Dreiser had also pointed out the similarities in behavior between humans and sea creatures in his digressions about the lobster and the squid and about the black grouper in *The Financier*. Of course, these examples are simple literary metaphors that Dreiser employed to furnish naturalistic support to his speculations on human behavior and cannot be compared to Loeb's rigorous experiments and observations on lower animals. Loeb might well have accused Dreiser of anthropomorphizing in these cases; Loeb frequently criticized Darwinian zoologists for applying human behavioral characteristics to lower animals.[24] Nevertheless, the two men shared an interest in the behavior of lower animals and in the clues to human nature that they revealed.

Dreiser's attraction to Loeb's mechanistic writings may be further explained by the scientific confirmation that Loeb's experiments seemed to lend to certain of Dreiser's preexisting ideas. In his four novels published between 1911 and 1915, especially in *The Financier* and *The Titan*, Dreiser began to refer to "the very chemistry of life" (*The Titan*, 113) and to assert that "the most noteworthy characteristic of the human race was that it was strangely chemic" (*The Titan*, 18). These allusions to chemistry illustrate Dreiser's continuing urge as a realist to attempt to explain and interpret life and humankind, particularly the temperament and behavior of his characters according to the latest scientific theories. Cowperwood's dynamic personality emits "a mysterious vibrating current that was his chemical product, the off-giving of his spirit battery" (*The Titan*, 25), while his mistress is described as "an unstable chemical compound" (*The Titan*, 213). The vocabulary of chemistry, however, most frequently appears in association with sexual passion. Sexual attraction is described as "a chemic perturbation in his blood" (*The Titan*, 306), sexual longing is "a chemic agony" (*The Financier*, 364), and sexual relationships are "chemic unions" (*The Titan*, 149) or "chemical affinities" (*The "Genius"*, 151). The chemical determinism underlying human passion is used as a justification of Cowperwood's hedonistic morality against the more orthodox morality of society:

> Those so fortunate as to find harmonious companionship for life should congratulate themselves and strive to be worthy of it. Those not so blessed, though they be written down as pariahs, have yet some justification. And besides, whether we will or not, theory or no theory, the basic facts of chemistry and physics remain. Like is drawn to like. Changes in temperament bring changes in relationship. Dogma may bind some minds; fear, others. But there are always those in whom the chemistry and physics of life are large, and in whom neither dogma nor fear is operative. (*The Financier*, 131)

With almost every use of this "chemic" prose, Dreiser describes behavior that overpowers a character in spite of the better judgment of reason, conscience, or convention. In *The "Genius"* Suzanne Dale reflects on the imprudence of her affair with Witla, concluding that her attraction was caused by "some chemistry of the blood, causing her to make a fool of herself, without having any real basis in intellectual rapprochement" (710), while in *Jennie Gerhardt* Lester Kane, in spite of his social, intellectual, and economic superiority to Jennie, is "nevertheless, instinctively, magnetically, and chemically drawn to her" (*Jennie Gerhardt*, 124). In addition to characterizing behavior that is beyond individual control, these "chemical" references also describe behavior that is beyond human understanding, conduct that springs from the inscrutable realm of the unknowable, passion driven by "the mystic chemistry of our being, . . . that incomprehensible chemistry which we call *life* and personality" (*The Financier*, 187) or "that subconscious chemistry of things of which as yet we know nothing" (*The Titan*, 253).

Dreiser's habitual use of the word "chemic" has drawn frequent comment. His friend Louise Campbell stated that "chemical attraction" was "a favorite phrase of his to account for an inexplainable situation." James T. Farrell noted that "his 'chemisms' are overall generalizations of impulses of which the character is not aware. In this respect Dreiser asserted a biological determinism, which in terms of our present state of knowledge about man, is crude." Another critic has stated that these "chemic" references "are best taken as metaphor. . . . [As explanations] they are inadequate."[25] Dreiser's references to the chemistry of human nature and behavior in these novels are certainly unsatisfactory as explanations of the motivations underlying his characters' actions, but they indicate that even before his first exposure to Jacques Loeb's work, he was at least aware of and had himself vaguely absorbed the mechanistic philosophy that viewed humankind as a complex chemical formula obeying the same laws of chemistry and physics that ruled all nature.

The most likely source of Dreiser's knowledge of mechanistic thought prior to his discovery of Loeb was a book by Ernst Haeckel, Germany's most well-known evolutionary biologist in the late nineteenth century.[26] Haeckel's very popular *The Riddle of the Universe at the Close of the Nineteenth Century* (1900) was designed as "a general survey of the actual condition of our knowledge of nature and its progress during the present century." Dreiser was no doubt attracted by the intelligible style (not to mention the title) of the English translation of this popularization. In addition, he no doubt felt at home with the evolutionary content running through much of the book that so echoed many of the ideas he had encountered in Huxley, Tyndall, Darwin, and especially Spencer. Haeckel resided in the same evolutionary universe that Dreiser had been introduced to in *First Principles*, applying the theory of evolution not only to the organic realm of life but to the inorganic realm of substance. He proclaimed that the law of evolution "dominates the entire universe, and that the world is nothing else than an eternal 'evolution of substance.'" This vision of cosmic evolutionary process led Haeckel to the same humbling and terrifying conclusion about the insignificance of humanity that Dreiser had reached after reading Spencer. "Our earth shrinks into the slender proportions of a 'mote in the sunbeam,'" Haeckel declared:

Our own "human nature," which exalted itself into an image of God in its anthropistic illusion, sinks to the level of a placental mammal, which has no more value for the universe at large than the ant, the fly of a summer's day, the microscopic infusorium, or the smallest bacillus. Humanity is but a transitory phase of the evolution of an eternal substance, a particular phenomenal form of matter and energy.

Even Haeckel's discussion of ethics merely duplicated what Dreiser had encountered in *The Data of Ethics*. Haeckel directly acknowledged Spencer's theory of ethical instincts, drawing the same distinctions in survival value between the "concurrent impulses" of egoism and altruism: "egoism secures the self-preservation of the individual, altruism that of the species which is made up of the chain of perishable individuals."[27]

The Riddle of the Universe, however, would prove much more valuable to Dreiser than a mere accessible recapitulation of the evolutionary ideas he had encountered over a decade earlier; for Haeckel's work was the first prolonged explanation of mechanistic science and philosophy that Dreiser would absorb. One of Haeckel's principal arguments throughout *The Riddle of the Universe* is that because both organic and inorganic matter are composed of the same basic atomic building blocks, the study of life must follow the same scientific principles that govern the study of all nature.[28] Because "the study of ponderable matter is primarily the concern of chemistry," Haeckel attempted to interpret all functions of life, from the primitive processes of sensation, respiration, and movement to the complex processes of consciousness, memory, and rational thought, in terms of the findings of nineteenth-century chemistry:

> The phenomena of the lowly psychic life of the unicellular protist and the plant, and of the lowest animal forms—their irritability, their reflex movements, their sensitiveness and instinct of self-preservation—are directly determined by physiological action in the protoplasm of their cells—that is, by physical and chemical changes which are partly due to heredity and partly to adaptation. And we must say just the same of the higher psychic activity of the higher animals and man, of the formation of ideas and concepts, of the marvelous phenomena of reason and consciousness; for the latter have been phylogenetically evolved from the former.

Chemical explanations of human nature, then, abound throughout the book. Psychological processes are described as the result of "psychoplasm" ("chemical analysis proves it to be a body of the group we call protoplasmic bodies, the albuminoid carbon-combinations which are at the root of all vital processes"), while the process of heredity, still a mystery, must eventually be reduced, "like all other vital phenomena, to exclusively physical and chemical processes, to the *mechanics of the protoplasm*" (Haeckel's emphasis). Sexual passion and reproduction, activities frequently described as "chemic" in Dreiser's fiction, are twice described by Haeckel as the result of "erotic chemicotropism."[29]

Dreiser had the highest regard for Haeckel's *The Riddle of the Universe*. In a 1921 letter to his friend Ed Smith, Dreiser revealed, "I read Haeckel, and have for years, (re-read) with unwearied interest." A year earlier he had encouraged Helen Richardson to read the book, and he reported in his journal that she was "enjoying it very much." In 1927 he ranked the book among the eleven of the world's best books.[30] Late in his life many of Dreiser's philosophical conclusions seem to have been inspired by the scientific and theological speculations that he found in Haeckel (see Chapter 6). His first reading of *The Riddle of the Universe*, however, was significant in introducing Dreiser to the basic ideas of mechanistic science that were circulating in German scientific circles. The large body of evolutionary thought that accompanied Haeckel's mechanistic outlook made the book a perfect vehicle for transporting Dreiser from the ideas of Herbert Spencer to those of Jacques Loeb.

In spite of Dreiser's fascination with Loeb's writing and his common interests in the subjects of Loeb's research, he did not attempt to correspond with or meet Loeb until 1919. By that time, his interest in mechanistic science had been expanded through his friendships with Dr. A. A. Brill and Edward H. Smith.

Ed Smith and his wife, Edith deLong Smith, were two of Dreiser's closest friends in Greenwich Village in the late 1910s. Dreiser served as the best man at their wedding, and he frequently attended their parties, social gatherings of the artistic and intellectual lights of the Village scene. During one such occasion in 1918, Dreiser met Dr. Abraham Arden Brill, the Austrian-born psychologist who was most responsible for presenting Freud's theories to America.[31]

Brill received his Ph.D. in 1901 at New York University and his M.D. at Columbia University's College of Physicians and Surgeons in 1903. By 1918, when Dreiser met him, he was the chief of the psychiatry clinic at Columbia as well as a lecturer in psychoanalysis and abnormal psychology at N.Y.U. Brill's most notable contribution to American psychology, however, commenced in 1909, when he began to translate Freud's major works from German into English. Beginning with Freud's *Selected Papers on Hysteria*, Brill brought Freudian theory to the attention of American psychologists and influenced a group of Greenwich Village writers who followed the cult of Freudianism for a generation after World War I.[32]

Dreiser was immediately impressed with Brill, and the two became friends. Dreiser considered Brill a modern "Socrates" or "Diogenes with his lantern—but not looking for honesty—instead understanding." Brill gave him a copy of his *Psychoanalysis: Its Theories and Practical Applications*, a summary of psychoanalytic theory, illustrated by many case histories of patients who had come under Brill's care. Dreiser was particularly moved by these stories, confessing that they had "the appeal of great tragedy for me":

> I feel as though I were walking in great halls and witnessing tremendous scenes. Life as revealed thus is sad to me—in view of all the obvious and yet unseen pitfalls through which we move. "The blind leading the blind." Again a book like this and the wisdom of Freud—is like a master with a key who unlocks subterraneous cells and leads forth the hoary victims of injustice.

Brill replied, "That my book should have produced that depressing effect on you is not bad. Such depressions are usually very transitory." He suggested that Dreiser's new awareness of the complexities of the psyche would undoubtedly result in "a greater penetration of human life than you have given the world thus far."[33]

Brill exposed Dreiser even further to Freud's ideas by encouraging him to read Freud's *Three Contributions to a Theory of Sex*, *Totem and Taboo*, and *The Interpretation of Dreams*, as well as H. W. Frink's *Morbid Fears and Compulsions*. Years later, Dreiser stated that he would never forget his first exposure to these works:

> At that time and even now quite every paragraph came as a revelation to me— a strong, revealing light thrown on some of the darkest problems that haunted and troubled me and my work. And reading him has helped me in my studies of life and men. I said at that time and I repeat now that he reminded me of a conqueror who has taken a city, entered its age-old hoary prisons and there generously proceeding to release from their gloomy and rusted cells the prisoners of formulae, faiths and illusions which have racked and worn man for hundreds and thousands of years. And I still think so.[34]

In spite of this high praise for Freud's work, Dreiser never became as fascinated by Freudian theory as many of his literary colleagues. Nor did he ever submit himself to psychoanalysis, unlike many other residents of the Village, where psychoanalysis became an intellectual fad. Although he did employ some Freudian elements in *An American Tragedy*, his portrayal of Clyde Griffiths was not a consistent Freudian portrait and his experimentation with literary techniques like stream-of-consciousness were minimal. His caution about the Freudian interpretation of human nature probably arose from the mechanistic criticisms of Freudianism, of which he was very aware through Loeb and Smith. The elements that he did cull from Freudianism were those that supported his continuing rebellion against the forces of traditional morality and those that reconfirmed his deterministic point of view.

For instance, in 1919 Dreiser wrote an essay, titled "Neurotic America and the Sex Impulse," in which he employed Freudian theory and terminology to attack the widespread suppression of sex in America by a group of "preachers and pretending thinkers." No doubt when Dreiser wrote this piece, he had in mind those moralists who had attempted to censor or ban *The Titan* and *The "Genius"* and who had been responsible for the near-suppression of *Sister Carrie* years earlier. Dreiser believed that "the impulses we are trying to suppress are, this side of excess, perfectly normal, while the thing we think we want is an infantile conception of life and its processes, unsuited to thinking men and women." The sex impulse was a "chemical force" within human beings that could not be totally suppressed. "It is a fire, a chemical explosion, really." The result of the moralists' attempt to suppress this internal chemical force was that "this country, taken as a whole, is as much a victim of deep-seated neurosis relating to this impulse as any." He noted with irony that in every town in America where churches preached their "lofty code of ethics and morals," there were also many places where neurotic behavior exhibited itself in the sale of pornography and the practice of prostitution.[35]

While Freud supplied Dreiser with some new scientific ammunition to fire at the Comstock Society and other agents of censorship, he also gave added support to Dreiser's mechanistic reading. For Freudian theory has a deterministic streak running though it, not only in its assertion that our unconscious desires, over which we have no control, play an important role in determining our conscious wills and behavior but also in its assertion that "chemisms" are responsible for the sex impulse.[36]

Like Loeb, Freud had been educated in Germany during the period when the mechanistic school had been revolutionizing German physiology. He had been a student of animal physiology for six years under Ernst Brücke, whose influence brought Freud to recognize the physico-chemical nature of the sex impulse. In *Three Contributions to a Theory of Sex*, Freud wrote that "we may now believe that in the interstitial tissues of the gonads special chemical substances are produced which, taken up in the bloodstream, permit the charge of definite parts of the central nervous system with sexual tension."[37] He referred to these chemical substances as "der

Chemismus," rendered by his English language translator, A. A. Brill, as "chemisms." Ellen Moers has noted that while Dreiser may have encountered the word in his reading as early as 1902, the first use of "chemism" in his writing occurred around the time of his reading Freud's *Theory of Sex*. The usage of the word by an authority no less than Sigmund Freud (or at least its use by his translator, Brill) gave Dreiser the sanction to employ this peculiar idiom whenever he wished in the future to refer to the physico-chemical conception of human nature that was contained in mechanistic philosophy.[38]

At the same time that Dreiser was linking Freud's chemical explanations of the sexual impulse to Loeb's physico-chemical explanations of human behavior, his mechanistic studies were furthered by his conversations and correspondence with his friend Edward H. Smith. In 1919, Smith met Dr. Max G. Schlapp, a professor of neuropathology at New York University's medical school. Schlapp was an advocate of the mechanistic point of view and had very definite opinions about "the chemical causation of abnormal behavior" that he wanted to put into printed form. Smith befriended Schlapp and, as Dreiser wrote, "presently appeared not only as this medico's public sponsor but scriptic interpreter." Smith and Schlapp soon began collaborating on a book called *The New Criminology*, a summary of Schlapp's theories about the role of the endocrine glands in producing normal and criminal behavior.[39]

Smith's wife died suddenly in early 1919, and thereafter he frequently visited Dreiser, who helped Smith through the shock of her death. During these visits, Smith began to inform Dreiser about Schlapp's theories. "There was some talk, of course, of endocrine glands and their social meaning," Dreiser reported, and he was no doubt very familiar with the material in the book when it was finally published in 1928.[40]

Schlapp was a mechanist who, like Loeb, believed that "the human being is a series of connected machines" and is composed of "a number of cell groups, which correspond roughly to the parts of a machine" (84–85). Just as each machine in a factory must function efficiently and in harmony with the others to create its normal finished product, Schlapp maintained that each cell group or organ within the body must function correctly and in rhythm with the other organs to produce normal behavior. The breakdown of the machinery of the body was, according to Schlapp, the cause of abnormal behavior. Like Loeb, he complained that Freudian interpretations of abnormal or criminal behavior were too theoretical and imprecise. He and Smith wrote that when

> the psycho-analyst comes to tackle the fundamental problem of abnormal behavior he lapses into a sad metaphysic. What must ultimately be explained in terms of physics still dwells with him in a metaphysical world. His explanations are modal instead of causal; he deals in symptomatology rather than etiology. He belongs, in other words, to the passing school. (26–27)

Schlapp felt that all human behavior could be studied in mechanistic terms, and that abnormal behavior was caused by "a Criminal Imperative, an inner drive which impels these forbidden and extraordinary human acts" and could be "completely accounted for under physico-chemical laws" (28).

Schlapp studied the functions of the endocrine glands, whose secretions, he believed, were the chemical determinants of behavior. If these glands secreted too much or too little of their chemicals into the bloodstream, the body was thrown into a state of chemical imbalance. Emotional shocks or stresses could cause the glands to react excessively and thereby create this imbalance. Schlapp postulated that "the diffident, the gentle, the unselfish, the refined and the sensitive" as well as "the insatiable and irrepressible adventurers and conquerors of the earth" were "creatures not of the will but the helpless mechanical products of inner secretions. . . . Cowardice and courage, dullness and genius, sloth and aspiration are alike only chemical sublimates" (99).

Schlapp maintained that it was a feeble-minded type who most commonly exhibited criminal behavior. Prison statistics as well as common sense observation revealed "that many offenders are mentally deficient in gross and palpable ways, that still more are of low intellectual power and that the great majority of convicts are from the stupid, the unlettered and debased ranks" (149). Feeble-minded children, as well as the more serious congenital defectives such as Mongoloid and cretinous children, were born with an endocrinological imbalance. Schlapp argued that such children were born with this imbalance because of

> a chemical absence or disbalance in the mother, which caused the selective inhibition of the formative process in the cells of the foetus. In other words, the brains and other essential parts of the nervous system in such children were already retarded prenatally because the mother's system was out of chemical balance and the cells improperly nourished. (112–13)

The typical mother of the feeble-minded individual was the woman who was exposed to the daily shocks and stresses of modern life and whose glands reacted excessively to cause a chemical imbalance. According to Schlapp, "It is the women who . . . enter into competition with men or are subjected to the strains and stresses of life who become the mothers of these uncounted defectives, insane and criminal individuals who are the scourge of the world and a torture to themselves" (133). Schlapp here reveals himself as a colleague of those physicians who in the late nineteenth and early twentieth centuries attempted to use the sanction of medical science to remind women of their primary role as mothers and to warn them that their growing presence in activities outside the home imperiled the very health of the race.[41]

Schlapp maintained that these feeble-minded individuals, or "deficients" as he called them, lacked a moral sense of what was right or wrong, or, in terms less moral and more mechanistic, lacked the ability to distinguish between "lawful and unlawful conduct or harmless and harmful acts." He declared that, to most deficients, "one deed is about equal to another and any discriminations in the nature and quality of acts must be dictated by considerations of immediate personal advantage" (155). Such a feeble-minded deficient was not only capable of abnormal behavior, but was often driven to criminal behavior including murder:

> He conceives a hatred for some person who stands in his way or who has done him a real or fancied injury. The concept of killing this enemy comes into his mind. Such ideas occur to all men at times. . . . The normal man rejects the idea almost as quickly as it is formed. . . . But the man capable of murder is disturbed in his glands, cells and nerve centers. The concept of killing is rapidly followed by another concept of the manner of carrying out the deed. Perhaps he thinks of a revolver, or a poison phial or a knife. The concept of a plan comes to him and the concept of a concealment, a flight and an escape. No doubt he struggles back and forth, drawn to his victim and away from the deed of blood by the contentions of his emotions and of his inhibitory brain parts. This very struggle works him up the more. The time comes when he can no longer resist. The idea has taken possession of him. He makes his plans, always under strong emotional excitement, lies in wait, strikes the blow and makes an attempt to divert suspicion from himself. (202–3)

Although *The New Criminology* was not published until 1928, it seems obvious that Dreiser was familiar with Schlapp's theories by the time that he wrote *An American Tragedy* in 1925. Perhaps it is too strong to suggest that Dreiser's portrait of Clyde Griffiths is a literary case study of Schlapp's mentally deficient murderer, but there are strong parallels between the description of murder quoted above as an act beyond the will or total responsibility of the individual and Dreiser's presentation of Clyde as a weak-willed mechanism, driven by social, sexual, and chemic forces beyond his control. That he recognized the parallels between his fictional murderer and Schlapp's real-life murderers is further revealed in the title of Dreiser's 1928 *Herald Tribune* review of *The New Criminology*: "American Tragedies."[42]

Dreiser's increasing interest in mechanistic philosophy finally led him to seek an introduction to Jacques Loeb in 1919, the very year that he was reading Freud and beginning to discuss Schlapp's theories with Smith. In early April he asked H. L. Mencken, "Do you know Jacques Loeb? If so would you give me a letter of introduction to him." Because Mencken was unacquainted with the eminent scientist, Dreiser himself wrote a brief letter to Loeb on May 29:

> Dear Mr. Loeb,
> Several years ago I read your book on the Mechanistic Interpretation of Life. I have been wondering if, since then, you have developed much additional data and if these are to be found in any published form. I will appreciate information.[43]

Dreiser's letter reached Loeb at Woods Hole, where he was conducting his summer research at the Marine Biological Laboratory. Loeb was delighted with Dreiser's interest in his work. "It is, naturally, a gratification to me," he wrote, "that you should take an interest in my work, which, as a rule, is not relished by the majority of literary people on account of the frankly mechanistic or chemical conception of life expressed in my writings." He recommended two of his recent books to Dreiser: *Forced Movements, Tropisms and Animal Conduct* (1918), a book "on Animal Conduct, which of course also holds for human conduct," and *The Organism as a Whole* (1916), which "explains the harmonious character of living organisms on a physico-chemical basis." He also invited Dreiser to visit him and observe his experiments when he returned to the Rockefeller Institute in the fall. "It would give me great pleasure to meet you personally, since I have followed your literary career with special interest. Needless to say, I am not a romanticist in literature."[44]

Although Dreiser read Loeb's two recommended books, as well as another, *Comparative Physiology of the Brain and Comparative Psychology* (1900), he did not call on Loeb in the fall; in October Dreiser left New York and moved to California, where he lived for the next three years. Yet their correspondence continued. Dreiser once asked Loeb to recommend a "clear readable summary of the Science of Human Behavior—to date," confessing to Loeb his difficulty in understanding much of the scientific literature that he encountered: "I am without scientific training and only a good writer can interpret science for the layman. I find no difficulty in reading and following you—but so often writers present their data so poorly that it is slavery to follow them."[45]

Loeb replied that "no exact work has been done on human behavior. The psychiatrists, of course, have to deal with the subject but their work is more or less of an amateurish character." Loeb complained about "the wave of Freudianism," which, unknown to him, had somewhat swept up Dreiser through Brill's influence:

> While in all of these hypotheses there is some basis of fact, the methods are so amateurish and crude that nothing permanent has or can come of it. Unless we get exact methods such as I have tried to introduce in the form of the tropism theory in lower animals, we have to be satisfied with admitting our igno-rance. . . . This condition of affairs makes one wish that one could come back to life in a thousand years, but alas, such possibilities exist only in mediumistic circles.[46]

When Dreiser returned to New York from California in October 1922, Loeb once again invited him to pay a call on the Rockefeller Institute. There, in January 1923, Dreiser met Loeb for the first time and began a series of visits during which he observed at first hand the experiments on animal tropisms and parthenogenesis that he had discovered in Loeb's books for the past eight years. He met other investigators who, like Loeb, believed that experimentation and exact measurements were the only methods that would yield true knowledge of the processes of life; among those whom Dreiser met were W.J.V. Osterhout and Boris Sokoloff, who would be responsible for Dreiser's visit to the Marine Biological Laboratory at Woods Hole a few years later. But the most important aspect of these visits for Dreiser were his discussions with Loeb about the physico-chemical basis of human nature. Loeb's view of the universe corresponded with the pessimistic, deterministic outlook Dreiser had picked up from his evolu-tionary readings. The scientist assured him that "all is accidental" and that there was "no thought, no plan—no intelligence" in the universe. He expressed fears to Dreiser, however, that reactionary vitalists and metaphy-sicians were presently renewing their efforts to discredit the mechanistic point of view. He foresaw a "great danger of dark ages returning" and suggested to Dreiser that the "intelligentsia ought to hold together in a kind of brotherhood."[47] Loeb evidently felt the need to popularize the message of mechanistic philosophy beyond his scientific circle, and sensing that he had found a powerful, sympathetic ally in the literati, he flattered

Dreiser, catered to his hunger for information, and invited him to return to the Rockefeller Institute. Dreiser's visits continued for the next year until Loeb's death in February 1924, and his discussions with Loeb were valuable for providing the mechanistic motivations he employed in his characterization of Clyde Griffiths in *An American Tragedy*.

*   *   *

The first indication in Dreiser's writing of his renewed interest in mechanistic determinism appeared several years earlier in his characterization of another chemically driven murderer in a play titled *The Hand of the Potter*. The main character of the piece is a young man named Isadore Berchansky, who is "badly compounded chemically." Berchansky sexually molests and kills the eleven-year-old daughter of one of his neighbors and eventually commits suicide rather than allow himself to be driven to repeat his horrible crimes. Dreiser completed the play in late 1916 and showed it to Mencken, who correctly recognized that the play was "loose, elephantine and devoid of sting." He accused Dreiser of having written it simply to test the moralists who were constantly waiting to pounce on his work. The play was not produced on the stage for two years and did not appear in print until 1919. In the epilogue of the 1919 published version, Dreiser made several changes and additions that underlined explicitly the influence of the mechanistic science that he had been studying.[48]

At the close of the play, several reporters at the scene of the suicide debate over the nature of Berchansky's crimes. One reporter, who is the spokesman for Dreiser's mechanistic views, reveals that he has

> been readin' up on these cases for some time, an' from what I can make out they're no more guilty than any other person with a disease. Did ye know, aither ave ye, that there's something they've called *harmones* which the body manufactures an which is poured into the blood streams of every waan ave us which excites us to the m'aning ave beauty an' thim things—"sensitizes" is the word they use. Now if a felly is so constituted that he has more ave that an' less ave somethin' else . . . he's likely to be like that. He can't help it. There's something in him that pushes him on in spite of himself.

Through the reporters' continuing discussion about Berchansky, Dreiser expresses his belief that moral notions about good and evil must be altered in the light of the findings of mechanistic science:

Don't be so cocksure in your judgments of who are the good an' who are the bad in this world. Facts an' proofs are naht aal on the surface, by any means. . . . Sometimes I think we're naht unlike those formulae they give ye in a chemical laboratory—if ye're made up right, ye work right; if ye're naht, ye don't, an' that's aal there is to it. . . . It's a great force about which we know naathing as yet an' which we're just beginnin' to look into—what it manes, how it affects people.[49]

These fragments of dialogue are typical of the additions Dreiser made to the final act of *The Hand of the Potter* in his 1919 version. Dreiser's deterministic point of view, embracing the rejection of the traditional concepts of good and evil and the denial of free will and responsibility that he had first internalized during his reading of evolutionary philosophy, was now blatantly proclaimed under the heady influence of his new absorption in mechanistic thought. Adopting Loeb's physico-chemical variation on Spencer's theory of ethics, Dreiser now maintained the conviction that human ethical instincts were inherited in the form of chemical compulsions that forced most humans, with the exception of a number of ethical mutants, to act in ways that were beneficial to their fellow species. In 1918 Dreiser wrote that "once this purely mechanistic theory or proof is accepted, all the ethic and unethic functionings of life become plain and understandable enough." He became impatient with those who confused these instinctual compulsions with ideal moral concepts of right and wrong; in 1920, for instance, he replied irritably to a correspondent that "we have no knowledge of any goods or evils existing outside of our chemico-physical plasm here. Read Haeckel, Crile, Loeb. You are mixing up religious balderdash with chemical and physical facts or laws."[50]

Between the writing of *The Hand of the Potter* in 1916 and the appearance of *An American Tragedy* in 1925, Dreiser's sketches, essays, and letters are full of references to his increasingly mechanistic orientation. In 1917, for instance, he wrote in his autobiography that his brother, the songwriter Paul Dresser, whose life Dreiser regarded as a failure, reminded him of the

unknown Miltons and Caesars walking obscure ways in obscure places. For here was one of those great Falstaffian souls who, for lack of a little iron or sodium or carbon dioxide in his chemical compost, was not able to bestride the world like a Colossus. (And how narrowly many others miss infinitely better fates than are actually theirs!) . . . A little more selfishness, a little more iron or licithin, maybe; as it was, with these missing, he could only sing, jest and grow fat.[51]

In the manuscript of *Dawn*, Dreiser at one point directly stated the Loebian mechanistic conception of the human species, complaining that "man as a chemic animal has been completely lost sight of. . . . [Man] *is* a chemic animal, reacting constantly quite as chemical and physical bodies do to laws." In an essay on ethics probably written in 1919, he expressed the same outlook: "[Man] is a chemical compound, bottled and sealed in realms outside his ken and placed here willy-nilly but subject to the laws of his own substances and such others as govern them." In a 1919 sketch of the marriage of Ed Smith and Edith deLong, he expressed once again his belief that the chemical composition of each individual determined his or her moral destiny; he suggested, in wording that reveals his growing acquaintance with the ideas of Freud and Schlapp, that "a little more or less of one or another gland juice would turn a Lincoln, say, into a small-town loafer and joke!" And in a 1924 letter that displays the influence of his conversations with Loeb, he expressed his displeasure with vitalist interpretations of human behavior, such as the existence of an entity corresponding to "mind," and embraced Loeb's chemical theories of tropistic responses as the true determinants of behavior. "So called *mind* seems to me for the most part an illusion. The actions of men have little to do with it or its primary principle—logic. In fact men act & react by some system of responses— chemic or psychic which has nothing to do with what we have been dreaming of as mind."52

Dreiser believed that the strongest chemical compulsion of human nature was the sexual impulse. Years before he had read Loeb or Freud, Dreiser suggested the chemical nature of sexuality when he wrote in *The Financier* that "a love affair . . . was little less or more than a drop of coloring added to a glass of clear water, or a chemical agent introduced into a delicate chemical formula." He came to believe, after reading Loeb and Freud, that the chemical reactions that expressed themselves in love affairs came to equilibrium after a time, ending the attraction of the partners for one another. "The duration runs from three months to three years. If two persons remain together after that, it is because of some other reason." Dreiser was not so timid to deny that he himself was driven by this sexual chemistry, and he once explained his own frequent love affairs with numerous women through this compulsion. "It's not my fault," he claimed. "You walk into a room, see a woman and something happens. It's chemical. What are you going to do about it?" His frank admission of sexual varietism in *Dawn*, written in 1917 before he met Brill, reads less like the confession of a prisoner of Freudian compulsions and more like the rationalizations of a victim of Loebian tropisms:

> For the second, third and fourth decades of my life—or from fifteen to thirty-five—there appeared to be a toxic something in form itself—that of the female of the species where beautiful—that could effect veritable paroxysms of emotion and desire in me, and that over distances of time and space. The mystery! The subtleties of physics and chemistry behind it! . . . We call it love. A word! Any other label that implies a chemical formula such as a human temperament, embodied as flesh and displayed as a design, can evoke, in another such form, emotion and so release and exchange tides of desire and sensual relationship, would do as well. The form of a woman is the best expression of that design or geometric formula, and the word "aphrodisiac" (Aphrodite) the best expression of the power of that form or formula upon its companion formula, the male.[53]

The mechanistic point of view that Dreiser embraced in the early 1920s found its finest expression in *An American Tragedy*, which was published in December 1925. In this novel, Dreiser combined his conception of the individual as a seeking, hungering mechanism of desire with an indictment of those aspects of American society that encouraged greed, the lust for power, and social and economic inequality. For the tragedy of this novel was that Clyde Griffiths's insatiable hunger for social position and wealth

> was really not an *anti-social* dream as Americans should see it, but rather a *pro-social* dream. *He was really doing the kind of thing which Americans should and would have said was the wise and moral thing for him to do had he not committed a murder.* His would not ordinarily be called the instinct of a criminal; rather, it would be deemed the *instinct of a worthy and respected temperament.*[54]

For over thirty years preceding the writing of *An American Tragedy*, Dreiser had noticed consistent patterns in a group of highly publicized murder cases. This set of murders involved young men of low or medium economic status who murdered those individuals who in some manner stood in the way of their marrying into a higher social class. Many of the cases involved a young man who murdered a former lover (sometimes a pregnant girlfriend) who would not set him free to marry his newer, wealthier lover. In each of these cases—in the Carlyle Harris case of 1894, the Roland Molineux case of 1899, the Chester Gillette case of 1906, the Dr. Bennett Hyde case of 1909, the Clarence Richesen case of 1911, and the William Orpet case of 1916—Dreiser found examples of young men who had murdered to secure the opportunity to advance to a position of social and economic power.

In examining and comparing these cases, Dreiser concluded that underlying each of the murders was the pursuit of the American dream:

> It seemed to spring from the fact that almost every young person was possessed of an ingrowing ambition to be somebody financially or socially. In short, the general mental mood of America was directed toward escape from any form of poverty. This ambition did not imply merely the attainment of comfort and the wherewithal to make happy one's friends, but rather the accumulation of wealth implying power, social superiority, even social domination.

In such a society where the accumulation of wealth obsessed so many youths, Dreiser observed that the quickest way to rise economically was to marry wealth. "In short, we bred the fortune hunter de luxe," he wrote. "Fortune-hunting became a disease."[55]

Of all the cases that he studied, Dreiser decided that the case of Chester Gillette most closely suited his needs for the novel he wanted to write. Gillette had been raised in the Midwest by poor, street-preaching parents. As a young man, Gillette was extremely ambitious in wanting to better his social position, but he was "not sufficiently developed mentally" ever to achieve the dreams of affluence that drove him. In 1906 he came east to work at a collar manufacturing plant owned by his wealthy uncle in Cortland, New York. He believed that "if in some fashion he could connect himself with the superior life of this uncle, he would naturally pass from a lower to a higher social and financial state." Gillette became romantically involved with a young girl named Billy Brown, who also worked in the factory. In time this girl became pregnant and demanded that Gillette marry her, although by then he had met many of his uncle's wealthy acquaintances and had fallen in love with a daughter of one of Cortland's finest families. His opportunity to marry wealth was blocked by the demands of marriage from a poor, working-class girl, and the potential loss of the American dream created in him

> a state to which he was socially and emotionally fearfully opposed, one which was sufficient, probably, to have affected his powers of reason. It could, and probably did, absolutely befuddle and finally emotionally derange a youth who because of his romantic dreams, and more, because when subject to them he was also subject to those dreadful economic, social, moral and conventional pressures about him, was finally driven romantically mad and brought to the point of committing a crime that was so terrible to the world.[56]

Chester Gillette drowned Billy Brown in the Big Moose Lake in upstate New York, was quickly apprehended by the local authorities, was placed on trial and found guilty, and was sent to the electric chair in March 1908.

Dreiser's description of Gillette's tragic dilemma, written almost ten years after publication of *An American Tragedy*, reveals elements of both Loeb's and Schlapp's views on ethical and criminal behavior. Loeb had maintained that ethics were inherited just as other human physical characteristics were passed from parent to child. Under certain economic and social conditions, however, Loeb warned, "individual mutants" could appear in whom the "desirable instinct" to behave in a proper manner would be lost. For Dreiser, Chester Gillette was such a ethical mutant, warped by "the general social and financial attitude of Americans—their dreams of grandeur, all based on financial achievement."[57] While this "American dream" did not corrupt the moral behavior of every ambitious individual in the society, Gillette's tragedy was that he was simply not mentally endowed to pursue his dream along socially recognized pathways of achievement. In fact, Dreiser seemed to regard him as the type of mentally deficient, feeble-minded criminal whom Schlapp claimed lacked a moral sense and ultimately landed behind prison bars. Dreiser, however, posited a variation of Schlapp's theories in accounting for destructive behavior like that of Gillette. Shortly before the publication of *The New Criminology*, Dreiser had a sharp disagreement with Schlapp's co-author, Ed Smith, over the degree of importance that social forces played in producing the internal imbalances that resulted in criminal behavior. While Dreiser fully accepted the important role of "glands + their defects or changes," he claimed that "back of them lie the *social accidents* which produce the defective glands" (emphasis added). In other words, Dreiser wished to emphasize the role of cultural determinants over that of genetic determinants in molding criminal behavior, stressing environmental factors such as the "economic, social, and political conditions or ignorance and superstition" as Loeb identified them, which could unbalance the delicate mechanism of the individual. Smith strongly disagreed: "Gland and nervous disorders, including insanity, are the proximate, immediate and psychological cause of such acts. Social accidents are the secondary causes." Smith hoped to minimize their difference of opinion, maintaining that they only "disagree in terms here, not in essence," but for Dreiser the difference was significant to his understanding and interpretation of Gillette's murderous actions and to his portrayal of Clyde Griffiths in *An American Tragedy*. For while Gillette possessed the "immature and more or less futile mind" of a mental deficient, according to

Dreiser it was the materialistic, acquisitive society that Gillette inhabited that proved "destructive to his reasoning powers." The final responsibility for the murder of Billy Brown lay not only in the mechanistic mysteries of human nature but also in the corrupting greed and economic inequalities of American society that unbalanced the chemical formulae within the individual. *An American Tragedy* reveals that Dreiser's naturalism not only consisted of a mixture of cosmic and chemical determinism but also included a form of social determinism as one of the factors that destined individual fates. Not only did this social determinism shift responsibility for crime from the individual to society, but it also allowed the possibility of reforming the corrupting influences within society. "Indeed," Dreiser wrote years later, "not only is crime actually induced, as I see it, by the economic inequalities of our present social order but also it most certainly could be lessened."[58]

In *An American Tragedy* Chester Gillette becomes Clyde Griffiths and Dreiser retells this dark story of the American dream turned American compulsion. In creating the character of Clyde Griffiths, Dreiser drew on documentary sources about Gillette and the other murderers whom he had studied, as well as incorporating both his personal recollections of his rebellious, troubled brother, Marcus Romanus (Rome) Dreiser and the self-consciousness of his own sexual and status appetites. But in addition, this complex fictional creation, which one scholar has referred to as the "Everyman of desire,"[59] displays Dreiser's understanding and utilization of Loeb's theories of tropistic behavior and the possibilities of mutated ethical instincts, Freud's theories of "chemisms" and the sexual impulse, and Schlapp's theory of the endocrinologically unbalanced "deficient" murderer.

From the time of his youth in Kansas City, Clyde Griffiths is "constantly thinking of how he might better himself, if he had the chance; places to which he might go, things he might see, and how differently he might live, if only this, that and the other things were true" (14). Clyde is tortured by his parents' poverty and by the affluence of the other boys his age whom he sees around him. "If only he had a better collar, a nicer shirt, finer shoes, a good suit, a swell overcoat like some boys had! Oh, the fine clothes, the handsome homes, the watches, rings, pins that some boys sported; the dandies many youths of his years already were" (19). Dreiser suggested that Clyde's dreams of wealth are warped by his poverty; "for his ideas of luxury were in the main so extreme and mistaken and gauche—mere wanderings of a repressed and unsatisfied fancy, which as yet had had nothing but imaginings to feed it" (35). Clyde displays the same hedonistic cravings that drive most of Dreiser's protagonists; the difference is that, unlike Carrie, Cowperwood, or Witla, Clyde is a loser in the Spencerian universe of struggle, and his weak personality or lack of force determines his inevitable failure. The tragedy of Clyde Griffiths and his real life counterpart, Chester Gillette, was very similar to the tragic predicament of human existence that had concerned Dreiser in Pittsburgh and New York in the 1890s, when he first read Spencer and Darwin; it was the tragedy of the "unfit" individual, who was driven by internalized social values to achieve, but who was destined by innate biological inabilities to fail in the competition for power, prestige, and pleasure.

While still in Kansas City, Clyde becomes fascinated with his rich uncle in New York whom he has never met; he imagines that "he must be a kind of Croesus, living in ease and luxury there in the east" (17). When Clyde eventually journeys to New York to seek employment at his uncle's shirt factory, he hopes that one day he will become part of the wealthy social world that his Eastern relatives inhabit. He goes so far as to prepare himself for his dreamed social rise by learning how to swim and row, because "if by chance he should be taken up by the Griffiths, he would need as many social accomplishments as possible" (255). Ironically, it is these abilities to swim and row that allow him eventually to plot Roberta Alden's drowning, a murder that he believes will lead him to his dream.

Clyde is not only driven by his desire to achieve wealth and social position; he is also driven by "chemisms" of the sexual impulse. Early in the novel, Dreiser blatantly displays his "chemic" conception of love and sex in his description of the seduction of Clyde's sister, Esta. "Not unlike her brother," Esta is attracted "to love, to comfort. . . . Within her was a chemism of dreams" that was beyond the understanding or approval of her parents. She is motivated by "the force and meaning of that chemistry and urge toward mating which lies back of all youthful thought and action" and by "those rearranging chemisms upon which all the morality or immorality of the world is based" (20). Within a week of meeting a young man "of compelling magnetism," the "chemic witchery was accomplished" (21), and Esta soon finds herself pregnant and abandoned. Following this virtual explosion of chemicals in the first pages of the novel, Dreiser is mercifully more frugal with his chemical references to romance and love. His descriptions of Clyde's sexual cravings, nevertheless, are occasionally expressed in such "chemic" prose and are almost always described as impulses beyond his control. "His was a disposition easily and often intensely inflamed by the chemistry of sex and the formula of beauty. He could not easily withstand the appeal, let alone the call, of sex" (239). One of his chief motivations is to find "a free pagan girl," and "he could scarcely wait until opportunity should provide him with the means of gratifying himself in this way" (70). Several women become involved with Clyde early in the novel, one of whom has "something heavy and langorous about her body, a kind of ray or electron that intrigued and lured him in spite of himself" (205). But it is Roberta Alden, an employee at the Griffiths factory, who first fulfills Clyde's dreams of sexual pleasure. Between Clyde and Roberta, there exists "a chemic or temperamental pull that was so definitely asserting itself, [that] he could no longer keep his eyes off her—or she hers from him" (254).

Sondra Finchley, however, is the fulfillment of Clyde's twin hungers for social status and for sexual gratification. Sondra was a "newer luminary—he could scarcely see Roberta any longer, so strong were the actinic rays of the other" (315). Sondra, in spite of her superior social position and the potential disapproval of her parents, is overcome by "the most destroying aspects of the very profound chemistry of love" (421) and is drawn romantically to Clyde. When she agrees to marry him, the thought is "like some sweet, disarranging poison to Clyde. It fevered and all but betrayed him mentally" (425). In spite of his obligations to Roberta, Clyde confesses that "I couldn't resist her [Sondra]" (683).

Yet all Clyde's seeking is destined for failure because of his mental deficiencies. Clyde's personality is described as "a temperament that was as fluid and unstable as water" (309), and he possesses "mental and material weaknesses before pleasures and dreams which he could not bring himself to forego" (466–67):

> For to say the truth, Clyde had a soul that was not destined to grow up. He lacked decidedly that mental clarity and inner directing application that in so many permits them to sort out from the facts and avenues of life the particular thing or things that make for their direct advancement. (169)

As defined by Dreiser, Clyde's personality seems to be a mixture of on the one hand the feeble-minded deficient of Schlapp and on the other hand the neurotic personality of Freudian theory, a personality dominated by the instincts of the id and incapable of sublimating desires into constructive, socially accepted actions. Once or twice in the novel, Dreiser suggests that the problem of Clyde's mental make-up is one of inheritance. His family is "one of those anomalies of psychic and social reflex and motivation such as would tax the skill of not only the psychologist but the chemist and physicist as well, to unravel" (13). Clyde's father in particular seems to display much of the mental weakness that the son possesses. Asa Griffiths is described as "one of those poorly integrated and correlated organisms . . . with no guiding or mental insight of his own" (13) and is "poorly knit mentally as well as physically" (172). Although his mother is much sturdier and more practical than her husband, Clyde's "emotionalism and exotic sense of romance" are derived "more from his father than from his mother" (14).

Dreiser's debt to Sigmund Freud reveals itself in the Freudian terminology that occasionally bursts forth from his pen, and much more significantly in the manner in which Dreiser handles Clyde's conception and planning of Roberta's murder. Dreiser's use of Freudian catch phrases usually appears in the introductory descriptions of lesser characters, or at a moment in the narrative when the author pauses to reflect on the motivations of such a character. For example, Clyde's Kansas City girlfriend, Hortense Briggs, who takes advantage of Clyde's naive adoration to enlarge her wardrobe while promising never-to-be-fulfilled sexual favors, takes pleasure in thinking that "he was suffering from *repressed desire* for her all the time that she tortured him . . . , a *sadistic trait* which had for its soil Clyde's own *masochistic yearning* for her" (107). The Reverend Duncan McMillan, who attempts to aid Clyde in grappling with the question of guilt at the novel's conclusion, is introduced to the reader as "possessing a highly poetic and emotional though so far *repressed and subliminated sex nature*" (777). The most prominent detail in Dreiser's description of Orville W. Mason, the district attorney who prosecutes Clyde, is his broken nose, a facial disfigurement that has left him somewhat unattractive to women and has resulted "in what the Freudians are accustomed to describe as a *psychic sex scar*" (504—emphases added). Such Freudian ornaments in Dreiser's descriptions seem to be the author's sincere but strained attempt to cloak his characters in psychological realism, as well as an attempt to establish to the reader the author's own authority as a psychic interpreter of the strange processes of the human mind.

Dreiser was much more effective in using Freudian ideas to overcome a central problem that he faced in constructing the novel: how to present Clyde's plotting of Roberta's death while still limiting or deflecting from his protagonist the total responsibility for the crime. Dreiser's strategy was to divide Clyde's personality into two opposing components that seem to resemble two of the three Freudian systems that define the personality: a dark subconscious id that encourages him through six chapters to commit murder, and a slightly more conscious superego, a reserve of ethical values that admonishes him to avoid such a horrible act. The thought of murder first enters Clyde's mind when he reads a newspaper account of a double drowning at a nearby lake. Immediately on learning that only the woman's body had been recovered while the man's body was still missing, Clyde begins to consider the possibility of devising a similar "accident" with Roberta. His superego at once exhorts him to reject such a plot. "The mere thinking of such a thing . . . was terrible, and he must not, he must not, allow such a thought to enter his mind. Never, never, never! He must not" (440). Although he tries to drive this gruesome scheme from his mind, "at moments the solution suggested by the item in *The Times-Union* again [thrust] itself forward, psychogenetically, born of his own turbulent, eager and disappointed seeking. And hence persisting" (463).

Clyde's evil subconscious voice from the id eventually assumes the hallucinatory form of a "Giant Efrit," a fairy tale genie who,

> now abhorrent and yet compelling, leering and yet intriguing, friendly and yet cruel, offered him a choice between an evil which threatened to destroy him (and against his deepest opposition) and a second evil which, however it might disgust or sear or terrify, still provided for freedom and success and love. (464)

Although his moral conscience tries to force him to defy the "Efrit of his own darker self" (472), Clyde, "because of flaws and weaknesses in his own unstable and variable will" (467), is unable to resist the suggestions and commands of his id. His ego, the active Freudian component of the personality that translates the impulses of the id into socially acceptable action, is so weak and underdeveloped that he can neither sublimate the id's primitive instincts for sexual pleasure and physical comfort nor resist the evil plot that the id has suggested to achieve these goals. Clyde proceeds with the step-by-step preparation of the murder like a victim of possession or like a puppet, carrying out the commands of an evil master in a passive, helpless manner; even as he telephones Roberta to arrange their final fateful meeting, "it seemed as though the Giant Efrit that had previously materialized in the silent halls of his brain, was once more here at his elbow—that he himself, cold and numb and fearsome, was being talked through—not actually talking himself" (471).

At the climactic moment when Clyde rows Roberta out to the middle of the Big Bittern Lake, where he has planned to drown her, Dreiser presents the final showdown between the warring factions of Clyde's personality. For a moment there is a "balanced combat" between his sub-conscious impulse ("a harried and ruthless and yet self-repressed desire to do—to do—to do") and his ethical impulse ("a chemic revulsion against death or murderous brutality that would bring death"). It is interesting that Dreiser here seems to lean away from Freud's concept of the superego, a matrix of *learned* social values and ideals that inhibits the compulsions of the id, and relies instead on a more mechanistic, Loebian force, an *innate*, chemical imprint that operates as an ethical imperative to block, tempo-rarily at least, the evil impulse of Clyde's id. At the moment when Clyde could consciously determine his fate, he is powerless to act, caught in a catatonic state between a subconscious command and a chemical instinct, or in Dreiser's words, "a static between a powerful compulsion to do and yet not to do" (491–92).

Although Dreiser did his best to illustrate that Clyde has no free will at that moment, and although the tragedy that follows is portrayed as an accident, it seems that the author intended finally to present Roberta's drowning as the result of some final triumph of Clyde's evil subconscious. For when Roberta, sensing that something is terribly wrong with Clyde, crawls across the boat to aid him, he reaches up to push her away from him. Although he shoves her away "not even then with any intention to do other than free himself of her—her touch—her pleading—consoling sym-pathy—her presence forever—God," he strikes her on the face with a "camera still unconsciously held tight." He hits her "with so much vehe-mence" that her nose and lip are badly cut, and as he rises to apologize for this blow, "so accidentally and all but unconsciously administered," the boat overturns. In the water, Clyde's subconscious voice returns for the last time, whispering:

> Is not this that which you have been thinking and wishing for this while—you in your great need? And behold! For despite your fear, your cowardice, this—this—has been done for you. An accident—an accident—an unintentional blow on your part is now saving you the labor of what you sought, and yet did not have the courage to do! But will you now, and when you need not, since it is an accident, by going to her rescue, once more plunge yourself in the horror of that defeat and failure which has so tortured you and from which this now releases you? (493)

As Roberta struggles helplessly, Clyde continues to lack the free will to act; however, while his frozen will had moments earlier prevented him from actively murdering her, his inactivity now passively causes her death. Considering the success of Clyde's subconscious voice in compelling his passive complicity in Roberta's death, as well as the earlier unconscious holding of the camera and the brutal force with which he struck her, it seems unlikely that Dreiser desired to portray the drowning as a "pure" accident, but rather as the final triumph of the dark, uncontrollable impulses of Clyde's id.

At the end of the novel, after he has been found guilty of murder and is awaiting his imminent execution, Clyde grieves in his jail cell over the inability of his saintly mother and his spiritual advisor, Reverend McMillan, to comprehend the underlying motivations and compulsions that led him to his ghastly crime. In an anguished, unspoken plea, Clyde questions whether "no one [would] ever understand—or give him credit for his human—if all too human and perhaps wrong hungers—yet from which so many others—along with himself suffered" (805). Dreiser believed that such a tormented prayer would be answered only when Americans abandoned their traditional moral conceptions of deviance and criminality and adopted the more precise methods of scientists like Loeb, Freud, and Schlapp.

Dreiser's compassion for the losers and victims of the social struggle for existence had its roots in his own childhood poverty and in his encounters in the ghettoes of Pittsburgh and New York in the 1890s. His reading of evolutionary philosophy, in addition, had given him the tragic vision that the majority of human beings were biologically predestined to fail in the competition for power, prestige, and pleasure. By the 1920s, as he began to lend his pen and his prestige to reform movements dedicated to uplifting those losers and victims, Dreiser sensed that not only could science identify the causes of human suffering and tragedy; his reading in mechanistic science had given him a strengthened faith that science could also alleviate such conditions. His essays in that decade often reveal a nearly utopian faith in the potential of science to interpret human behavior and to solve the mysteries of human nature:

> The more we know, exactly, about the chemic, biologic, and social complexities by which we find ourselves generated, regulated, and ended, the better. Man has never progressed either self-defensively or economically via either blind faith or illusion. It is exact knowledge that he needs.[60]

Since modern science had shown that the human being was nothing more than a mechanism operating according to the same physical and chemical laws of nature by which the entire physical universe was governed, the spiritual myths and metaphysical illusions of the past were no longer relevant explanations of human nature. "The hour has struck," Dreiser declared in 1923, "when man must divorce himself from religious and philosophical theory."[61] In their place, the objective, rational methods of science had to be substituted:

> Close the churches, and open scientific laboratories that seek to know the secrets, if not the meaning of life and its creative forces—and see how much more quickly we shall come by wisdom and beauty; how much more valuable and helpful our relations with our fellow beings will be.[62]

With the interest in criminal behavior and mental illness that accompanied the creation of *An American Tragedy*, and through the mechanistic theories that he encountered that touched on these subjects, Dreiser became convinced that it was essential for Americans to replace their severe moral judgments on deviant behavior with a more humanitarian, enlightened understanding of the causes behind such aberrations. He believed that the only useful work in aiding or rehabilitating "the defective, the insane, the criminal, the deficient or others who, for some reason or another, limp in the rear of the ranks" was currently being performed not "by Christians, but by up-to-the-minute, generous-minded, warm-hearted sociologists and economists, trained in the exact truths of science, and not in the wornout and threadbare dogmas of the churches." Only these few social scientists who were educated in the illuminating findings of mechanistic science, Dreiser believed, could comprehend that "man becomes criminal not because he 'got in the wrong crowd,' as the religionists would say, but by the same impulse that the moth is drawn to its destruction in the flame."[63] The solution to understanding or preventing such "American tragedies" as Clyde Griffiths or Chester Gillette lay only in the scientific investigation and eventual comprehension of the forces underlying human behavior.

In the previously mentioned 1928 review of *The New Criminology*, Dreiser recommended Schlapp's book to "all priests, ministers, prison reformers, parole and pardon boards, judges, lawyers, doctors and the moralists and religionists generally of my day." The establishment of moral and legal justice, Dreiser seemed to suggest to these guardians of social order, could only be accomplished when the innate compulsions that drove people and the external, social forces that warped their ethics could be comprehended and accepted. True justice would not condemn a Clyde Griffiths or a Chester Gillette for behavior for which they were not responsible, and society could not fairly demand the penitence of such "American tragedies." Instead, Dreiser advised, "Society should ask forgiveness. Perhaps God also."[64]

This final, curious comment, with which he ended his review, reveals that Dreiser did not entirely absorb the materialistic presumptions of mechanistic science. For while mechanists like Loeb hoped to remove supernatural explanations from the understanding of life processes, Dreiser obviously continued to maintain a belief in the existence of a God that had created the mechanistic nature of living beings. During the same period in which he was attracted to mechanistic philosophy, Dreiser's conviction in an unscrutable, overseeing power that was ultimately responsible for determining the individual's destiny continued to develop. In these same years, his fascination with occult and parapsychological phenomena intensified and much of his minor work became increasingly preoccupied with supernatural themes. A conflict between science and the supernatural or between reason and feeling, therefore, was developing in his thought, a conflict that would soon frustrate Dreiser in his search for answers to "the mystery and wonder and terror of life."

1. Young Dreiser (middle row, third from left) during his year at Indiana University in 1889–90, prepared for one of Albrecht's geology field trips. His friend Ratliff is sitting directly beneath Dreiser. Used by permission of the Theodore Dreiser Papers, Special Collections, Van Pelt Library, University of Pennsylvania.

2. Dreiser in his study in 1918. Used by permission of the Theodore Dreiser Papers, Special Collections, Van Pelt Library, University of Pennsylvania.

3. Jacques Loeb in 1923, the year in which Dreiser finally met him at the Rockefeller Institute. Used by permission of the Marine Biological Laboratory Archives.

4. Calvin Bridges, with whom Dreiser formed a close friendship during his 1928 and 1929 visits to the Woods Hole Marine Biological Laboratory. Bridges, who treated Dreiser to boating excursions around the Woods Hole area, is shown here beside his rowboat in 1918. Photo by Tove Mohr, provided courtesy of Garland E. Allen.

5. Dreiser and Charles Fort at Dreiser's home, Iroki, in Mt. Kisco in October 1931, seven month's before Fort's death. Used by permission of the Theodore Dreiser Papers, Special Collections, Van Pelt Library, University of Pennsylvania.

6. Woods Hole, Massachusetts, in the 1920s. The recently completed Lillie Wing of the Marine Biological Laboratory is the large building in the center of the photo. Used by permission of the Marine Biological Laboratory Archives.

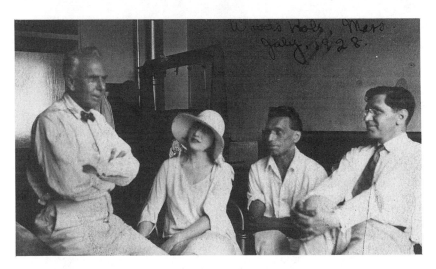

7. Dreiser and Helen Richardson during their first visit to Woods Hole in 1928. Listening attentively are two of Dreiser's scientist-acquaintances, Boris Sokoloff (left) and L. V. Heilbrunn. Used by permission of the Theodore Dreiser Papers, Special Collections, Van Pelt Library, University of Pennsylvania.

8. Dreiser and George Douglas beside the artificial fish pond in Douglas's back yard, where Dreiser loved to relax and contemplate the "pattern of the life process." Used by permission of the Theodore Dreiser Papers, Special Collections, Van Pelt Library, University of Pennsylvania.

9. Dreiser at Iroki, wandering in the midst of one of his proofs of the Creator's existence—wildflowers. Used by permission of the Theodore Dreiser Papers, Special Collections, Van Pelt Library, University of Pennsylvania.

4. Science and the Supernatural

H. L. Mencken published a collection of essays in 1917 called *A Book of Prefaces*, which contained one of the first critical evaluations of Dreiser's place in American letters. In this essay, Mencken identified what dozens of critics would later recognize as a major contradiction in Dreiser's personality and writing:

> One-half of the man's brain, so to speak, wars with the other half. He is intelligent, he is thoughtful, he is a sound artist—but there come moments when a dead hand falls upon him, and he is once more the Indiana peasant, snuffling absurdly over imbecile sentimentalities, giving a grave ear to quackeries, snorting and eye-rolling with the best of them. One generation spans too short a time to free the soul of man.

Mencken greatly admired Dreiser's work as a realistic novelist and student of scientific thought, but strongly objected to and severely criticized Dreiser's "other half," which "more than once, seems ready to take refuge behind an indeterminate sort of mysticism, even a facile supernaturalism."[1] What Mencken recognized was Dreiser's intense interest in the occult, his fascination with the inexplicable, his awe and fear of "the unknowable." This absorption in the supernatural, which is almost totally absent in the stark materialism of his first six novels and which seems so far removed from a realistic or mechanistic orientation, was, nevertheless, increasingly manifest in much of the minor work, such as the poetry, plays, essays, and sketches that Dreiser wrote after 1915 as he became more involved with "the mystery and wonder and terror of life."

Mencken recognized that Dreiser's childhood in the small towns of Indiana and the influence of his family were greatly responsible for the creation of his friend's "unfortunate" superstitious side. Dreiser himself confessed "a deeply-rooted vein of superstition which was one of the few traits of temperament my father and mother possessed in common and which was the heritage of most of their children." In his autobiography he recounted numerous tales of family superstitions and visitations from strange spirits. One evening shortly before she met her future husband, Dreiser's mother was visited by thirteen mysterious dancing lights, which she interpreted as a sign of the thirteen children she would bear. A few years later, after giving birth to the first three of her children, she saw three lights bobbing and dancing in the night sky outside her brother's farmhouse. "Right away," Sarah Dreiser later reported, "I knew that those were my three children and that they were going to die!" When within a few years this premonition had come true, Dreiser's mother broke down and prayed for forgiveness for her sins, promising God that she would do anything, carry any burden, even bear ten additional children—as eventually came to pass. His father, Dreiser claimed, also believed in spirits, most of them evil, and frequently sent for the local priest to sprinkle holy water about their house to exorcize whatever supernatural malevolence might have been lurking.[2]

Dreiser's youth was surrounded with tales of occult events. His sister once revealed to him that at the very moment of his birth, "three maidens (graces, shall we say?), garbed in brightly-colored costumes" came dancing through the Dreisers' front door, found their way up to the bedroom where Sarah Dreiser lay in childbirth, circled the room laughing, and then left by the back door. When the new-born Theodore proved to be a sickly infant, his mother turned for a supernatural cure to "an old German woman, a feeble and mysterious recluse who was regarded in the neighborhood as, if not a witch, at least the possessor of minor supernatural and unhallowed powers." The old woman prescribed that the child be exposed to the curative rays of the full moon. "Leave his head and face uncovered," she instructed, "and stand so that the light will fall slant-wise over his forehead and eyes. Then say three times: '*Wass ich hab, nehm ab; was ich thu, nehm zu!*'" Sarah Dreiser performed this ritual for three nights, without her husband's knowledge, and to her amazement Theodore was fully recovered in a few months.[3]

These events were typical of the family atmosphere that Mencken identified as the inescapable source of Dreiser's interest in the supernatural. "Struggle as he may, and fume and protest as he may," Mencken complained, "he can no more shake off the chains of his intellectual and cultural heritage than he can change the shape of his nose. . . . Briefly described, [that heritage] is the burden of a believing mind, a moral attitude, a lingering superstition."[4]

In the years of their friendship, Mencken strove to keep the realist half of Dreiser cultivated. By criticizing Dreiser whenever he speculated about the supernatural in his writing, by correcting mistakes in scientific or medical fact that occasionally surfaced in his work, and by warning him against the quacks with whom he seemed so frequently to associate, Mencken struggled almost as a kind of "realist conscience" for his occasionally fanciful friend. In 1918, for instance, Mencken complained to Dreiser about an embarrassing display of medical ignorance that had revealed itself in a short story titled *Free*. In this story, a woman dying of a heart lesion is treated with injections of horses' blood, because it is "better, thicker than human blood—not so easily bled out of the heart." Mencken blasted Dreiser for this absurdity: "Who in hell was your medical consultant in 'Free'? Some 3rd ave. abortionist, I do suspect." He sarcastically pointed out that a transfusion of horses' blood would poison the patient, and he offered assistance to Dreiser on such matters of information in the future. "Come to the old reliable Dr. Mencken when you want pathology. Forty years uninterrupted practise in private diseases. . . . No publicity."[5]

On another occasion Mencken advised Dreiser that a doctor who was treating him for lung problems was a medical fraud. Dr. Albert Abrams had invented a machine called the oscilloclast, a small box that sent out vibrations according to the principle of E.R.A. (electronic reaction of Abrams). These vibrations allegedly could both diagnose and treat the illnesses of Abrams's patients. Abrams reaped a small fortune from his patients and from a cult of devoted physicians who leased their own oscilloclasts from him. In 1920, while living in California, Helen Richardson, Dreiser's most recent but most lasting female companion, had been suffering from a stomach ailment. George Sterling, a poet and critic with whom Dreiser was friends, insisted that Helen travel to San Francisco to be treated by his acquaintance, Dr. Abrams. Dreiser and Helen visited Abrams and were "impressed with his amazing energy and vibrant personality." After both underwent diagnostic tests with the oscilloclast, Abrams pronounced that Helen had sarcoma and Dreiser had tuberculosis. He prescribed a series of treatments with the oscilloclast, and after several months of therapy from an Abrams associate in Los Angeles both Helen and Dreiser reported that they were feeling much better. "Helen appears to be entirely well," Dreiser wrote to Llewelyn Powys, who was also being treated for tuberculosis by Abrams. "All the symptoms have disappeared and she is as healthy as ever." Abrams eventually came under attack from the American Medical Association and *Scientific American*, and Mencken decided to visit Abrams when he was in San Francisco in 1921 to investigate the claims of Dreiser, Powys, and Sterling. "He made a rather indifferent impression on me—the usual Jew doctor," Mencken reported to Dreiser. "He can't do the things that Sterling says he can do; no one can."[6] Dreiser, nevertheless, continued his daily therapy with the oscilloclast until he was certain that his lungs were cured.

By criticizing the errors in Dreiser's fiction and warning him away from quacks like Abrams, Mencken was attempting to sustain Dreiser's realistic, scientific point of view. But what most disturbed Mencken and what he most frequently criticized was Dreiser's preoccupation with occult phenomena. In spite of Mencken's sarcastic remarks, Dreiser became increasingly interested in the supernatural. He frequently patronized fortune tellers, attended seances, and divined the future on Ouija boards, all peculiar activities for one who championed the materialistic tenets of mechanistic philosophy.

Dreiser had been fascinated by mind readers and magicians since his days as a reporter in St. Louis in 1893, when he interviewed several spiritualists, who amazed him by their ability to read his mind. "It gave me an immense kick mentally," he wrote of one encounter, "one that stays by me to this day, and set me off eventually on matters of psychology and chemic mysteries generally." One of these mind readers, Jules Wallace, made such an impression on him that Dreiser immortalized him seven years later as one of the patrons of Fitzgerald and Moy's in *Sister Carrie*.[7] In Pittsburgh in 1894, while he was still a reporter, Dreiser was amazed by the feats of a magician who called himself Hermann the Great. While Hermann assured Dreiser that his magical powers were mere tricks that anyone with the proper knowledge could perform, Dreiser believed that Hermann was secretly possessed of real "wild talents" but denied them in public to protect himself from "reprisals that might follow superstitious opposition to any such talents."[8]

Dreiser believed in the existence of a supernatural world and was always willing to experiment with various means of making contact from our material world. In the winter of 1915–16, Dreiser and several friends—including John Cowper Powys, the English novelist, poet, and mystic—gathered around a Ouija board on several occasions. The Ouija reported to the group that the Great War would conclude on 11 February 1918, when the Kaiser would be poisoned by his cook, and that America would remain neutral for the remainder of the conflict. The spirit of the board also confirmed the meaninglessness of leading a moral life, as well as the absence of evil and the lack of design or controlling intelligence in the universe, topics that Dreiser no doubt introduced into the group's conversation with the Ouija.[9] Dreiser also dabbled in communicating with the supernatural through seances. Once, at a seance at Upton Sinclair's home in California, Dreiser was "amazed and surprised as the medium told several astounding things. Things that he could not have known." During this seance, the medium at one point divined that a man from Ohio named Charles Yost was "in the spirit world," trying to deliver a message to his son. The revelation astonished Dreiser, who years earlier had known a newspaperman named Charles Yost in Fayette, Ohio. After the seance Dreiser wrote to Yost's family asking if he was still alive. When Yost answered that he was very much alive, Dreiser, perhaps with a little disappointment, replied, "I am so glad that you are still among the living."[10]

In addition to mind reading and communication with the spirit world, Dreiser believed that certain gifted individuals possessed powers such as teleportation and levitation, powers that John Cowper Powys personally demonstrated to him. Powys once claimed that he could project "the essence if not the substance" of himself over a great distance, and offered to prove this ability to Dreiser. He instructed Dreiser to be alone in his room at midnight and to look for a sign. Dreiser reported:

> Almost precisely at the hour of twelve, within a minute or two either way, first his eyes and then his face and shoulders and arms appeared, as though he were standing directly before me, looking down at me. I was not so much amazed as particularly arrested by the peculiarly penetrating look which was in his eyes at the time, as much as to say, "You see? What did I tell you?" Then it was gone.[11]

But it was the alleged powers of fortune tellers that most fascinated Dreiser. He often asked friends to direct him to seers whom they patronized, and he frequently visited fortune tellers during periods of crisis in his personal life. For instance, in 1900, after Doubleday had accepted the manuscript of *Sister Carrie*, Dreiser claimed that a "tenth sense" told him that something would go wrong with the publication of the novel, and that he should consult a seer. "'Go to a fortune teller' was a phrase repeatedly whispered in my ear. 'She will tell you something.' I went so far as to ask the negroes working for us here where a seeress lived, but neglected to seek the 'Old Mammy' pointed out." Although he did not follow through on this occasion, in the future Dreiser frequently consulted fortune tellers. In his portrait of "Giff" in *A Gallery of Women*, Dreiser revealed his belief in seers and his relationship with a particular Greenwich Village interpreter of dreams, palms, tea leaves, and coffee grounds. Jessie Spafford, a one-time resident of a Canadian insane asylum, made several predictions in 1917 about Dreiser's career which came true and which stirred his curiosity about "the scientific or philosophic or material or spiritual significance of forecasting in general." Mencken, who found Dreiser's belief in Spafford's sibylline abilities amusing, was merely curious whether "a dollar's worth of counsel on the Irish sweepstakes" would be a worthwhile investment.[12]

For Dreiser, occult phenomena like these were more than merely the "guesswork or the sly deductions or trickeries of money-seeking charlatans." They were links to the "unknowable" that had devastated and terrorized him in his first encounter with Herbert Spencer. For example, in reflecting on Jessie Spafford's prognostications and on the other occult experiences of his life, Dreiser wrote:

> They did and do suggest something which all science, if not philosophy, may deride, yet for me remains a strong possibility. And that is that beyond the material or electrical face of life—its remotest and most abstruse and to me quite mystical atoms or etherons or quantums—moves something which, if not less mystical, is still less divisible and quite possibly more real—an all-pervasive intention or plan, if not necessarily wisdom.[13]

The fact that the supernatural became a more frequent subject in his minor works after 1915 suggests that Dreiser was growing more comfortable with his contemplations of the "unknowable."

What is curious about the timing of this developing preoccupation with the supernatural is that it coincides exactly with the period of Dreiser's discovery of the work of Jacques Loeb and the growth of his attraction to mechanistic philosophy. It also corresponds, however, to the period in Dreiser's life when he first experienced the bizarre, supernatural writings of Charles Fort. In order to understand the shifts that were taking place in Dreiser's attitudes toward both science and the supernatural, it is enlightening at this point to examine Charles Fort's work, which in many ways reflected or possibly even influenced Dreiser's ideas.

*   *   *

Charles Hoy Fort devoted much of his life to collecting citations of strange unexplained phenomena and stringing them together in a series of unusual books about the supernatural, written in a language and style that can only be described as free association. A generation before "UFO" and "Bermuda triangle" became part of the language and before Immanuel Velikovsky and Erich von Däniken published their cosmic speculations about worlds in collision and visitations from alien gods, Charles Fort was speculating about these same subjects, writing controversial books and outraging scientists. Dreiser was Fort's closest friend and proved indispensable in getting Fort's works into print. One of Fort's most energetic critics, however, was Dreiser's realist-conscience, H. L. Mencken. Mencken tried to convince Dreiser that Fort was "enormously ignorant of elementary science, particularly biology" and that his books were "full of stupid stuff." Dreiser, however, respected Fort's writing and identified strongly with his theories. Dreiser once confessed, "Always he was one who seemed to be talking with my own voice, with my own moods."[14]

Fort was born in Albany, New York, on 6 August 1874 to a wealthy grocer and his wife. As a child, he was captivated by nature and spent hours collecting minerals, shells, and bugs, shooting and stuffing birds, and continually classifying and rearranging his collections in good amateur-naturalist fashion. As a young man, he worked on the *Albany Democrat* and the *Brooklyn World* as a reporter, then edited the short-lived *Woodhaven Independent*. In 1894, living on an income of $25 a month supplied by his grandfather's will, Fort began a two-year journey that took him across the United States and then to Scotland, Wales, England and South Africa. When he returned in 1896, he married Anna Filing in New York City and, living in near poverty, earned a meager income working at menial jobs in hotels and writing short stories.[15]

After reading several of Fort's sketches in the newspapers in 1904, Dreiser contacted him to invite him to submit short stories for *Smith's Magazine*, which Dreiser was then editing. Fort appeared one day at Dreiser's office and pulled several crumpled manuscripts of stories out of his coat pockets. Years after their first meeting, Dreiser wrote, "When I see [Oliver] Hardy I see Fort as he was then—that unctuous, ingratiating mood, those unwieldly, deferential, twittery mannerisms were Fort's then." Marguerite Tjader later described Fort as a short, rather unattractive man, "dark with a greasy complexion, scant black hair brushed over a round dynamic head. His hands were fat and protruded from filthy shirtcuffs under a dark nondescript suit. In spite of all this, there was something fascinating about him; he seemed utterly alive, carefree and all-knowing, as he talked."[16]

Dreiser bought several short stories and published them in *Smith's*. He had only the highest praise for Fort's fictions, calling them "the best humorous short stories that I have ever seen produced in America. They were realistic, so wise, so ironic, and in some ways, so amusing and in their way beautiful."[17] Dreiser promoted Fort's talent to other New York editors, and within a year Fort was also publishing in *Tom Watson's Magazine* and *Popular Magazine*. Then, on the verge of making a successful living from writing, Fort suddenly announced that he no longer wanted to write fiction and moved to a new address, losing contact with Dreiser for several years.

While editing *Broadway Magazine* in 1907, Dreiser decided to locate Fort to encourage him to submit some stories to the magazine. He found Fort and his wife living in a small, dirty apartment in the Hell's Kitchen section of New York. Dreiser attempted to lure Fort back to short story writing by offering much higher rates of payment from *Broadway* than he had been able to pay as editor of *Smith's*, but to Dreiser's surprise Fort insisted that he could not return to writing stories. He was too busy collecting data for a book that would be totally unlike anything he had yet written.[18]

Dreiser lost contact with Fort for several more years until May 1914, when Fort wrote, asking Dreiser to sponsor him for library privileges at the New York Public Library. Dreiser wrote back, teasing Fort about the years of research he had spent on his book-in-progress. He asked if this work was to be "an encyclopedia Fortiana." Dreiser signed the necessary form to give Fort his library privileges and mockingly encouraged him to continue to

> consume more data to your own confusion. Eat libraries and suffer eventual encyclopedic apoplexy. Stuff in world histories and choke on a world diction-ary. You will be no wiser. And meanwhile fare well for two more years—unless perchance I look you up in person. May you swell with information until you burst.[19]

It seems likely that Fort's request for sponsorship may have given Dreiser the inspiration just a few months later to apply for his own study room at the library, where he began to "stuff" himself with books on mechanistic research.

In less than a year Fort delivered to Dreiser the manuscript of the mysterious book called "X" that he had been researching and writing for the past eight years. Dreiser was immediately captivated by what he read:

> I had not read three paragraphs before I said to myself, this is not only beautiful, it's wonderful. . . . It was then for the first time, that I fully understood why it was that he had decided to waste no more time on fic-tion. . . . It was so strange, so forceful, so beautiful that I thought that whether this was science, or apocryphal and discarded, it was certainly one of the greatest books I have ever read in my life.

Because Fort eventually destroyed this manuscript, Dreiser's descriptions of "X" are the only available accounts of Fort's first discourse on unexplained phenomena:

> Strange arresting explanations and deductions from a thousand sources that I had never contemplated as sources—newspaper clippings, published but ignored data of the most amazing kind from the world's scientific journals—French, Chinese, Russian. . . . There was a vessel-like mechanism with great wheels of fire that passed before the eyes of ship-masters in various parts of the Pacific. There were recorded foot prints of an immense giant in some northern snow field—a record not reported in a newspaper but in some scientific journal of standing. Here and there and everywhere were rains of blood that fell in the exact dimensions of certain artificially marked out areas. Somewhere in space about us were forces as intelligent and as practical as ourselves.[20]

Intertwined within this catalogue of bizarre incidents, Fort wove a unifying hypothesis that claimed to account for all these mysteries. Fort proposed that our material world was not real, but merely an illusion projected from someplace (called X) in space:

> Fort, in his book, saw certain rays, only he did not call them X or Cosmic, for X was the mysterious something from which these rays were emanating. But what these rays did, and wherein it was that their wonder and power lay, I will try to show. These rays were the emanation of something that was capable *through them as a medium* of creating *us*, you, me, all animals, plants, the earth and its fullness, its beauty and variety and strangeness, its joy and sorrow and terror as well as the ecstacy of this thing we call life in all its variety and scope. And it did this quite as we, by the means of light and photography, throw a moving picture on a screen, the sensitive chemicals of a photographic film and the light that causes that film first to receive an impression of something and later to retransmit it as seemingly the very substance of reality. Only to X, the earth is the sensitive film and its speeding rays the light of the modern film camera.[21]

Dreiser was astounded by Fort's manuscript. That his life and the world around him could be an illusion designed and manipulated by superior beings on another world was an unforgettable, visionary proposition for Dreiser. "We are such stuff as moving pictures are made of," he wrote ecstatically, "and the rays pouring from X, made us seem to be as we seem to be. When I sensed the imaginative power of such a concept, I was in a worshipping state of mind. True or false, marvelous." Here was really little more, however, than Spencer's nineteenth-century concepts of cosmic determinism and the "unknowable" dressed up in a gaudier twentieth-century, science-fiction variation. The basic difference, and one that was probably important for Dreiser, was that in the place of the Spencerian universe of random chance and purposelessness that he had construed from his reading of *First Principles*, the Fortean universe postulated superior beings or intelligent forces that created and ruled human existence. This fanciful speculation struck Dreiser as so unique and imaginative that he employed the same notion as the central idea of a short play, "The Dream," which he published several years later in *Hey Rub-a-Dub-Dub*.[22]

Dreiser offered to use his influence to secure a publisher for Fort's work, predicting that "it ought to sell a hundred thousand." He took the manuscript to Macmillan's, Harper's, and Scribner's as well as to his own publisher, John Lane. All refused to publish it. When he tried to interest *Popular Science Monthly* in Fort's work, Waldemar Kaempffaert, the editor, replied sharply, "A vast amount of reading has been done which has not been correctly applied." And when Dreiser showed the manuscript to one of the editors of the *Scientific American*, he reports that the editor

> blew up in my presence. And how! He almost choked as he told me that it was an outrage for Fort, an uninformed fool or dunce to go gathering so-called data that no scientist would accept, and then dare offer it as a book. He said that it was an insult to show him such a thing.[23]

Undaunted by Dreiser's failure to find a publisher for "X," Fort began to do research on a second book about a hidden civilization called "Y." " 'Y''s got me," he reported to Dreiser. "Beyond the Arctic there is a great civilization; . . . for many years, guards, say in flying machines, from that civilization have been watching our Arctic explorers, keeping out of sight, but spying, and discouraging if not openly attacking." The idea of "Y" came to Fort after he read Americus Symmes's *Theory of Concentric Spheres*, a nineteenth-century piece of geographic speculation that conjectured the existence of large openings at the two poles, which led to a series of concentric spheres inside the earth. Fort was also inspired after discovering reports that Arctic explorers had sighted balloon- or kite-like vehicles on their expeditions. While Dreiser was still seeking a publisher for "X," Fort sent him the manuscript of "Y." "Brace up," Fort jested. "This is only the beginning. . . . 'Z' hasn't even been heard from. You have at least one thing to be thankful for—I might have begun with 'A.' " Once again, Dreiser was astounded by Fort's manuscript and offered to find a publisher for both "X" and "Y." He declared that Fort was "out-Verning Verne. Talk about scientific imagination."[24]

Fort, however, was growing discouraged by Dreiser's failures on his behalf, especially after Dreiser had failed to interest even his new publisher, Horace Liveright, in printing "X" and "Y." Fort requested the return of the manuscripts and, to Dreiser's horror, destroyed them. "After sending 'Y' to you," he wrote to Dreiser, "I went on collecting data, and now have so many more matters of evidence that I want to write the whole thing over."[25] From Dreiser's descriptions of these lost manuscripts, it can be assumed that these two works followed the same basic formula as that used in Fort's four later published books. It was an eccentric formula that was understandably suspect to publishers, who doubted the sales potential of works that did not fit into any conventional genre.

Fort's formula was first to catalogue dozens of scientific anomalies, documented but baffling phenomena that defied any sort of logical explanation. Scientists tended to ignore reports of showers of blood or alien flying objects because they did not fit into their system of explanatory paradigms that defined what was seen as physical reality and suggested what was possible or impossible in the universe. Fort, therefore, regarded himself as the champion of these discarded or "damned" phenomena, rescuing them from obscurity. "Everywhere is the tabooed, or the disregarded," he complained. "The monks of science dwell in smuggeries that are walled away from event-jungles."[26] The second consistent pattern of the Fortean formula was to present some general hypothesis, generally outrageous and improbable, that drew together and accounted for his collection of oddities. Fort was creating works that, intentionally or not, parodied the basic principle of logic he had assigned to modern science. They are classic examples of warped inductive reasoning, of deriving a general theory from a group of specific facts while ignoring or disputing all other experience of reality that does not correspond with the theory.

It was these wild theories and the twisted reasoning behind them, rather than Fort's catalogue of scientifically unexplainable phenomena, that most likely outraged popular science publishers like Kaempffaert. For the more mainstream publishers like Liveright or Lane, the problem was simply how to classify Fort's books for the public. The books could not be marketed as non-fiction, since they contained so much imaginative fantasy. They were not classifiable as science fiction or even fantasy, since they lacked the narrative elements of plot and character and read like factual monographs. And there was the additional problem of Fort's nearly unreadable style.

In spite of his two failures in the publishing world, Fort, nevertheless, produced a new manuscript called "The Book of the Damned," which he asked Dreiser to promote to the publishers. This newest work was a compilation of the citations of weird phenomena that he had been collecting for the past ten years from various libraries around New York City. He took notes on small slips of paper, which he classified under assorted headings and filed in hundreds of pigeonholes built around his desk. By the time he was writing *The Book of the Damned*, Fort had some 40,000 notes divided into 1,300 categories of unexplained phenomena. He once described his method of research:

> I undertook the job of going through all scientific periodicals, at least by way of indexes, published in English and French, from the year 1800, available in the libraries of New York and London. As I went along, with my little suspicions in their infancies, new subjects appeared to me—something queer about some hailstones—the odd and unexplained in archeological discoveries, and in Arctic explorations. By the time I got through with the "grand tour," as I called this search, . . . I was interested in so many subjects that had cropped up later, or that I had missed earlier, that I made the tour all over again—and then again had the same experience, and had to go touring again—and so on—until now it is my recognition that in every field of phenomena . . . is somewhere the unexplained, or the irreconcilable, or the mysterious—in unformulable motions of all planets; volcanic eruptions, murders, hailstones, protective coloration of insects, chemical reactions, disappearances of human beings, stars, comets, juries, diseases, cats, lampposts, newly married couples, cathode rays, hoaxes, impostures, wars, births, deaths.[27]

In the opening lines of *The Book of the Damned*, he described his unusual data:

> A procession of the damned.
> By the damned, I mean the excluded.
> We shall have a procession of data that Science has excluded.
> Battalions of the accursed, captained by pallid data that I have exhumed, will march. You'll read them—or they'll march. Some of them livid and some of them fiery and some of them rotten.

In this book Fort documented hundreds of strange events including huge stones that had fallen from the sky, some of which had inscriptions carved in them, sightings of cylindrical flying vehicles, brightly glowing clouds at night, unscheduled eclipses of the sun, and showers of fishes and frogs. All these events could be explained, according to Fort, by the existence of the "Super-Sargasso Sea," a region high in the earth's atmosphere where the laws of physics do not apply. Trapped in this region were "things raised by this earth's cyclones: horses and barns and elephants and flies and dodoes, moas and pterodactyls" as well as "derelicts, rubbish, old cargoes from inter-planetary wrecks; things cast out into what is called space by convulsions of other planets, things from the times of the Alexanders, Caesars, and Napoleons of Mars, Jupiter and Neptune." In addition, buoyed in the Super-Sargasso Sea were other worlds with names like Genesistrine, Azuria, Monstrator, and Elvira, which at times navigated themselves to within a few miles of the earth's surface. Fort not only suggested that beings from some of these worlds were in communication with certain groups of earthlings, but that all human experience is controlled for some inscrutable purpose by super-aliens from these worlds. "I think we're property," Fort speculated in a mood of cosmic determinism.[28]

Early in 1919, Fort handed Dreiser the completed manuscript of *The Book of the Damned*. Once again Dreiser was impressed:

> Wonderful, colorful, inspiriting—like a peak or open tower window commanding vast realms. "Inter-planetary trade routes, super sargasso seas,—the foot prints of sidereal visitors in a special sense." My hat is off. All of your time has been admirably spent. This book will be published and I offer my services to that extent as a tribute.

This time Dreiser acted more forcefully to get Fort's book published, applying pressure on his publishers, Boni and Liveright, to accept *The Book of the Damned*. Horace Liveright read the manuscript and told him that the book would be a commercial failure. But when Dreiser threatened Liveright, "If you don't publish it, you'll lose me," the publisher chose to print a small edition of Fort's book in the spring of 1919, rather than lose the prestige of publishing Dreiser.[29]

With his first book finally in print, Fort continued his search for "taboo" data for his next book. "I've gone on working," he informed Dreiser, "collecting more data, because I'm a thing of inertia. In the past two weeks, I've exhumed some stuff that ranks with the best in the 'Damned.'" But gradually Fort realized that he had exhausted the collections of the New York Public Library and the other libraries in the region, and in May 1920 he announced to Dreiser, "Forces are moving me to London. Annie and I sail on the 27th."[30] Financially independent now from the money he received in the wills of his late uncle and brother, Fort left to continue his research at the British Museum for six months. He was so overwhelmed by the data that he found in London that he and his wife returned to live there for four years from 1923 to 1926 and for another two years from 1927 to 1929.

During the period of his London residence, Fort did not correspond with Dreiser and became increasingly reclusive. "He liked solitude," Anna Fort told Dreiser. "He was a hermit. He did not want anyone to come in, and he did not want to go out." When a Philadelphia publisher wrote to Dreiser in an attempt to locate Fort, Dreiser replied:

> I am indeed sorry to have to report to you that I know absolutely nothing regarding his whereabouts.
> Like you, I am interested in him and uneasy, too, and should you locate him or learn anything regarding him, I would very, very much appreciate your passing this on to me.

In spite of Fort's growing solitary habits, when Dreiser visited London in 1926 and successfully tracked down Fort, who was living in a small, two-room apartment, Fort delightfully exclaimed that "life itself with all its component parts came in through the door when [you] appeared."[31]

In 1923 Boni and Liveright published Fort's second book, *New Lands*. In this work, Fort presented a collection of citations of astronomical and geophysical anomalies, such as the appearance of bright flashes on the surface of the moon and Mars, the transit of uncharted planets across the face of the sun, the failures of meteor showers or comets to appear at their calculated moments of arrival, unexplained explosions in the atmosphere, and frequent sightings of fantastic flying vehicles. Because astronomers had failed to account for so many aberrations in their system of defining the universe, Fort proposed an alternative system of "neo-astronomy" to explain and describe the universe:

> This supposed solar system—an egg like organism that is shelled away from external light and life—this central and stationary earth its nucleus—and around it a revolving shell, in which some stars are pores, or functioning channels, through some of which spray irradiating fountains said to be "meteoric," but perhaps electric—in which the nebulae are translucent patches, and in which many dark parts are areas of opaque, structural substance—and that the stars are not trillions nor even millions of miles away—with proportional reductions of all internal distances, so that the planets are not millions, or even hundreds of thousands of miles away.

While much of his system resembled the ancient Aristotelian conception of an earth-centered universe, Fort speculated further that within the "shell" that bounded our universe "the Geo-system is an incubating organism, of which this earth is the nucleus," and that this organism was developing according to an "underlying Schedule and Design, predetermined and supervised, as it were, by nothing that we can conceive of in anthropomorphic terms."[32] Once again Fort incorporated into his speculations a Spencerian element, the evolutionary development of the universe, but in place of the purposeless universe of chance that Dreiser had inferred from Spencer, Fort again postulated purpose and intelligence behind the evolutionary plan.

Fort returned to the United States in 1929, and his friendship with Dreiser strengthened in the next three years. Dreiser frequently invited Fort and his wife to Iroki, his country home at Mt. Kisco, where the two authors spent hours discussing cosmic phenomena. During the Christmas holidays in 1930, Dreiser visited the couple's small apartment and delivered $100 to Fort, who had exhausted his inheritances and was once again nearly penniless.

In 1930 Fort's new publisher, Claude Kendall, wrote to Dreiser, asking for opinions on Fort that could be used for promotional purposes on Fort's forthcoming book, *Lo!*, a study of theories and illustrations of the power of teleportation. Dreiser wrote to Fort, expressing his bewilderment that Kendall should want to publicize the work of such a master as Fort using the words of so ordinary a writer as himself: "You—the most fascinating literary figure since Poe. You—who for all I know may be the progenitor of an entirely new world viewpoint: You whose books thrill and astound me as almost no other books have thrilled and astounded me."[33]

In November 1930, Dreiser decided to take up the task of promoting Fort's reputation. He bought as many copies of *The Book of the Damned* and *New Lands* as he could locate and began sending them to influential critics like Walter Yust, Monroe Upton and Joseph Henry Jackson, and to his friends like John Cowper Powys, Edward McDonald, and Harry Elmer Barnes. On 25 March 1931, Dreiser sent his "prized" first edition copy of *The Book of the Damned* to H. G. Wells. Wells's reply to Dreiser was prompt and concise:

> I'm having Fort's *Book of the Damned* sent back to you. Fort seems to be one of the most damnable bores who ever cut scraps from out-of-the-way newspapers & thought they were facts. And he writes like a drunkard. *Lo!* has been sent to me & it has gone into my wastebasket.

Dreiser's sarcastic response to Wells' letter was intended "to get an additional rise out of him." He wrote, "At best your letter hands me a laugh. . . . As I see it, if you were still in the *War of the Worlds* or the *Doctor Moreau* frame of mind, you might readily see in this data a field for the activities of your always fascinating pen." Dreiser was actually quite angry with Wells for rejecting Fort and refused to participate in a dinner honoring the Englishman that October when he visited America.[34]

In 1932 Fort was preparing his final book, *Wild Talents*, which would expose the existence of uncanny parapsychological powers within certain humans:

> All around are wild talents, and it occurs to nobody to try to cultivate them, except as expressions of personal feelings, or as freaks for which to charge admission. I conceive of human powers that will someday transcend the stunts of music halls and seances and sideshows, as public utilities have passed beyond the toy-stages of their origins. Sometimes I tend to thinking construc-tively—or [of?] batteries of witches teleported to Nicaragua, where speedily they cut a canal by dissolving trees and rocks—the tumults of floods, and then magic by which they cannot touch houses—cyclones that smash villages, and they cannot push feathers.

While completing *Wild Talents*, however, Fort became seriously ill. His physical condition had been deteriorating for at least two years. Mistrustful of medical science, he refused to be hospitalized and died of leukemia on 3 May 1932, days before the publication of his final book.[35]

Dreiser continued to work as a popularizer of Fort even after the eccentric author's death. He tried unsuccessfully to interest Richard R. Smith, an editor with the Frederick A. Stokes publishing company, in buying the plates to Fort's four books and reissuing the books for two years, with all royalties going to Anna Fort. In addition, he put together a file of Fort materials collected from Anna Fort and Claude Kendall with the intention of writing several articles on Fort's personality and thought. But because he felt that he could never adequately capture Fort's essence Drei-ser never published any of these articles.[36]

*   *   *

It may seem difficult at first to understand the appeal of such an eccentric type as Charles Fort for a man like Dreiser, whose interests in scientific subjects was so great. Previous scholars of Dreiser's life and work have certainly ignored or minimized Fort's relationship with him. Those past scholars who considered Dreiser primarily as the producer of realist or naturalist literature must have felt that his friendship with Fort was merely one more unimportant whim in the life of a writer who seems full of contradictions. Even more recent scholars who have recognized and interpreted the spiritual, intuitive side of Dreiser have chosen to minimize their discussion of Fort as either a reflection of or influence on his ideas. Perhaps there is a reluctance to admit that Dreiser was so captivated by this indigent, eccentric, and possibly even mentally disturbed writer of trivial books that no one wanted to publish. Yet Dreiser regarded Fort as a genius— quite an evaluation from such a proud and even supercilious personality, who rarely recognized an acquaintance as a superior. In the unpublished essays that he wrote about Fort, Dreiser consistently portrayed the relationship between Fort and himself as that of a master to a student. "It was wonderful to feel so close to someone who was a master," he wrote, "who, like a gigantic lens seemed to gather some little spicules of light from the immensity and strangeness of a universe that was dark enough to me." This does not mean that Dreiser accepted literally everything that Fort wrote and said. He wisely realized that "1/2 of it is probably written with his tongue in his cheek" and that Fort's preposterous theories were often lampoons of scientific methods, logic, and hypotheses. Nevertheless, under the surface of silliness and pranksterism, Dreiser found some core ideas in Fort's work that were fascinating for him to contemplate. "Once Fort puts things in one's mind," he admitted, "they are there to stay. The problems, or perhaps I would better say, mysteries he chooses to pose are always amazing and, I might add, deathless in their hold on the mind."[37]

Dreiser's relationship with Fort was strengthened by a number of factors. In addition to sharing an interest in occult and parapsychological phenomena, Dreiser greatly admired and identified with Fort's nonconformist temperament. Dreiser praised him for the challenging attitude of his books, for his rejection of "accepted ideas," and for his imagination in suggesting unconventional alternatives:

> Although he was moved by the usual compulsions of human beings, he was continually questioning their appearances. Is it as it seems? . . . There are very few who can take the leap, even in imagination. Poe could. Hardy could. Swedenborg could. Certain sections of the romanticists could. And every now and then you come into contact with a temperament, shrewd, brilliant, exacting and truly skeptical, which can lift itself from the security of fixed ideas.

He also identified with the rejection Fort suffered as a result of this nonconformity. Recalling his own struggle years earlier over *Sister Carrie*, Dreiser wrote:

> Here I was coming with something that was not at all acceptable at that time, foreign to the mood of that time. . . .

And Fort, you see, was meeting the same reception. . . . Those whom he faced wanted books only about what was known or, better yet, accepted, at that time. In other words, and as in my case, there was no receiving station for his work, no office where it could be taken and understood for what it was worth, no door into a publisher's where he or it would be welcomed, in other words, no market.[38]

Considering the contrariness and obstinacy of Dreiser's personality, every attack on Fort from a Kaempffaert, a Mencken, or a Wells probably only increased his estimation and adoration of the maverick.

What was more significant in solidifying their friendship was their common philosophical outlook—a shared presumption of the "unknow-ableness" of life. Throughout Fort's books is the suggestion that life is a mystery and that the reality that we perceive through the senses is fantasy. "All appearances are illusions," Fort wrote. "No one with a microscope doubts this; no one who has gone specially from ordinary beliefs into minuter examination of any subject doubts this, as to his own specific experience—so then, broadly, that all appearances are illusions." According to Fort, our existence is a dream, and our lives are divorced from a reality that we once knew and that we struggle to remember. In a paragraph in *Wild Talents* that Dreiser marked in his personal copy, Fort elaborated this view:

I now have a theory that once upon a time, we were real and alive, but departed into this state that we call "existence"—that we have carried over with us from the real existence, from which we died, the ideas of truth, and of axioms and principles and generalizations—ideas that really meant something when we were really alive, but that, of course, now, in our phantom existence . . . can have only phantom meaning—so then our never-ending, but always frus-trated, search for our lost reality. We come upon chimera and mystification, but persistently have beliefs, as retentions from an experience in which there were things to believe in.[39]

Dreiser obviously shared Fort's vision of mystery and uncertainty. In a 1932 interview he echoed Fort's conception that the physical reality that we perceive around us is a deceiving phantasm:

We say that we know what we see, that we know what we think. But do we really? I don't know anything. I know that life is amazing to me, that I am going through an experience that seems like a dream. And it is a dream. It must be. If it has any reality, it is the reality of illusion. For I cannot see aught but illusion and principally frustrated illusion—the worried and fading characters of a bad or good dream, as you choose.

In such a world of illusion and doubt, it was certainly possible that such fantastic phenomena as mental telepathy, alien vehicles, showers of frogs, or even the Super-Sargasso Sea might exist:

> Since I have gone through life so far without any particularly valuable solution of anything that has occurred, and know really that behind me in the depths of time have passed billions and billions of people, creatures as confused and mentally defeated as myself, I am ready to at least meditate upon, if not accept, such items of strangeness as are suggested by Fort in his curious explorations.[40]

Beginning sometime around 1915, Dreiser's meditations on the mysteries of existence took on a different tone from the mood of hopelessness and despair that characterized his late-nineteenth- century reflections on Spencer's principle of the "unknowable." In 1894 Dreiser had been devastated by his interpretation of Spencer. "I felt the rhythm of life," he recalled of his reading of *First Principles*, "but the central fact to me was that the whole thing was unknowable—incomprehensible." Now, over twenty years later, he seemed increasingly to revel in the illusions of existence and in a mad universe full of Fortean riddles. "Give me, instead, sound and fury, signifying nothing," he wrote in *A Hoosier Holiday*, published in 1916. "Give me the song sung by an idiot, dancing down the wind. Give me this gay, sad, mad seeking and never finding about which we are all so feverishly employed. It is so perfect, this inexplicable mystery." This shift in Dreiser's attitude toward the unknowable seems to have been the result of a growing suspicion, one that he shared with Charles Fort, that there was a purpose to existence, that some sort of "super-personality" was using all living creatures for some larger, inscrutable process in the universe. In *A Hoosier Holiday* he announced his changing attitude:

> I once believed . . . that nature was a blind, stumbling force or combination of forces which knew not what or whither. . . . Of late years I have inclined to think just the reverse, i.e., that nature is merely dark to us because of her tremendous subtlety and our own very limited powers of comprehension; also that in common with many other minor forces and forms of intelligence— insects and trees, for example—we are merely tools or implements—slaves, to be exact—and that collectively we are used as any other tool or implement would be used by us.[41]

Ever since his reading of Huxley and Spencer, Dreiser had vigorously discarded and opposed the influence of conventional religion and morality. Yet, as Mencken suggested, the need to believe in some supernatural controlling power was a heritage from which Dreiser had never freed himself. He had never fully yielded to the materialistic atheism implicit in Huxley's agnosticism or later in Loeb's mechanistic philosophy. In fact, his pursuit of scientific knowledge about the origin and nature of life had largely been a quest for enlightenment about a greater universal experience of which human beings and their world were a part. It was, as Dreiser told Mencken, "a form of prayer." Charles Fort shared Dreiser's skepticism about traditional religious dogma. And yet Fort openly speculated in his books about humanity's relation to cosmic processes determined by supernatural forces. Dreiser was fascinated by these speculations, whether it was Fort's theory in "X" that life on earth was a cosmic motion picture projection from another world, or his hypothesis in *New Lands* that our portion of the universe was a super-embryo developing into some larger organism. "In this as in other of the several volumes by Fort," Dreiser commented, "he shows, and how clearly, how the most inexplicable things have happened time and again, how, for instance, superpersonalities have moved and effected things here on this earth that we do not understand."[42] Through these books and through his conversations with Fort in Greenwich Village, Hell's Kitchen, London, and Mt. Kisco, Dreiser encountered a counterbalancing influence to the mechanistic conception of an "accidental," purposeless universe that he was encountering through his reading and conversations with Jacques Loeb during the same period. Indeed, Dreiser's deep admiration for Fort's work may have encouraged him to begin to express his interest in the supernatural more frankly in his minor writings after 1915, the year when he first discovered Fort's supernatural speculations in "X."

Dreiser now shared the very idealist, Fortean view that humanity was merely a thought in the mind of "an omnipotent, omnipresent force which, embodying the possibilities of all forms, conceivable or inconceivable to us, extended itself, into what we see." Dreiser wrote on this theme in a 1919 essay called "Man and Romance":

> As one contemplates the amazing facts of astronomy it becomes clear that man can scarcely have as much significance as he imagines, scarcely more than a passing insect here, is little more than a method of some kind whereby something that is content to operate on this infinitesimally small orb is seeking to express itself here. He may be useful as a means of sensory enjoyment to something of which he is the material expression, a race-spirit or oversoul seeking to enjoy itself here via him, but scarcely more.

Dreiser also expressed a hypothesis similar to Fort's that humanity was collectively in an embryonic stage, developing into an unknown, more advanced organism. This theory fit nicely within the evolutionary context of Dreiser's thought, while still allowing him to incorporate his belief in the inscrutabliity of the purpose of existence. In *A Hoosier Holiday* Dreiser described this belief: "I am convinced that man *in toto*—the race itself—is nothing more or less as yet than an embryo in the womb of something which we cannot see. We are to be protected (as a race) and born into something (some state) which we cannot as yet understand or even feel."[43]

Implied in this conception was a sense of cosmic indifference toward the fate of the individual. The human race *as a whole* was developing, and the individual's destiny was insignificant to the ultimate fulfillment of the cosmic plan:

> We socalled individuals are probably no more than mere cell forms constructing something in whose subsequent movements, passions, powers we shall have no share whatsoever. . . . When one thinks of how little of all that is or will be one has any part in—are we not such stuff as dreams are made of, and can we feel anything but a slave's recognition?

For Dreiser, each individual's relationship to the developing organism that the human race collectively composed was analogous to the relationship of each individual cell or atom to the body of a human being that they collectively composed:

> We, as individual atoms, may never know, any more than the atoms or individual plasm cells which constructed us ever knew. But the race atoms are being driven to do something, construct something—(a race man or woman, let us say)—and like the atoms in the embryo, we are struggling and fetching and carrying.[44]

Dreiser was careful not to allow his readers to think that the "intelligence" or "superpersonality," of which we were the expression, resembled the conventional, moral conception of a personal God. His world view continued to deny concepts like the absolutes of goodness and evil, and he insisted that this larger intelligence around us was not the embodiment of truth or of good and evil, nor could it intervene on the behalf of any individual:

> Some undernourished, partially developed ion in you may cry, "The power which rules me is a devil." But you are not a devil. Nor does it necessarily follow that the thing that makes you is one. You really could not help that particular atom if you would. So over us may be this oversoul which is helpless in regard to us as we are in regard to our constituent atoms.[45]

In the same year that *A Hoosier Holiday* appeared, Dreiser published a collection of short plays called *Plays of the Natural and the Supernatural*, in which he further expressed both his fascination with the illusion and mystery of life and his belief in larger forces that somehow controlled or used humanity. The seven plays in this 1916 collection can be divided into three natural plays and four supernatural plays. The four supernatural plays are similar in structure; each play has a dramatic framework built around an event in the natural or real world (the accidental death of a deformed child, a medical operation, a slum murder, an organ recital). Each of these events is surrounded by invisible forces, spirits, shadows, or ghosts, which actually control or influence the outcome of the play.

In "The Blue Sphere" Dreiser dramatized the story of the Delavan family, whose three-year-old son, Eddie, is "a deformed monstrosity." During the play a "shadow," visible only to the child and represented on stage by "a soft, girlish figure, . . . trailing clouds of diaphanous drapery," lures Eddie to his death by waving a mysterious, illuminated sphere before his eyes. The "shadow" causes the child's mother unconsciously to leave the front gate of their yard open and to forget him for a few moments. Lured on by the hope of capturing the blue sphere, Eddie crawls through the gate, down the sidewalk, and onto the train tracks at the end of the street, where the "shadow" tosses the sphere into the child's arms at the same instant that he is struck by a train.[46]

The play "Laughing Gas" was based on dreams that Dreiser himself had experienced during two operations, when "under ether, certain characters appeared to me, acting in a particular way and saying various things to me which impressed me greatly at the time." In the play an eminent physician, Jason Vatabeel, undergoes a minor surgical operation and is anesthetized with laughing gas. During the operation it is discovered that the surgeon's assistants have not provided enough oxygen to revive Vatabeel when the operation is completed. As a result, there is a danger that he will regain consciousness while still under the effects of the laughing gas, go into a fit of laughter, and rupture his incision. In a dream, various spirits appear to Vatabeel, taunting him with the mysteries of the universe and with his own insignificance. One of these spirits, Demyaphon, a personification of laughing gas, tells Vatabeel that he will be forced to laugh, although he may die if he does:

> You think of forces as immense, silent, conglomerate, without thought, humor or individuality. I am a force without dimension or form, yet I am an individu-

ality, and I smile. (A sense of something—vast and formless—cynically smil-
ing comes over Vatabeel, though he cannot conceive how. He is conscious of a
desire to smile also, though in a hopeless mechanical way). I am laughing gas,
for one thing. You will laugh with me, because of me shortly. You will not be
able to help yourself. You are a mere machine run by forces which you cannot
understand.

In spite of the efforts of the surgeons and assistants, Vatabeel awakens in a
fit of laughter, nearly killing himself. Yet fate is kind this time, and he is
allowed to live with a new awareness of his determined existence.[47]

"In the Dark" is a grisly tale of a slum neighborhood's discovery of a
brutal murder and of the apprehension of the murderer by the police.
Throughout the play, a set of spirits run through the neighborhood,
screaming the news of the murder and invisibly leading the police to the
murderer and the body. All the while, the wraith of the victim also travels
through the neighborhood, bemoaning his loss of life and his confusion
about his new existence.[48]

"The Spring Recital" tells the story of an organ recital held in a church
on a spring evening. The musician-minister is irritated that an audience of
only four have appeared to hear his recital. Yet, unknown to anyone, the
minister's music conjures up a group of hamadryads and fauns, as well as
the ghosts of three Egyptian priests of Isis, a monk from the age of the late
Roman empire, and a Reformation-era English minister. The mythological
characters dance and play musical instruments throughout the recital, while
the ghosts of the men of religion express surprise that the "awe of religion"
has persisted into the twentieth century. They also reveal their sorrow that
they can no longer participate in the beautiful illusion of life. The ghost of a
tramp, recently deceased, enters the church and taunts the ghosts of the
religionists about the folly of what they had preached during their earthly
existence and about how the afterlife is not at all what they had proclaimed
that it would be.[49]

These brief experiments in drama were Dreiser's first fictional attempts
to deal with the supernatural, a subject that he had avoided in his previous
novels and short stories. They contain many of the themes of his earlier
writing: the folly of conventional religion and morality, the lack of individual free will, humanity's seeking, hungering nature, and the unknowableness of the ultimate meaning of existence. For the first time in his writing,
however, Dreiser was groping with the idea that behind the physical reality
of human existence, intelligent forces or shadows were manipulating everyday experience and using humanity for some inscrutable purpose.

Four years after the publication of *Plays of the Natural and the Supernatural*, Dreiser published a collection of philosophical essays and sketches called *Hey Rub-a-Dub-Dub*. The collection was appropriately subtitled *A Book of the Mystery and Wonder and Terror of Life*, for the theme of the inscrutability of life's ultimate meaning, a combination of Spencer's "unknowable" and Fort's "phantom existence," runs through most of the essays. The most obviously Fortean-influenced piece in the collection is a short play called "The Dream." Years after he published it, Dreiser acknowledged his debt to Fort's "X" manuscript in inspiring the play:

> So impressed was I by all this that shortly after I read his book I had a dream which seemed in no indefinite way to confirm it. After arising from that dream, some months or weeks after I had read the book, I immediately sat down and wrote a one act interpretation of it, using Fort's theory as a thesis or backbone of the action.[50]

The main character of the play is George Syphers, a chemist whose opinions about the universe coincide exactly with Fort's theories in "X":

> All life, as we know it, is based on the cell—cell origination, cell multiplication, cell arrangement. . . . The whole thing may have been originated, somehow, somewhere else, worked out beforehand, as it were, in the brain of something or somebody and is now being orthogenetically or chemically directed from somewhere, being thrown on a screen, as it were, like a moving picture, and we mere dot pictures, mere cell-built-up pictures, like the movies, only we are telegraphed or telautographed from somewhere else, like those dot pictures that are now made electrically, built up dot by dot, millions of them coming rapidly by wireless or wire being thrown on a screen of some kind.[51]

Syphers wishes to pursue research in this direction but does not have the money to fund such a project. Depressed and frustrated at his inability to pursue his theories, he falls asleep one night in his small apartment and dreams an incredible dream.

Syphers finds himself on a battlefield, where a group of soldiers is attacking him. He suspects that he is dreaming but tries to escape because he is uncertain whether this dream is not really his only world of existence. When the soldiers finally capture and shoot him, the dying Syphers takes comfort that he is waking from a dream. But one of the soldiers taunts him:

> Well, you're a fool! Wait! You may be waking into another state, but you'll be dead to this one. But we won't. Ha! Ha! We'll still be here, alive. (To the second dream soldier.) He thinks he's not real. He thinks we're not real. He thinks he's not going to die, but wake up into something else! Ha! Ha! . . . When he passes out of this won't he be dead to this, though?[52]

Syphers awakens, wondering whether he really has died from another existence. He resolves to devote his life to solving this mystery. By coincidence at the very same moment, he receives a telegram informing him that his late uncle has willed him $300,000. Syphers realizes that he now has the financial means to pursue his research, but gradually concludes that he should use the money to marry his girl and live comfortably instead. As a result, humanity would continue to exist in darkness.

With the publication of *Hey Rub-a-Dub-Dub*, several of Dreiser's friends became alarmed with his increasing fascination with the supernatural. Edward H. Smith wrote, warning Dreiser of the tendencies that he saw in his recent work:

> I fear me, and with very deep concern, that Theodore Dreiser's mind turns ever a little more toward metaphysical symbols and signs. I shudder at your interest in that awful mess of twaddle which Fort made into a book. I tremble at the Christian Science fugue in the end of *The "Genius"*. Your plays of the supernatural rather appal [sic] me. I find you playing more and more with metaphysical terms and ideas—perhaps unconsciously—in much of your later work. (*Hey, Rub*; one or two stories in *Free and Others*, a few phrases in your astounding introduction to Odin Gregory's play.)

Smith repeated Mencken's observation that Dreiser's family and youth had much to do with this tendency. "I dread the spectacle of age and suffering breaking out the props under you and letting you drop into the mystical latrine. You have suffered much. You have a religious parentage. Men do not leap out of such trends in a single generation."[53]

Mencken was also worried by Dreiser's metaphysical speculations. He thought that *Hey Rub-a-Dub-Dub* was a awful book, both "unintelligible" and "unintelligent," and that it would appeal only to "the defectively educated." Mencken added sarcastically that the book would probably enhance Dreiser's reputation, since "it pays now and then to mystify the public. It (the public) always confuses the unintelligible with the superior."[54]

Dreiser denied that he was becoming metaphysical or, even worse, religious. He was merely "very curious as to how and why we come to be where and as we are today. I doubt if any healthy person differs with me as to that." As to the poor reviews that *Hey Rub-a-Dub-Dub* had received, he claimed, "I am not at all disturbed by such things. I know whereof I speak when I say that *Hey, Rub* contains the substone of a new and better philosophy, something on which can be reared a sounder approach to life than is now voiced. Some one is going to come along who will get it and make it very clear." And finally, about Mencken's criticism of his interests in the mysteries of life, Dreiser wrote:

> He has no least interest in anything save the visible face of life. The invisible mechanism with which science is always concerned interests him not at all, or so little that it may be dismissed as negligible. Anyone with these defects would never get me. . . . The man does not understand me and now, after years I begin to suspect that he can't.[55]

As Dreiser's friendship with Charles Fort developed and strengthened and as his attention turned increasingly toward "the mystery and wonder and terror of life," it is plain that Mencken's influence as a "realist-conscience" lessened on him, that their friendship became filled with tension, and that Dreiser's philosophical realism was shifting toward a more idealist position. Even after Dreiser's death, Mencken continued to complain that Dreiser's more idealist tendencies had driven the wedge that split their relationship. In a letter written a month after Dreiser's death, Mencken explained to Helen Dreiser that "I could never, of course, follow him into his enthusiasms for such things as spiritualism, Communism and the balderdash of Charles Fort." A year later, in his curious 1947 eulogy for Dreiser, Mencken publicly proclaimed his disdain for Dreiser's idealist enthusiasms in a more contemptuous restatement of his 1917 *Prefaces* observation:

> He renounced his ancestral religion at the end of his teens, but never managed to get rid of it. Throughout his life it welled up in him in the form of various fantastic superstitions—spiritualism, Fortism, medical quackery and so on— and in his last days it engulfed him in the form of Communism, a sort of reductio ad absurdum of the will to believe. If he had lived another ten years, maybe even another five years, he would have gone back to Holy Church—the path followed before him by many other such poor fish, for example, Heywood Broun.

Obviously, Mencken's bitterness at Dreiser's intellectual betrayal lived on well after the latter's death.[56]

Dreiser's growing idealism naturally had a direct influence on his estimation of science and on the manner in which he would regard science for the rest of his life. For if our existence was an illusion and reality was merely the phantom projection of an intelligence that was unknowable, how could human observations and logical deductions ever be trusted to recognize anything reliable about the universe?

Once again, Charles Fort shared the suspicion of the value of science that was intensifying in Dreiser's thought. If there is one theme that runs through Fort's books, it is an antagonism toward modern science. He constantly mocked scientists for ignoring or denying the existence of his "taboo" or "damned" data. Fort believed that the hypotheses that he constructed to account for his data were no more ridiculous than some of the latest theories of modern science:

> The science of physics, which at one time, was thought to have disposed of werewolves, vampires, witches, and other pets of mine, is today such an attempted systematization of the principles of magic, that I am at a loss for eminent professors to be disagreeable to. Upon the principles of quantum mechanics, one can make almost any miracle, such as entering a room without penetrating a wall, or jumping from one space to another without transversing the space between.

Fort claimed that science was guesswork as long as it dealt with less than "ideal certainty," and that the "attempt to take the principle of uncertainty—or the principle of unprincipledness—into science is almost the same as would be an attempt by theologians to preach the word of God, and also include atheism in their doctrines."[57]

Fort argued that science, like religion, created systems of belief by which its devoted disciples explained the nature of existence. "Religion is belief in a supreme being," he wrote. "Science is belief in a supreme generalization. Essentially they are the same." His anger at science was aimed at its dogmatism. Science, like religion, believed that it was the revealer of "immortal Truth," and the "theologians of Science" were always quick to destroy any theories or to ignore any evidence that contradicted their conceptions of the universe. But Fort believed that there was no Truth that we could discover, that Truth was merely the vague memory of an ideal that we had experienced in another existence. "He was constantly a rebel," Dreiser wrote, "against the tendency of religion, philosophy and science to make a consistency out of the universe, a consistency which can be maintained only by systematically ignoring an enormous group of natural phenomena."[58]

Dreiser would gradually develop the same dissatisfied attitude toward science as he realized that scientists did not share his interest in the supernatural. He eventually grew impatient because they refused to investigate the mysterious, occult phenomena that so fascinated him. As early as 1909 in an essay on spiritualism, Dreiser called for research on that subject:

> If there is anything in it, out with it, and let us all be admitted to the evidence of the fact. Only so the world progresses. And only can we come to a better understanding of what we ourselves are, of what we are going to be, and what and whence come the things of which we are a part.

A few years later, Dreiser's autobiographical protagonist in *The "Genius"*, Eugene Witla, makes a similar request as he reflects on the earlier success of an astrologer to foretell his future:

> Did any of the so-called naturalistic schools of philosophers and scientists whom he had read know anything at all? They were always talking about the fixed laws of the universe—the unalterable laws of chemistry and physics. Why didn't chemistry and physics throw some light . . . on the truthful prediction of the astrologer, on the signs and portents which he had come to observe for himself as foretelling trouble or good fortune for himself.

Almost two decades later he was still challenging the scientific community to study occult phenomena. "Why not give the world a kick, offer it something new," he pleaded, adding that a scientific investigation of "Hindoo" or African magic would be "a damned sight more important than some of the things they do study, and certainly just as practical." Until scientists turn their attention to a subject like clairvoyance, "we shall have 'chance' and 'accident' as the explanation and the future of life, its visibility and hence predictability to some, denied." Occasionally Dreiser even offered a possible explanation for some mysterious phenomena that he hoped some investigator would follow up. He suggested, for example, that parapsychological powers such as telepathy might be analogous to the nonverbal communication of certain animals. This possibility had occurred to him after reading the work of the French entomologist Jean Henri Fabre, who had shown that certain females of a species of black butterfly could attract male butterflies from distances of up to one hundred miles:

> And in connection let us talk of mental telepathy. I know personally many scientists who will not listen to any talk of mental telepathy and who insist that it does not exist; it has not yet been proved. Yet, . . . I doubt if they will contradict Fabre, but they won't admit that the same things happen between people.[59]

Dreiser's impatience and criticisms of the scientific community thus came to resemble Fort's attacks on the self-imposed limitations of scientific investigation. Dreiser felt that scientists were "pointing pole-star wise" in one direction, without turning their heads to take in a broader picture. They were "people peeking through a crack or keyhole," concentrating on insignificant little studies of "how" the processes of nature operated, instead of opening the door to discover answers to the larger questions of "why" things were as they were. In *Dawn*, he complained:

A physicist will tell you, for instance, that our glorious sunsets are accidents of dust, and a geologist will report that all scenery, as we know it, is chance, never to appear perhaps anywhere again. Well, then, what of geology or scenery, or the minds that rejoice in them? Of what import, other than knowing the how of it, which is certainly not much, as one may easily note for himself, for one science or another leads into this or that abstraction, and at their remote ends point to what? Order? Morality? Persistence? The significance of man? Who will venture to say so? Rather is it not plain that here at least the blind lead the blind, or the dreamers the dreamers, and we stand as ever in the past on the shore of the unknowable.

Dreiser claimed that science was losing much of its significance for him, because it could not or would not give him answers about the mysteries of life:

> I cannot feel . . . that a greater knowledge of chemistry or physics or mathematics is to solve anything in so far as the totality of the universe is concerned. . . . Hence as for speculations, developments, of the science of this and the art of that, to me they are only partially valuable, and at that only as passing curios or toys.[60]

Many of Dreiser's poems from this period reflect his frustrated yearning to know the unknowable as well as his disappointment over the lack of answers that science had provided. In "The Sailor" he metaphorically identifies science as the compass that guides his voyage through life but that offers no knowledge of his ultimate, mysterious destination:

> There are rumors of dark shores—
> Of lands of evil,
> Of coasts of disillusion—
> But my compass points straight.
> I hold by my all-seeing God,
> My all-knowing science.
> And yet—
> And yet—
> These bits of inexplicable seaweed!
> That something
> That may be drift of what?—
> There in the dark?
> Illusion?
> Unreality?

In yet another poem, "The Timekeeper," he ponders the mechanistic, clockwork nature of life while lamenting the inability of science to discover the purpose of the timepiece:

> Thrum, thrum, thrum,
> by night and day,
> the mystery of it,
> here, in my breast, and every other.
> Salt, sodium, carbon,
> in strange action and reaction,
> in that narrow box, the heart.
> Outside the world, the noises of the street,
> stars overhead
> (thrum, thrum, thrum)people,
> pathetic, seeking animals.
>
> Perk as one will, pry like a rat,
> with telescope and microscope,
> deeper, deeper still,
> thought, inspiration yield one nothing.
> (Thrum, thrum, thrum.)
> Only this pulse and movement,
> only these waves that flash and change,
> action and reaction within this narrow house,
> For whom? what?
> Why?[61]

Dreiser, who had never adopted the purely materialistic outlook of mechanistic science, was now developing the view that emotional and intuitive responses to nature were just as important, if not more important, than scientific analyses of it. "The limits of the senses" was a phrase that began to appear more frequently in his philosophical writings, suggesting that Dreiser believed that without some means of extrasensory vision, human comprehension of nature would be incomplete and frustrated. For example, in discussing Sir James Jeans's *The Universe Around Us*, he wrote:

> Its enormous calculations have an airy unsubstantiality which may mean anything or nothing, because after all, like yourself and myself, he is using our five senses, elaborated as they may be by implements of various kinds, and I am not sure that these in themselves constitute the sum total of sensitivity or

response in nature. I know only that I respond in various ways with the five that I have, but around me and beyond me, lie nothing but mysteries which, instruments or no instruments, I have not the slightest ability to solve—nor have I found others who have.

If the testimony of human senses and intellect were limited in what they could reveal about the meaning of life or about the relationship of humanity to the forces that determined its existence, perhaps, Dreiser suggested, people must begin to seek answers by an additional means of perception that all other living creatures on earth possessed in common. "Why billions of trees, flowers, insects, animals, all seeking to feel, unless feeling without so-called reason is the point? Why reason anyway? And to what end?"[62]

Dreiser himself understood that by embracing feeling and intuition as methods of perceiving nature, he could no longer be considered within the philosophical boundaries of realism. He admitted as much in *Dawn*, when he wrote:

> For all my modest repute as a realist, I seem, to my self-analysing eyes, somewhat more of a romanticist than a realist. The wonder of something that I cannot analyse! The mystic something of beauty that perennially transfigures the world. The freshness of dawns and evenings! The endless change of state and condition in individuals! How these things grip and mystify! Life itself so unstable, water-slippery, shifty, cruel, insatiate, and yet so generous, merciful, forgiving.

The "other half" which Mencken had recognized and warned of was taking over in Dreiser's thought. "There is vastly more intuition in him than intellectualism," Mencken had written, and "his ideas always seem to be deduced from his feelings." Dreiser confirmed Mencken's analysis in 1933, when he proclaimed that "there is a great deal to be said for non-science or non-truth."[63]

5. Science as a Religious Quest

By the late 1920s, Dreiser was once again in intellectual turmoil. The frustrating implications of Spencer's "unknowable" were now forcefully apparent to him. By that time Dreiser had come to recognize the limitations of science in addressing the ultimate questions that he wanted answered. In his own words, science had shown him "how" nature operated; he wanted to know "why" nature existed. Science had been interesting and useful to him in explaining much of the *process* of life, but as he approached the seventh decade of his existence, he was becoming more impatient in seeking answers about the *purpose* of life. As his mind turned more in the direction of metaphysical and spiritual problems, he began to recognize that because its method relied on empirical observation and because its subject was therefore limited to the observable, material universe of substance, science was frustratingly inadequate as a means to probe the unknowable, immaterial realm of the mystery, wonder, and terror of life.

Baffled and annoyed at the philosophical dead end to which science had carried him, he wrote his oft-quoted "Statement of Belief," which was published in September 1928 in *Bookman* as part of a series of philosophical statements by "America's leading authors." The essay seems almost curt or angry in its brevity and overflows with the intellectual frustration that Dreiser felt at that time; he allowed a six-sentence paragraph to stand as his philosophical testament:

> I can make no comment on my work or my life that holds either interest or import for me. Nor can I imagine any explanation or interpretation of any life, my own included, that would be either true—or important, if true. Life is to me too much a welter and play of inscrutable forces to permit, in my case at least, any significant comment. One may paint for one's entertainment, and that of others—perhaps. As I see him the utterly infinitesimal individual weaves among the mysteries a floss-like and wholly meaningless course—if course it be. In short I catch no meaning from all I have seen, and pass quite as I came, confused and dismayed.[1]

This statement reveals the continuing dominance of both Spencer's conception of the "unknowable" and Fort's vision of the illusion of life in Dreiser's thought at the time of its composition. The tone of the piece, however, reeks with sullen pessimism; this is Dreiser at his darkest and moodiest. In place of the optimistic, nearly utopian claims that characterized his declarations about science earlier in the decade, this 1928 statement seems almost an atavistic retreat to the deeply fatalistic determinism that had characterized Dreiser's initial reaction to Spencer in 1894. Noteworthy is the lack of praise, let alone mention of science in this statement, suggesting that the value of scientific research and conclusions had lowered considerably in his estimation or at least was undergoing a significant reevaluation. It is the painful, final sentence of this testament that is most revealing of Dreiser's frustrated state of mind in 1928. In spite of all the knowledge and inspiration that Dreiser had drawn from his study of scientists and their work, he had found "no meaning" from his quest for answers to the mystery of life.

Determined to overcome this melancholy of confusion and dismay, Dreiser embarked on an intensified search for understanding almost immediately following the composition of his "Statement of Belief." Rather than abandoning science as a worthless means of enlightenment, Dreiser plunged even deeper into the most intensified period of his scientific self-education. Frustrated by the refusal or inability of scientists to devote themselves to the supernatural realm that lay just beyond the material realm of their investigation, Dreiser took it upon himself to learn as much about modern scientific knowledge as he could comprehend in order to reinterpret that knowledge in the light of the intuitive conception of the universe that was becoming more prominent in his thought. In a 1939 interview, Dreiser recalled that beginning in 1928 "I began to re-educate myself—I had only one year of college. I studied science and philosophy, visited laboratories, talked with a lot of people who knew about such things."[2] Commencing with his three-week visit to the Marine Biological Laboratory at Woods Hole in July 1928, and culminating with his month-long stay at the Carnegie Biological Laboratory at Cold Spring Harbor in July and August 1937, Dreiser began a ten-year scientific exploration for enlightenment about the mysteries of existence.

Dreiser's quest to know the unknowable dominated much of his creative energy during this period. Only four books by Dreiser were published in these ten years: a collection of biographical sketches (*A Gallery of*

Women, 1929), a volume of prose and poetic sketches (*My City*, 1929), a book of socio-political criticism of American capitalism (*Tragic America*, 1931), and his autobiography (*Dawn*, 1931) which he had actually composed over a decade earlier. Fiction was now unimportant or impossible to produce as long as the ultimate meaning of existence was unclear; the next Dreiser novel would not appear until the year after his death. Instead, much of Dreiser's interest and energy between 1928 and 1937 would be devoted to gathering the nuggets of scientific information needed to lend an aura of empirical support to his increasingly anti-empirical interpretation of the universe, as well as to the giant philosophical book, *The Mechanism Called Man*, with which he hoped to climax his quest. While his "philosophy" would rely most heavily on his artist's imagination and intuition, Dreiser was ever concerned to fortify his speculations with the authority of science.

At first glance, it may seem contradictory that Dreiser turned to science during this period in search of support for his philosophical ideas. Dreiser had concurred with the Fortean proposition that reality or nature was an illusion and that science was therefore incapable of *directly* perceiving the supernatural forces that had created reality. To know the unknowable, therefore, required the extrasensory powers of intuition and feeling, while the ordinary five senses of empirical observation were almost useless. Dreiser expressed this belief when he wrote that

> our five senses are not enough to tell us whether these forces are the emanation of a conscious divine brain far greater than our own, or merely fortuitous. . . . With the universe as vast as it must be, it is ridiculous to think that we in this little earth could have the facilities to even begin to suspect the nature of this acting force or intelligence.

Nevertheless, an important dimension of Dreiser's "philosophy" in the 1930s would continue to rest on what he learned from science. Although his strengthening conviction in the existence of a supernatural, creative force was based on his increasing reliance on feeling and intuition, his explanation of the relation between the creative force and its creation would continue to rely on the mechanistic conception of life that he had acquired from Jacques Loeb and other scientists:

> I hold that life as we see or sense it with our several senses—in other words, the physical aspect of the world with all of its flora and fauna as well as its universal aspect—is no more than a mechanism through which something that is not a mechanism, but that can, at will, embody or disembody itself mechanistically, expresses itself and that we, along with all things so embodied or expressed, are

an integral fraction of that primal essence: "In the beginning was the Word and the Word was made flesh"—or stone or oxygen or hydrogen or protoplasm or suns or sidereal systems.

Dreiser believed that through the study of life and the universe, science was examining the ordered, mechanistic processes by which this supernatural creator expressed itself in the material world. He hoped that by immersing himself in scientific investigation, he might *indirectly* gain some insight into the essence of this supernatural force:

> Man is permitted to study his relationship to this vast process and its relationship to us for, as Max Planck has asserted, "We ourselves are a part of nature and therefore part of the mystery that we are trying to solve. . . ." [We] are not trying to solve its mystery, but rather it through us (the mechanisms which it has created or at least which have come to pass through it) and *we* through or because of *it* (the motivation of us which it provides) are seeking to grasp the mystery not only of it, our creator, but of ourselves as a part of it—a fantastic procedure as you must see. For as a part of it, why should we know, sense—sense the oneness of it all and all of the processes of it all.[3]

By turning to science to gather supporting evidence for his "philosophy" and possibly to gain further insight into the ultimate mysteries of the universe, Dreiser was not contradicting Fortean ideas. In fact, Dreiser was adopting Fort's own research methods. Fort had spent years of research in gathering data (even if they were scientific anomalies), in order to build a pseudo-scientific foundation for his fantastic, speculative interpretations of the supernatural realm. Fort had believed that the study of the material universe, in spite of its illusory nature, could provide clues about the nature of the intelligence responsible for the material universe. Since the natural universe had been created as a "tool" for the purpose of some "superpersonality," Fort believed that the study of nature itself might reveal something about that purpose. In a letter to Dreiser, Fort had written that

> if X is acting upon us, or using us for purposes of its own, . . . that use could only be of our own natural tendencies, just as everything else that is used, is used by taking advantage of what, to some degree, it would do anyway. . . . Then, in the search for X, we should look, not for the strange, seemingly supernatural phenomena, but for things that we should have done anyway, but in a lesser degree, or things that we should only have tended toward doing.[4]

Fort was saying, in other words, that the study of the "tool" itself would reveal something about the purpose of the "tool" and the intent of the "toolmaker." The creative force was inscrutable to direct observation, but an indirect understanding of this force could be gained through careful study of the clues it left in creation. Although Dreiser had once chided Fort for his many years spent in "consum[ing] data" and "eat[ing] libraries," he now saw the value of collecting data that would lend support to his own fantastic, speculative interpretation of the universe. However, rather than isolating himself in dusty corners of libraries to read obscure journals as the introverted Fort had done, the more sociable Dreiser went straight to the source of his data: the scientific research laboratory.

* * *

His first contact in this period came in the summer of 1928 when he and Helen Richardson visited the Marine Biological Laboratory at Woods Hole, Massachusetts. They spent several weeks at Woods Hole at the invitation of Boris Sokoloff, a research physician and writer of fiction whom Dreiser had met at the Rockefeller Institute.[5]

The Marine Biological Laboratory at Woods Hole was founded in 1888 to provide American biologists a research and educational facility similar to European experimental research stations. Within a few years of its founding, it became a national center, uniting researchers each summer from college and university departments across the United States. When Dreiser arrived at Woods Hole in the summer of 1928, there were 323 research investigators and instructors, and 133 students, most of whom were teachers pursuing postgraduate study in biology. The main building at the center was the Lillie Building, a large new four-story structure, containing administrative offices, a library, seventy research laboratories, and an auditorium, where Dreiser would address an assembly of biologists shortly before his departure. There were, in addition, several other laboratory buildings, a mess hall, a club house, and several large dormitories.[6]

"Here all is charming," Dreiser wrote from Woods Hole, "the most sea-ee place I have encountered in America. . . . I am surrounded by nearly 300 biologists (ouch!) each one with a microscope or more." Dreiser had been fascinated with the ocean since he had first seen it in 1894, when he moved to New York from the Midwest, and the setting of Woods Hole enchanted him. "Today all is bright here—blue waters, white gulls, lovely sandy beaches. I have room 225 in the Marine Biological Laboratory from the windows of which I can see a part of this charming fishing town harbor."[7]

But it was the scientists and their research at Woods Hole that captured Dreiser's fullest attention. He arrived on July 2 at the height of the research season, when the greatest number of investigators were present. Dreiser wrote that he was "hard at work here extracting information from biologists. There are some 283—big & little—and I have uncorked about 12. But I am seizing on special cases." Interestingly, Dreiser found himself classifying the scientists by their religious or philosophical views about the universe. "They are not all mechanists," he wrote with surprise. "Some are agnostics, some mystics, some of a reverent and even semi-religious turn." He was most surprised to find even a Roman Catholic priest, the Reverend Anselm M. Keefe of St. Norbert College, doing research at the facility.[8] Surely this priest was a different species from the dogmatic, anti-scientific priests Dreiser recalled so unpleasantly from his childhood.

Among the biologists Dreiser "uncorked" were S. C. Brooks, a professor of zoology at Berkeley, Leonor Michaelis, the world-famous bacteriologist and biologist who was about to join the staff of the Rockefeller Institute, and Leo Loeb, a physiologist and the brother of Jacques Loeb. He became reacquainted with the physiologist W. J. V. Osterhout, who had taken over the head position of the laboratories of general physiology at the Rockefeller Institute after Jacques Loeb's death. And he initiated two long-lasting friendships with Robert Chambers of New York University and L. V. Heilbrunn of the University of Michigan. Both these men were researchers in cell physiology, an area that fascinated Dreiser. The uniformity of the cellular composition of all living material would in later years lend support to his belief in a creative plan that expressed itself in all life.

Dreiser's most significant friendship at Woods Hole, however, was formed with Calvin Blackman Bridges. Bridges was a member of one of the most important research teams in American science, the so-called "*Drosophila* group" led by Thomas Hunt Morgan. Between 1910 and 1915, T. H. Morgan and three of his Columbia University graduate students, Bridges, Herman J. Muller, and Alfred H. Sturtevant, had succeeded in showing that the chromosomes were the cellular mechanisms of inheritance. Through years of experimentation on and microscopic observation of the small fruit fly, *Drosophila melanogaster*, the Morgan group proved that there was a physiological mechanism that accounted for the abstract, hypothetical "factors" that Mendel had postulated fifty years before. Their findings were published in *The Mechanism of Mendelian Heredity*, which Jacques Loeb called "the most revolutionary development in biology in the twentieth century" and which earned the group the Nobel prize in physiology in 1933.[9]

Each summer from 1910 until the early 1940s, the Morgan team packed their *Drosophila* experiments into barrels and relocated to Woods Hole. In the summer of 1928, Dreiser met the Morgan group, observed and discussed their research, and initiated a lasting friendship with Calvin Bridges. A brilliant and highly precise investigator, Bridges was also a dynamic and amiable person who was always at the center of social activities at Woods Hole. He was a nonconformist who supported the political left and advocated free love. Each summer Bridges left his wife and four children behind in New York City and acquired a notorious reputation at Woods Hole for conducting private boat trips to the nearby islands accompanied by one of his many woman friends.[10]

Dreiser was attracted both to Bridges's unconventional personality and to his willingness to discuss for hours the questions that Dreiser posed to him. In one such discussion, Bridges tried to explain to him that science did not address itself to the ultimate questions that haunted Dreiser. Helen Richardson recalled that Bridges "endeavored to explain to Dreiser, who invariably asked the 'why' of the mysteries of life, that science was not concerned with the 'why' of anything. There was no legitimate 'why'. Only the 'how.'"[11]

Like Bridges, many of the scientists at Woods Hole enjoyed meeting Dreiser, showing him their experiments, and participating in "exciting discussions" with him. Helen Richardson reported that "they said he stimulated their imaginations in a way that a technical scientist might not, because he was not limited by any of the accepted scientific rules." An article in *The Collecting Net*, a weekly newspaper published by the staff of the Marine Biological Laboratory, noted Dreiser's ability to "uncork" the researchers with his stimulating questions:

> He has that rare talent . . . of asking questions which require hours of enthusiastic monologue to answer. Silent scientists have burst into profuse verbiage at his questions, to explain themselves. Timid scientists with inferiority complexes have talked of biological ambitions for hours at a time. Ordinary normal scientists have lifted their feet to the table, hunched themselves deep into their chairs and discussed pros and cons, past and future. Mr. Dreiser sits, profoundly interested, and listens.[12]

After three weeks of peering at "the fairyland which lies just below the microscope," of witnessing experiments frequently scheduled so that he could be present, and of attending the numerous parties and boating excursions that were usually arranged by Bridges, Dreiser returned to New York with Helen. He left Woods Hole impressed by the dedication and self-sacrifice of the researchers he had met. "Their approach to the mysteries of life," he wrote, "is one of the most hopeful things in connection with the human mind as it functions today," and he claimed that he had been "visited by an elation of spirit such as does not ordinarily befall me." He felt honored that he had been permitted "to breathe a freer mental or spiritual air than is breathed elsewhere in America at this time." The experience, he confessed, had made him "grow decidedly reverent."[13]

In the year following his first visit to Woods Hole, Dreiser corresponded with several of the scientists whom he had met. He wrote to John Churchman of Cornell University's Medical Laboratory, asking to visit Churchman's laboratory sometime when he was conducting his experiments on "the very remarkable and mysterious activities of nature." Churchman replied that he would give Dreiser a call if he ever discovered "any one of Nature's antics which seems to be sufficiently interesting." Robert Chambers, who was also associated with Cornell's Medical School, wrote to Dreiser, inviting him to attend a lecture on "Conditioned Reflexes of the Nervous System." Dreiser corresponded with S. C. Brooks of Berkeley, warning of the dangers of traditional religion to the mission of science: "Instead of science letting the Catholic Church make war on it," Dreiser suggested, "it ought to make war on the Catholic Church—openly and flatly." And Dreiser took time to read and comment on the literary efforts of two of his scientist friends. He wrote an enthusiastic introduction to Boris Sokoloff's collection of short stories, *The Crime of Dr. Garine*, but commented unfavorably on the manuscript of a poem by L. V. Heilbrunn, titled "Ode to the Spirit of Jewish Poetry," which he dismissed as "race wail stuff."[14]

Dreiser's memories of the peaceful days at Woods Hole in 1928 and his desire to reimmerse himself in the "reverent" atmosphere of scientific research led him to accept the invitations of Heilbrunn and Bridges to return to the Marine Biological Laboratory in August 1929. Here he once again circulated among the assembled scientists and posed his brooding questions about the mysteries of life. The Bridges-Dreiser debates continued, with the scientist once again struggling to convince the writer that he was asking the wrong questions of science. If science taught any lesson, according to Bridges, it was that there was no existence other than the reality of this life and that one must "*live* as fully as possible, in response to [the] stimuli of nature, whether you are studying them in the laboratory, or come upon them in life outside, particularly in the form of beautiful girls." Dreiser insisted that his strange experiences at seances and around the Ouija board had suggested to him the existence of supernatural controlling forces. "Pooh!" Bridges scoffed. "Learn more about science, and these things don't bother you." The scientist and the writer failed to convince one another, however, and their conversations "got nowhere, but circled pleasurably to their quick temperaments."[15]

The end result of Dreiser's conversations with Bridges and the other scientists during his two visits to Woods Hole was a final resignation that his acquaintances in science would never be interested in probing the ultimate questions that so fascinated him. While his observations of the ongoing research at Woods Hole stirred a reverence and "elation of spirit" akin to spiritual inspiration, his inability in his conversations with Bridges and the other researchers to perceive or evoke similar feelings in the scientific community stirred his frustration and irritation at the shallowness of science. That frustration and irritation is quite apparent in a philosophical essay that Dreiser composed shortly after his second Woods Hole visit.[16] The essay, titled "What I Believe" and featured in the November 1929 issue of *Forum*, is little more than an extended version of his 1928 "Statement of Belief." Present is the same Dreiserian rage at the inscrutability of the meaning of existence, but "What I Believe" differs from his earlier philosophical testament in that much of his rage is now openly directed at the scientific community.

Dreiser opened "What I Believe" with a declaration of his intense fascination with "the mystery of life": "Its inexplicability, beauty, cruelty, tenderness, folly, etc., etc.—has occupied the greater part of my waking thoughts; and in reverence or rage or irony, as the moment or situation might dictate, I have pondered and even demanded of cosmic energy to know *Why*" (279). Dreiser was forced to confess, however, that his quest for enlightenment thus far had been unfulfilled. "Here I sit at this particular moment," he wrote, "pen in hand and scribbling briskly concerning something about which finally I know nothing at all, and worse yet, about which no one can tell me anything, and yet wishing to know *Why*" (279). Dreiser then launched into his criticism of scientists like Bridges who insisted "there can be no *Why* but only a *How*, since to know *How* disposes finally of any possible *Why*" (279). He repeatedly assailed the inadequacy of scientific explanation of process that lacked explanation of purpose: "Here is no *Why*, only a *How*—and the ultimate basis of the *How* not known! Instead, only a chemico-physical process which requires endless observation and correlation but with no least belief that it can lead to more than a very limited knowledge of *How*" (281). Dreiser declared that he could no longer accept descriptions of "the will-less mechanism of the physicist and the chemist which just is and does, but without any traceable intention of doing so" (280).

Orthodox religion, on the other hand, was equally inadequate in providing answers about the mystery of life. Religious leaders continued to earn Dreiser's special wrath for promoting "an illusion of the rankest character" (319), which served merely as a "medicament" of escape for the masses, who were too weak to face the tragedy of life. Concerning the ultimate mystery of death, Dreiser complained that there was "no word of truth in regard to it all from either science or religion—but with science arguing eternal dissolution and religion barefacedly lying as to the what and how of the future" (317). Dreiser seemed preoccupied with the subject of his own death in this philosophical essay, and at one point offered a personal evaluation of his own place in the universal scheme of things:

> I really view myself as an atom in a greater machine, just as is the cell in the greater body of which it finds itself a part. . . . When I am dead, as I see it, I shall be dissolved into my lesser constituents; I shall then be, if anything, a part of universal force, but merged and gone forever. (320)

The scientists at Woods Hole, however, were not the only ones incapable of appreciating Dreiser's quest for answers about the mysteries of life. Dreiser's friends in the literary world were often even more critical of his interest in philosophy and his scientific search for confirmation of his ideas. Sherwood Anderson, for example, tried to lure Dreiser back to writing "the simple story of lives," reminding him of the "terrible loneliness of people in America" and suggesting that the "goddamn science and mechanical development you talk of doesn't help all this while the other part of your work . . . the telling of the story always does." Another friend, Louise Campbell, who had assisted him in editing *Twelve Men* and *An American Tragedy*, considered Dreiser's philosophical quest to be "naive and muddled"; in her opinion, "[Dreiser's] search for a formula to reorganize the universe led him, I believed, along paths I could not and would not want to follow." H. L. Mencken continued to criticize him for the growing supernatural and philosophical speculations in his writing, but Dreiser was no longer concerned with the complaints of "a critic with a purely materialistic approach to the world about him," for whom "a wall is a wall and a chair is a chair, and that's that."[17] But perhaps the most frustrating and angering rejection of his philosophic and scientific concerns by his literary colleagues occurred during Dreiser's involvement with the *American Spectator*.

George Jean Nathan and Ernest Boyd were the active editors of this new weekly literary newspaper, which began in late 1932. Eugene O'Neill,

James Branch Cabell, Sherwood Anderson, and Dreiser were to serve as unsalaried contributing editors. Dreiser saw this venture as an opportunity to popularize scientific and philosophic matters that were close to his own thinking. In a note to Nathan, in which he outlined "My Program for the *American Spectator*," Dreiser made clear that his vision of the newspaper included both "scientific presentation of something—preferably an examination of an important scientific fact or an interesting speculation" and "philosophic discussion of an abstraction after the manner of Santayana, Spencer, James, or whomsoever."[18] Dreiser wrote to his acquaintances in scientific research to encourage them to produce articles for the *Spectator*. He requested his scientist friends to introduce the publication to their associates and to encourage the latter to contribute articles as well. He even imposed upon one friend, Robert Chambers, to review several submissions for their scientific accuracy. He also sent out over a dozen letters to researchers with whom he was not acquainted, including Albert Einstein, from whom he requested "your comments or conclusions on any phase of life whatsoever."[19]

In spite of Dreiser's attempts to present the latest in scientific speculations in the pages of the *American Spectator*, Nathan and Boyd evidently had no intention of publishing such ponderous material. As early as December 1932, Dreiser sent the editors an article by Calvin Bridges with the recommendation that this piece was "the type of thing we should have more of, and it should get in soon." In March 1933, Dreiser pressed hard for the publication of an article by Sherwin F. Kelly called "Physicists Come to Earth." Dreiser called the article "a very interesting geodetic survey of the relation of physics to physical geography," but Nathan and Boyd rejected it because "it was heavy." Dreiser wrote apologetically to Kelly, complaining, "For some, to me, almost incomprehensible reason, I cannot get these people to agree that this sort of material falls in with the scope that promises the most success for the paper. With that conclusion, I heartily disagree. It should be published, but there is a fight here." By October, Dreiser's disagreement with the two chief editors had become even more heated; he accused them of being "intellectually unequipped" to appreciate "the mystical, esoteric and speculative in regard to life, its origins, its anomalies and anachronisms":

> And the worst of it is that you are satisfied that a magazine which would venture to present the astounding speculations and creative mentations of a man like Charles Fort, for instance, would be ridiculous and useless. . . . [W]hen it comes to the matter of original mentations or emotional reactions to mysteries in the field of science, . . . you find yourself shouting "Junk!"

Within three months of writing this angry letter, Dreiser resigned from the *Spectator's* editorial staff.[20]

At just this time, Dreiser began to consider writing his "book of philosophy." It was no coincidence that he wrote the first essays for *The Mechanism Called Man* so soon after his disagreements with Nathan and Boyd. Dreiser had always seen himself as a nonconformist, producing books that were "not at all acceptable" to the mood of the time. So the arguments and ridicule of his literary colleagues as well as his scientist friends only strengthened his stubbornness and confirmed his desire to produce a book that would "knock people's eyes out."[21]

Dreiser's decision to begin writing his philosophy at this time was probably also sparked by the loss of his friend Charles Fort. When Fort died in May 1932, Dreiser mourned the loss of not only a friend but also, in his opinion, a genius who had shaped his vision of the universe. He must have felt that by turning to work on a book of philosophy at this time, he would continue the expression of the Fortean ideas that had moved him so greatly. After he had published *Hey Rub-a-Dub-Dub*, his first collection of Fortean-influenced essays, Dreiser had claimed that the book contained the seeds of "a new and better philosophy" and that eventually someone would "get it and make it very clear."[22] Now, in 1934, he decided that he would be the one to give expression to these revolutionary ideas.

Perhaps the most important factor influencing his decision to write his personal philosophy at this time was Dreiser's friendship with George Douglas. While he was living in California in 1920, Dreiser had met the Austrian-born Douglas, who was the literary editor of the *San Francisco Bulletin*. A fast friendship was formed, and in the years that followed, he and Douglas frequently discussed his philosophical theories in their correspondence. In 1929 Douglas praised Dreiser's "What I Believe" essay as a piece of "keen insight and sound reasoning, no less logical and far more interesting because of its personal note." By 1934 Douglas was alone among Dreiser's close friends in responding sympathetically to his projected work of philosophy. "Psychic osmosis, almost a mystical form of it, characterized your very first letter," Dreiser wrote to Douglas, "for at the mere hint that I was attempting a philosophy you proceeded to interpret the thing I was doing,—the need and place for it under modern conditions,—in a, to me, beautiful, stimulating and at the same time almost amazing way."[23]

Because Douglas had provided him with "the only intelligent response that I have had so far," Dreiser decided to ask Douglas to assist him in producing his philosophy. "If we two were together somewhere," Dreiser suggested to him from New York, "you would be the most stimulating, illuminating and correcting force that I could have." Dreiser went so far as to ask Douglas to quit his job in California and to come live in New York, where he could support himself by writing magazine articles. Although Douglas wisely turned down this scheme, Dreiser continued to derive inspiration and support from Douglas's letters and finally traveled west himself to live with Douglas from May until August 1935.[24]

Dreiser's stay with Douglas was an intensely emotional and inspiring experience. The two men spent hours each evening discussing aspects of Dreiser's philosophy, studying the latest scientific texts, and reading Shakespeare, Keats, and Shelley to one another. Douglas had an ability to shape Dreiser's occasionally confused or vague ideas. Dreiser said that Douglas's insights into his philosophy were "about the same as if a person began, or no more than suggested, a campaign of some sort to a listener, who, before a portion of his thought was out, would spring to a black-board and outline the entire campaign." Besides the inspiration that he drew from Douglas's appreciation of his philosophy, Dreiser enjoyed the closer contact with nature available at Douglas's home. Helen Richardson wrote that whenever Dreiser took a break from the hard work of writing, "he would wander out to the garden at the rear of the house where there was an artistic fish pond. He would sit by the edge of it absorbed in watching the fish and the birds carrying out their pattern of the life process." After Dreiser returned to New York City in the fall, he wrote to Douglas that he deeply missed walking with him through the gardens, "watching the birds at the pool or the stars in the sky. . . . Hail George! Oh ho! I am grateful. And I could cry."[25]

In early 1935 Dreiser referred Douglas to two essays that he intended to use as two chapters in his book. These essays were "The Myth of Individuality," which had been published in the *American Mercury* in March 1934, and "You, the Phantom," which had appeared in *Esquire Magazine* in November 1934.[26] These two essays reveal that the materialistic, mechanistic conception of the universe that Dreiser had adopted from Haeckel, Snyder, and Loeb, while still prominent in his thought, had been adapted by his growing intuitive conviction in a creative, overseeing power and by the idealist, metaphysical ideas of Charles Fort.

Dreiser accepted the mechanistic conception of the universe revealed to him in his studies. But he denied the belief of mechanistic scientists that there was no creative or mental force permeating the mechanisms of nature. Perhaps he had Calvin Bridges in mind when he described the method and the conclusions of the mechanistic scientist as prying or peeping through chinks and mouse holes such as microscopes and telescopes, at the vast illimitable processes of nature or the universe without and about him. Yet, these, in turn, he described, and still does, as "mechanistic" and so decidedly not *mental* like himself, either in their content or result!

Dreiser strongly disagreed, proclaiming, "I can find nothing that is not mind, neither myself, nor any lesser or greater thing." He envisioned a cosmos of mental energy, some of which was "free moving . . . , or impulse," and some of which implemented itself to form material substance. Dreiser believed that this latter form of mental energy permeated the material universe by expressing itself as the "amazingly coordinated beings—or energy containers" that scientists called atoms. Using the atom as a constructive device, "this something seems also to desire to express itself in bird, flower, fish, insect, rock, gas, planet, and other forms. . . . In short, a universe (and of those there are many) seems to be one of its (in a very immense sense) forms or extensions." Because he was constructed of these atoms, Dreiser felt that he too was part of this universal mind:

> I am not so much an individual force but a mechanism for the mind and the intention of some exterior and larger mental process which has constructed me and those minor entities which help to make me what I am, but not, probably, for any individual purpose of my own, but rather, and quite obviously to me, for some purpose of its own.[27]

Dreiser expressed the idealistic conception of reality that had been central to Fort's vision of the illusion of life by suggesting that our material existence was merely an expression of the ultimate, conceptual reality made up of the thoughts of the creative, mental energy. Dreiser wrote, for example, that "the *man idea*" of the creative mind was "the only reality or actual man." Each human being was therefore "nothing more than the extension, nay, even a mimeograph copy of the man model." From this premise it followed than no human could possess individuality. The mechanistic unit called "man" was "manufactured by the billions" to serve the purposes of a larger mental process. Each unit was a "utensil" lacking individuality and was "no different in that respect from any chair set forth by a chair factory, or an automobile by an automobile plant." A human being possessed no individual or creative thought, because his or her thoughts were actually determined by the larger creative mind:

> Man is not really and truly living and thinking but, on the contrary, is lived and thought by that which has produced him. Apart from it . . . he has no existence—no thought one might conceive of as a thing apart. You are only thinking as Nature, life, or, as it is now called, Creative Energy, thinks.[28]

Douglas wrote that "The Myth of Individuality" was "a powerful essay and confirms a conviction of long standing that you are most lucid when most philosophical." He praised Dreiser for taking up this "most excellent project" and asked what outline he proposed to follow in setting forth his entire philosophy in *The Mechanism Called Man*. Dreiser replied that the opening chapter would be "The Essential Tragedy of Life," an essay that had previously been published in *Hey Rub-a-Dub-Dub* in 1920. The next chapter was to be called "The Myth of Reality," an essay into which "You, the Phantom" would be incorporated. The following chapters were to take up such mistaken human self-conceptions as "The Myth of Individuality," "The Myth of the Creative Power of Man," "The Myth of Free Will," and "The Myth of Death." The second section of the book would define "Some Attributes of a Creative Energy as Expressed Here on Earth." This section would elaborate on such topics as "The Reality of Change," "The Reality of Beauty," and "The Necessity of Secrecy."[29]

He informed Douglas that somewhere in the book he would also place a chapter entitled "The Present Limitations of the Race Mind," where he would once again elaborate on the limitations of scientific research. He claimed that "with the five or six senses that we have and their scientific extensions," humanity was incapable of understanding the true nature of the beginnings of the universe and life:

> Even if we were to reach the point where we could grasp the exact process by which Life on this earth began, still mentally we would not be anywhere, because all we would have would be a dynamic or electro-chemic or electro-physic explanation of "*how*" without the "*why*". How *why* is to be answered with the equipment we have is not clear and if it should come along in the process of change that the *why* could be discovered by some highly improved organism still that organism would not be man as we know him now.[30]

These comments reveal the lingering power of Spencer's "unknowable" in Dreiser's thought and the growing conviction that the testimony of the senses were inadequate to answer the questions that haunted him.

In spite of the limitations of science, Dreiser told Douglas that "I am still reading and collecting current scientific data and I swear if nothing else is growing my brain appears to be." He continued at this time to correspond with scientists, to visit various scientific laboratories, and to read extensively in both biology and physics. The result of these studies for Dreiser was that "a lot of things that I suspected in connection with this mortal scheme are being confirmed."[31]

Beginning in April 1935, Dreiser began a series of visits to laboratories around the country to observe scientific research and to gather information from eminent scientists to support his developing philosophy. On April 2, he visited the Rockefeller Institute of Medical Research, where he lunched with his friend W. J. V. Osterhout and with the head of the Institute, Simon Flexner. Dreiser questioned them about "the mystery of the Autonomic [nervous] System," about which he felt "something creatively astounding appears to be waiting for proper biological, chemical and physical attention." The autonomic nervous system was no doubt of interest to Dreiser because it is that part of the nervous system that controls the involuntary motor functions of the heart, lungs, intestines, glands, and other organs of the body. He considered the automatic processes of digestion, circulation, and respiration without the conscious willing of the mind to be only one more proof of our determined, mechanistic nature:

> The unconscious processes are plainly not under your conscious control. Your heart beats but you do not will it to do so. Your blood circulates, your nerves register, your stomach, liver, kidneys, lungs, and all your various glands that constitute and effect that astounding chemical synthesis which permits you to live, all work without your willing and without your knowledge.

When this system breaks down, Dreiser noted, the result is "a pain, an ache, a sense of nausea" or suffering that is certainly beyond volition. If the breakdown is beyond the repair of doctors or of the system itself, the result is death. "And yet you think of yourself as a free agent. As having free will—or a non-dependent power to go, do, be."[32]

Later in the month, Dreiser was in Chicago to give a lecture at Northwestern University. He took the opportunity to visit Harvey Brace Lemon and the Nobel laureate, Arthur Compton, both physicists at the University of Chicago, and he asked them to explain "the probable nature of the bridge between the ultimate physical atom or proton and the ultimate unit of protoplasm, or if not that then the physics of protoplasm." Dreiser's desire to know the precise means whereby inorganic materials combined into organic substance was fundamental in his philosophical quest to trace organic evolution back to its ultimate beginning—the first appearance of life. His fascination with microscopic, unicellular animals like the amoeba—"protoplasm in its humblest form"—had existed at least as far back as the writing of The "Genius", when he had quoted material from the biologist Gary Calkins on the habits of protozoa. The transformation of atoms and molecules into these primitive forms of life was "a mystery which offer[s] to the so-called evolved mind of man something so startling that it cannot grasp the 'how' let alone the 'why' of it, or whether it is pleasurable or the reverse, or 'thought' or what, and this in the lowest of the evolutionary forms." In speculating in his philosophy on the "hows" and "whys" of the mysteries of life's beginnings, Dreiser would rely on his intuition a great deal more than on what he learned from Lemon or Compton or the other physicists and biochemists whom he interviewed and read.[33]

Regarding the "how" or the process of protoplasm's origin, Dreiser speculated on the basic building blocks of the atomic elements, "93 all told, being attracted, gravitationally we say, although it might well be emotionally, the one to the other. Who knows what gravitation is?" He then briefly outlined the successive steps involved in atoms constructing cells, cells constructing tissues, tissues constructing organs, and organs comprising organisms, all proceeding "under creative direction—material or immaterial, or wisdom, as we think of it. . . . Mind? Universal mind? Most likely." In positing emotion, wisdom, and mind to the process of the creation of life, Dreiser was clearly envisioning the origin and evolution of life as the plan and achievement of a conscious, willing entity—a Creator that had set the entire process in motion billions of years ago. And he was fully aware that this proposal contradicted the materialistic orientation of Lemon, Compton, and his other scientific acquaintances:

> The form and technique of each particular species as you can for yourself see, having been most slowly evolved year by year, century by century, age by age, from protoplasm upward, it follows that the creative thought or compulsion must have centered there, or if not there, then in the force or forces that generated protoplasm. . . . And you are then compelled to ask, is there any thought in this?
>
> The answer of the physicist today at least, is, of course, *no*. And if no thought, then no conscious knowledge. Only a process which is not willed, but *is*.

Having listened to and learned as much as he could from his friends in the world of science, in his philosophy Dreiser would transcend the confines of the material universe that were the realm of science, to speculate on a spiritual realm that was unknowable to the methods of science.[34]

During the summer of 1935, while living with Douglas in Los Angeles, Dreiser had the opportunity to visit a number of scientists associated with the California Institute of Technology. Calvin Bridges and T. H. Morgan's *Drosophila* group had moved to Cal Tech from Columbia in 1928, and through Bridges, Dreiser was introduced to many of the researchers of that institution. Among those he met was Robert A. Millikan, the world-famous physicist whose work on the isolation of the electron had won him the Nobel prize in 1923. Millikan also discovered and named cosmic rays, an achievement that his biographer claims made him "with the exception of Einstein, the most famous scientist of his day in America. He was—a celebrity." Dreiser probably could not have approached anyone in the American scientific community who was more interested in the spiritual implications of scientific knowledge than Robert Millikan. Since the mid-1920s, in response to the attacks of fundamentalists on the "crass material-ism" of science, Millikan had engaged in a personal crusade to reconcile science with religion. In 1923, he wrote a statement, designed to counteract the image of spiritual shallowness connected with science, that was ul-timately signed by a number of leading scientists, as well as by sixteen Protestant theologians and Herbert Hoover:

> It is a sublime conception of God which is furnished by science, and one wholly consonant with the highest ideals of religion, when it represents Him as revealing Himself through countless ages in the development of the earth as an abode for man and in the age-long inbreathing of life into its constituent matter, culminating in man with his spiritual nature and his God-like powers.

This declaration of faith was a twentieth-century restatement of the natural theology of the eighteenth and early nineteenth centuries that had sought to prove the existence and discover the nature of God through the scientific study of the ordered processes of the universe that God had created. A few years later, Millikan proclaimed that the "God of Science is the Spirit of rational order and ordered development." Dreiser, whose philosophy was forming along the same lines of natural theology, was anxious to discuss the physicist's belief in "the *integrating factor* in the Universe which you seem to identify with mind, ideas and intelligence. In other words, . . . an ordered Universe." Dreiser was also coming to the conclusion that the harmony of chemical and physical processes throughout the universe was a proof of the existence of a conscious, willing creative power, and he hoped that Milli-kan's research would only reconfirm his conception of the "Oneness" of creation. "I would like to know," Dreiser asked, "if the result of your scientific labors so far justifies the assertion that the universe as thus far surveyed is truly cosmical, or, on the contrary, there is any evidence of disorder or chaos anywhere."[35]

At the time that Dreiser met Millikan, he had questions about "the principle of uncertainty," a physical law that had been a controversial development in nuclear physics ever since it was first proposed by Werner K. Heisenberg in 1927. The principle simply stated that it was impossible to determine the exact position and velocity of an electron, since the photons of ordinary light needed to observe or photograph an electron exerted a violent unpredictable force on such particles. Dreiser had briefly read about "the principle of uncertainty" in Fort's ridiculing comments in *Wild Talents* and in Millikan's "What I Believe" essay in *Forum*, and the phrase disturbed him because it seemed to imply disharmony in the basic structure of all matter, a circumstance that would contradict his belief in a created, mechanistic order underlying all nature. Seeking reassurance, Dreiser wrote to both Calvin Bridges and Millikan, asking "what is meant by the principle of uncertainty in connection with microscopic processes, and does that principle imply a possible irremediable disorder as opposed to order in the universe?" Bridges replied that "certain religiously-minded physicists" had attempted to use the principle of uncertainty to disprove mechanistic theories of the science and to assert that it opened the door to such vitalistic doctrines as free will and the existence of God. He ridiculed such speculation and assured Dreiser that "the universe has always been in order." Dreiser was no doubt relieved by Bridges' declaration of an ordered, mechanistic universe, although he did not share the latter's purely materialistic interpretation of the cosmos. Dreiser was closer philosophically to Millikan, who perceived the work of an immaterial designer in the harmony and order of the mechanistic universe, and who declared that the principle of uncertainty implied disorder only "to those non-physicists who have been worrying their heads over their inability to reconcile the principle of law with the facts of free will and responsibility." The mechanistic order of the universe having been reconfirmed to him, Dreiser wrote of the principle of uncertainty:

> We cannot predict anything certainly about an atom. Here chance seems to predominate. No law, whether of energy, mechanics, thermodynamics, or whatever, is sure to operate in any case. Here, then, also it would seem that instead of laws which operate with a large degree of uncertainty, it would be better to assume that there are a number of causes which are operating according to their laws but which we do not know.[36]

Dreiser rejected the seeming existence of chance in subatomic movements and instead simply placed the problem in the realm of the unknowable beyond our current perception or understanding.

Bridges also arranged for Dreiser to visit the Mount Wilson observatory that summer. There he met the distinguished astronomer Edwin P. Hubble and his research assistant, Joel Stebbins. Dreiser confided to Stebbins that "among scientists, astronomers, because of the all-inclusiveness of their observations and speculations, have long since taken on, to me, a relatively sacerdotal character." He was overwhelmed by the wonders of the universe that he saw through Mount Wilson's telescope, and he was moved by Stebbins's "personal and poetic and affectionate response to the night sky outside, and your illuminating explanations and deductions. Awe and reverence, as you well know, walk deep with understanding. I felt the three transfuse in all that you had to say." The "awe and reverence" that the contemplation of the universe aroused in Dreiser produced some of the most overtly devout prose in his philosophy. His reflection, for example, on the great unity implied by the shared atomic composition of both the protoplasm of life that he observed through the microscope and the suns of gigantic sidereal systems that he witnessed through the telescope exemplifies the spiritual serenity that Dreiser drew from his scientific studies:

> As the Hindus so grandly phrased it—"Brahma is in all things. He is also without." . . . All are blood and brother, father and daughter to the lowliest as well as the greatness. For what is an island universe but an accretion of atoms. And what is the lowest and (to bring in man as witness as well as measure) its, to him (perhaps to nothing other), meanest and most offensive creation—cancer germ, or murder-fever, plague virus, or gluttonous lust—but some compound or dilution of its own deathless energy or substance. "I and my father are one" cries the new testament of Jesus. And the laboratories of science can say no less, confirming by chemical and physical experiment that which all, had they eyes to see and ears to hear, could see and hear of themselves.[37]

Returning to New York in the fall, Dreiser continued his visits to scientific laboratories. In November he wrote to the General Electric Company, requesting information about "the scientific laboratory demonstration that accompanied the Magic Kitchen display, in San Diego," which he had visited while living with Douglas. The head of G.E.'s Publicity Department replied by inviting Dreiser to visit their research laboratory in upstate New York. On December 19 he took the train to Schenectady, where he was met by two of G.E.'s chemists, William D. Coolidge and the Nobel prize-winning researcher Irving Langmuir. After touring the research facility, he bombarded Coolidge and Langmuir with questions about nuclear physics. Fascinated by Langmuir's research at the Schenectady laboratory, Dreiser continued his discussions with the chemist a month later when the two met for lunch at the Chemist's Club in New York City. One of the areas of nuclear physics about which Dreiser questioned Langmuir was the subject of absolute zero, the hypothetical point at which all molecular motion ceases. "At absolute zero," he asked, "what happens to the interior content of the atom? to electrons, protons and their movements? Or is this unknown?" These inquiries seem to have been related to Dreiser's concern over the conservation of energy and how that principle related to the ultimate nature of death. In the section of his philosophy dealing with "The Problem of Death," Dreiser wrote:

> Death is held by some to be nothing more than a cessation of impulse on the part of energy, which now moves to construct something and now rests—the power to rest or to construct being ever present; the power to cease absolutely or disappear completely, which would be death, being absent.
> This power on the part of energy to move to combine or construct or to rest seemingly ranges between an absolute zero of cold, 284 degrees below Fahrenheit zero, and 15,000,000 degrees of heat above, which, according to such physical knowledge as at present holds, may be looked upon as "absolute heat."
> But energy itself at absolute zero does not cease or die.

Dreiser asserted here that the energy of molecular motion is not destroyed, but simply assumes a dormant state at absolute zero (which is actually at a much colder -459.67 degrees Fahrenheit than Dreiser reported). He was curiously restating the principle of the conservation of energy, the nineteenth-century discovery that recognized that the total amount of energy in a physical system can be neither increased nor diminished, but can only change form. The significance for Dreiser's "philosophy" is suggested by its introduction into the chapter on "The Problem of Death"; it relates to his developing notion of an afterlife. Dreiser would become convinced that upon death, although his material body would decay, the indestructible energy within the atoms that constructed him would continue to exist, thus yielding an afterlife of sorts:

> if when you die the atoms or electrons of which you are composed should disintegrate, which would mean that they would change into pure energy, and if—and this is a purely speculative idea of my own—this energy should, for some reason, coagulate as a force, you would, thereby, become an immense power or unit of energy capable (assuming that thought is a phase of energy, which many now believe), although bodiless, of continuing to think—imagine the possibilities of observation, conclusion, interest—assuming that there were endless other such disembodied and yet *thinking* units of energy to be observed by you!—perhaps even confer with! Imagine![38]

In May 1936 Dreiser lectured at Purdue and took the opportunity to visit the university's physics laboratory under the directorship of Karl Lark-Horowitz. He listened attentively to Lark-Horowitz's speculations on "some theory of atomic combination" that explained "the close similarity of the crystalline form of snow, diatoms, and vitamin B2." Although the scientist may have illuminated him on the principles of molecular construction, Dreiser seems to have been more concerned with the spiritual significance of the repetition of form in so many of nature's creations:

> Why should there be such a variety of forms? And why should there appear to run through them all a kind of unity, as if they were all expressing some one thing? Creative energy, say. And why should it be that everything appears in some form or other? . . . Why are so many forms round? Why are large bodies round? And why are some forms crystalline and angular? . . . Why does a snow crystal have its fragile complex design and the beauty of that? And why should Vitamin H crystals sometimes appear like snow crystals? . . .
>
> How very mysterious are these forms! The endless, ceaseless mystery of them, within and around us. And yet seem to us now as if they were all constructed on one principle and permitted by one thing! And yet the wonder and mystery of them remains.[39]

Repetition of form implied "principle" or design to Dreiser, and perceiving design, he suggested that there must be some sort of a designer. This "argument from design" was hardly an original philosophic insight on Dreiser's part, for it had been the cornerstone of natural theology for the century and a half preceding Darwin. Dreiser's increasing reliance on this argument, however, is interesting in revealing the pre-Darwinian foundation on which much of his final philosophy would rest.

During this same Midwestern trip, Dreiser visited the Cleveland laboratory of George W. Crile at Western Reserve University. Dreiser had been aware of Crile's mechanistic research since the mid-1910s, when he had read Crile's *Man—an Adaptive Mechanism*. In his previous book of philosophy, *Hey Rub-a-Dub-Dub*, Dreiser in several essays referred to Crile and Loeb as the leading mechanistic scientists on whom much of his own thought was based. At Crile's Cleveland Clinic, the scientist discussed his latest mechanistic theories with Dreiser and gave him a copy of his newest book, *The Phenomena of Life*. Crile's mechanistic generalizations in this book that "the central fact regarding living organisms is that they are transformers of energy" and that the living cell "was a bipolar mechanism or an electric battery, the nucleus being the positive element, the cytoplasm being the negative element" were assertions that excited Dreiser and tended to provide scientific sanction to certain of his speculations. *The Phenomena of Life*, Dreiser wrote to Crile, "has reinforced my own feelings and deductions in regard to nature and man and has clarified for me many points as to the reactions of human beings which have always puzzled me." In his philosophy, Dreiser would echo Crile's conclusions concerning the mechanistic nature of life, writing that "every living being, and even man himself, is but a transformer of energy, changing the energy derived from the earth and air and sun into mechanical motion, nervous energy, and heat." Describing Crile as "an American scientist of no little standing," Dreiser reported that "George W. Crile has dogmatically asserted that life is electricity." Dreiser then followed this statement immediately with an inquiry concerning the inscrutable power that he believed lay behind the mechanism of life. "But what is Electricity?" he asked. "The final all or a mere phase or expression of it [the final all]?"[40]

In October 1936, Dreiser visited Clark L. Hull, the president of the American Psychological Association and the head of Yale's Institute of Human Relations. In a *New York Times* account of Hull's address to the Association, Dreiser had read about the psychologist's aim to "bridge the chasm of scientific thought between tiny electrons and the intellect of man." Hull had urged his colleagues to study the processes of the mind through the methodology of mechanistic science and to throw off philosophical fetters such as psychic and spiritual interpretations. He demonstrated to his colleagues an electrical machine that duplicated "many of the complicated mechanisms of human or animal behavior," such as the ability to remember and forget. Dreiser wrote to Hull to ask if it would be possible to see this machine, adding, "I am very much inclined to believe in a mechanistic conception of things in general, and I have often thought that such a machine as you describe would some day be developed." Hull sent Dreiser material about the "artificial mechanisms" and invited Dreiser to New Haven to discuss his mechanistic theories of human behavior. Hull's thinking machine may have stimulated the same reaction in Dreiser that the "Differential Analyzer" of Vannevar Bush provoked several years later. After reading about this forerunner of analog and digital computers, Dreiser described it in his philosophy: "You place a problem (an intricate problem, not just a sum) in one of the machines, do a little something with the gears and levers, and out comes the answer." Dreiser's attention here was captured not merely by the fascinating abilities of the mechanism, but by the analogy that it furnished for his conception of the mechanistic universe: "But back of the machine is the man's mind that made it, and back of the man's mind was the evolutionary processes that evolved it. And back of the evolutionary processes were matter-energy-space-time. And back of matter-energy-space-time—?" The answer to this Socratic question that Dreiser wanted his reader to provide was obviously "universal mind." In one of the many variants of the "argument from design" that he employed throughout his philosophy, Dreiser suggested that the existence of a machine must always assume the existence of a mechanic or engineer who designed and constructed the mechanism. "Doesn't mechanism imply something that is not mechanical," he argued, "—the other half of something we call mechanical but out of which mechanism comes."[41]

Dreiser's visits to these various scientific laboratories around the country in 1935 and 1936 were supplemented by his reading of dozens of books on biology and physics in the same period. The studious Dreiser reported to Mencken, with whom he had reconciled after an eight year silence, "I'm so busy getting an education that I never have an hour any more for idling just to be idling."[42]

Dreiser's studies at this time began with a rereading of the works of Jacques Loeb. In February 1935 he ordered copies of *The Organism as a Whole*, *The Dynamics of Living Matter*, and *Forced Movements, Tropisms and Animal Conduct* from Loeb's publishers. At the same time he wrote to Mencken, asking if he was aware of any further work that had been done along mechanistic lines since Loeb's death:

> Have his deductions ever been gainsayed? Has Loeb's tropistic data—his demonstrated heliotropisms, geotropisms, galvanotropisms ever been questioned? Have these been brilliantly enlarged upon or summarized by a particular person? I know there is plenty of work pointing in this direction but are you familiar with any one single luminous work?

Dreiser wrote a similar letter to Calvin Bridges only one month later, asking, "Does your work and that of Morgan and others in any way conflict with Loeb's mechanistic interpretation of life?" Loeb's mechanistic philosophy was obviously an important supporting foundation for the philosophy that Dreiser was intending to write. These letters to Mencken and Bridges were an attempt to make certain that the very mechanistic foundation of his philosophy would be consistent with the latest in scientific research. Mencken replied, "So far as I know, there has never been any serious refutation of Loeb's books. His discovery that eggs could be fertilized artificially seems to me to be one of the really great biological discoveries of the last fifty years." Mencken believed that the bluntness of Loeb's political and anti-religious statements had cost him some acclaim. "There was a faction that didn't like his inconvenient plain speaking. . . . Old Loeb's agnosticism and irreverence made him many enemies, and so there has been some disposition to pooh-pooh him." Mencken concluded, nevertheless, that "no one has ever really disposed of him." Dreiser was no doubt also pleased when Bridges replied, "when I grew up at Columbia, J. Loeb was one of the biological heroes of the time and still holds his place. Later work has extended but not contradicted his results—so far as I know." With this endorsement from Bridges, Dreiser felt that he could then recommend Loeb's books to his collaborator, George Douglas:

> The more I examine the various scientific attempts at an interpretation of life, the more I respect and admire Loeb. He has not been superseded—he has not even as yet been approximated. . . . Of all the scientific reading that you could do at present, I think the reading of Loeb would prove the most profitable.[43]

In addition to rereading Loeb's books, Dreiser read T. H. Morgan's Nobel lecture on "The Relations of Genetics to Physiology and Medicine." The essay, according to Dreiser,

> fills in exactly what I want to know about the latest in genetics, and particularly, in regard to the genes. As in the case of the physics of protoplasm, I notice that the line between matter and energy, is lost or not to be determined. This seems to unite the two worlds, and on the plane of immensely creative intelligence.[44]

Dreiser also studied Harvey Brace Lemon's *From Galileo to Cosmic Rays*, an undergraduate-level physics textbook, which Lemon sent to him after his visit to the University of Chicago. Lemon had intended the text to appeal to the general reading public by designing it as "a book with continuity, . . . for reading from cover to cover within a reasonable time." Dreiser wrote Lemon that he "read and understood and what is more enjoyed" the book. He then asked Lemon to restate his theory about "a standardized form of life origination on millions of possible planets throughout our own little illimitable universe," a theory that the two had discussed when they met. "I ask this because I have always been fascinated by any and every demonstration of the mechanistic nature of life." Because he imagined a universality of mechanistic order and process, Dreiser found it only logical that the origin of life on our world was being mechanistically repeated on innumerable other worlds. In his philosophy, he meditated briefly on the incomprehensible and unknowable forms of life that had likely evolved in the vast reaches of the universe:

If the various universal elements and the chemicals into which they can be broken down are as endless as they appear to be, and a portion of them, with solar and sidereal light added, can, on this minute earth, bring into the vision and so the sensitivity of man all of the innumerable forms he is already dimly aware of, what possible approximation of the further creative powers of these same, as they might manifest themselves in the endless reaches of space, could be made by man with his limited sensory capacities?[45]

Dreiser also read Alexis Carrel's *Man, the Unknown*, which was published in 1935 and quickly became a best-seller. Carrel had been connected with the Rockefeller Institute of Medical Research as a research physician since 1906, and it is likely that Dreiser had met him on one of his visits to that institution. *Man, the Unknown* is Carrel's critique of twentieth- century Western civilization and modern science. He wrote that while science had achieved many accomplishments, it had done very little to improve the potential of humankind. He complained that "the conquest of the material world, which has ceaselessly absorbed the attention and the will of men, caused the organic and spiritual world to fall almost into complete oblivion." In a section that must have disturbed Dreiser, Carrel declared that the mechanistic conception of life was to blame for much of the spiritual bankruptcy of modern society: "The illusions of the mechanists of the nineteenth century, the dogmas of Jacques Loeb, the childish physicochemical conceptions of the human being, in which so many physiologists and physicians still believe, have to be definitely abandoned." Dreiser, who found spiritual inspiration in the mechanistic conception of life, was disappointed by Carrel's attack on mechanistic science. After reading *Man, the Unknown*, Dreiser's evaluation of Carrel was that "if this is his measure, he is smaller than I thought." Dreiser simply dismissed Carrel's criticisms, finding renewed confirmation for his mechanistic beliefs in George Crile's *The Phenomena of Life*. Dreiser wrote to his recent acquaintance, Crile, expressing his enthusiasm over the book and comparing it favorably to Carrel's work:

It impressed me as much as any scientific writing I have read in years. I could not help comparing it with Carrel's *Man, the Unknown* and decided that except for the exactness of his biological knowledge, his book offered no solution whereas your deductions seemed to be exactly in line with the mechanistic reality we call life.[46]

In addition to his own "research," Dreiser occasionally paid several women assistants to read scientific literature and to mark sections that might support his philosophy. For instance, he gave *Man, the Unknown* and a book on "the latest survey of scientific achievements" to Esther McCoy, a frequent research assistant, with instructions to examine the book "with an eye to The Mechanism Called Man, The Myth of Free Will, Good and Evil, the Wisdom of the So-Called Unconscious, the Myth of Individual Thinking, etc. etc. Return books and copied quotes to me." On another occasion, he instructed McCoy to find a copy of *Beauty* by George Santayana: "See if he interprets beauty mechanistically & give me some exact quotations—if any." A few months later, Dreiser had her investigating the psychology of color, in an attempt to find answers to such questions as

> what colors seem to be consistently with what emotions—for example, hate and love, sorrow and joy? Is there anything inherent in color . . . that seems to be able to arouse emotion, or, on the other hand, is it purely because of connection in experience of certain colors with certain emotions . . . ? Does color have more connection with emotion than the sensory reactions?

In addition to Esther McCoy's research, Dreiser had several other assistants, including his full-time secretary, Harriet Bissell, checking science articles in newspapers and magazines for any useful information. For a number of years she clipped appropriate articles from *Reader's Digest* until Dreiser canceled his subscription in 1942 because of "its anti-Russian and pro-Fascist articles."[47]

While Dreiser was busy with this popular science reading, he continued to correspond frequently with George Douglas. After the summer of 1935, which he had spent with Douglas, Dreiser had planned to move permanently to California to be close to his collaborator. "We plan to move back to L.A.—most surely," he wrote to Douglas in January 1936. "How I wish I could spend more days with you. I have almost enough material for all—all of the topics I want to deal with." Two weeks after he wrote this letter, Dreiser received a shocking telegram from Douglas's daughter: "Father died suddenly this afternoon from heart attack. His death was peaceful and without warning."[48]

Dreiser was devastated by Douglas's death. Douglas had perhaps been his closest friend at that time, and Dreiser wrote that the loss "hurts beyond belief." He must have been haunted by Douglas's words in confessing his sorrow and pain at Dreiser's return to New York at the end of the previous summer: "Parting from a friend like you [is] much like a parting by death. There is no essential difference, he said, since there can be no assurance of another meeting. A friend absent is really a friend who has passed away."[49] Douglas's death, however, also had a crippling effect on the writing of *The*

Mechanism Called Man. Although Dreiser continued his investigations of scientific research for the book, he had lost a collaborator whose editorial skill and ability to sharpen his unfocused thoughts would have been essential to the work's production. The result was that Dreiser's "philosophy" was never published in his lifetime. Instead, he left behind several crates of loosely organized notes and comments, which later scholars arranged along the lines of Dreiser's proposed outline and published in 1974 as *Notes on Life*.

      *   *   *

    When Sherwood Anderson asked Dreiser in late 1935 why he had abandoned fiction and was wasting so much time studying science, Dreiser replied, "What I am really doing, is seeking to interpret this business of life to myself. My thought is, if I ever get it reasonably straight for myself I will feel more comfortable." This revealing statement indicates that Dreiser's quest for understanding was actually a deeper quest for tranquility. The fruits of his research were not merely a cold, intellectual knowledge of the processes of nature, but a deeper, emotional fulfillment. "Science," Dreiser insisted, "is certainly not dull, lifeless, nor even mechanical in a narrow way. I think the reason people reject it is because they haven't got the capacity to see how enormously rich, mysterious, varied, and in fact, entirely satisfactory in an emotional way, science as such can be."[50] In his many meetings with prominent American scientists and in the many works of science that he read, Dreiser had been seeking knowledge that would aid him in answering such questions as the nature of his creator, the purpose of his existence, and the meaning of death. In effect, Dreiser had been attempting unconsciously to fill in details of theology in what had previously been his personal, dogma-free religion. His quest for scientific understanding had been a part of a larger quest for spiritual enlightenment.

    There is of course little that is ultimately scientific about the interpretation of existence that Dreiser was building in *The Mechanism Called Man*. The speculations and fancies of his "philosophy" were drawn directly from his artistic imagination and intuition. The role that science played in his imagination, however, was a powerful sanctioning role. Science had established its authority to Dreiser in the 1890s, when the evolutionary scientists and philosophers had provided him an intellectually and emotionally satisfying interpretation of the poverty, struggle, and helplessness that he saw, felt, and feared at that time. Having discovered enlightenment on the social and personal problems and questions facing him in the late Gilded Age, Dreiser maintained his faith in science in the 1930s as he wrestled with more ultimate, but still very personal, metaphysical and spiritual problems and questions. "He was searching for *facts*," wrote Dreiser's literary secretary, Marguerite Tjader,

> —in chemistry, in biology, in astronomy, in psychology—not only for them-selves, but to be able to transmute them directly into philosophic truths, or particles of truth which, he hoped, would eventually make up answers, or some of the answers to the questions he had endlessly asked. How? Why? Perhaps, as he seemed to envision, there would be just One, great unified Answer. And with it, he would astound the world. . . . The final word had not been said. But he longed, and in his longing, almost *prayed* to say it.[51]

Dreiser's "philosophy" was based first and foremost on what he in-stinctively felt. The authority of science was then called upon secondarily to fortify or sanction his speculations. The testimony of the senses, as orga-nized and professionalized in our civilization into the institution of science, was recruited to confirm Dreiser's a priori, extrasensory conclusions. Drei-ser confessed as much in his letter to George Crile, disclosing that *The Phenomena of Man* had "reinforced my own feelings and deductions in regard to nature," or in his letter to George Douglas, confiding that, as a result of his scientific research, "a lot of things that I suspected . . . are being confirmed." His method was again revealed in his instructions to his secre-taries to glean his science books for grains of usable information that would fit the Dreiserian interpretations of free will, good and evil, or the wisdom of the unconscious. Esther McCoy's assignment to find "some exact quota-tions" in Santayana's *Beauty* to support a mechanistic conception of beauty once again exemplifies Dreiser's exploitation of outside authority to rein-force his own authority as interpreter of the cosmos. Because science wielded such overwhelming authority in the thought of modern civiliza-tion, as well as in Dreiser's imagination, scientific authority was naturally the most desirable and most consistent sanction he appropriated for his "philosophy."

Dreiser fully believed, however, that he was building a philosophy on a solid foundation of scientific fact, meaning that his exploitation of science was not a conscious one. He had not yet realized that he was giving his own instincts, feelings, and emotions priority in his interpretation of nature. That awareness was finally reached in an epiphany of insight that he attained at the climax of the ten-year period of his scientific education that has been de-scribed in this chapter. In July 1937, Dreiser visited the Carnegie Biological

Laboratory at Cold Spring Harbor. He spent several weeks at the Long Island research station with his secretary, Harriet Bissell, at the invitation of Calvin Bridges and W. J. V. Osterhout, who were conducting research there that summer.[52] Dreiser's stay at Cold Spring Harbor brought him the recognition that his interest in science had been a spiritual quest, and resulted in a final turning point in the development of his thought.

Dreiser was tormented by a number of personal problems at the time of his Cold Spring Harbor visit. Helen Richardson had recently left him because of his innumerable affairs with other women. His financial situation was deteriorating, partly as a result of a lawsuit he had lost to his former publisher, Horace Liveright, who had sought the return of over $12,000 in advances for a novel that Dreiser had never produced. And finally, the deaths of Charles Fort and George Douglas, his two closest intellectual companions of the past decade, were perhaps forcing Dreiser to face the fact of his own mortality. At Cold Spring Harbor, Dreiser wrote that "I am hiding myself away from the world for a time for the very good reason that its noise and flare . . . and unending questioning and argument have about worn my nerves to shreds." Seeking asylum from the emotional and financial stresses that were tearing at him, he retreated to the "simple, almost monastic atmosphere" of Cold Spring Harbor:

> It is so charming here. These people! These scientists! How sincere! How self-sacrificing! How completely respectable! After the scramble for inanities and trivialities—the money standard of values—to come here to find them ideally set aside. . . . A lovely, clean, courteous world of thought. . . . I am deeply respectful.[53]

Dreiser was pleased to find that most of the researchers at Cold Spring Harbor accepted the mechanistic conception of life, sharing his belief "that man and every animal and bird and fish and insect and tree and flower is a machine." He spent his days "bothering and catechizing those who would endure to be bothered and catechized by one as technically uninformed as myself." Dreiser's spirits were gradually lifted by the activity and ideas around him, as well as by the hope that his direct contact with ongoing scientific research might provide some small clue to solving the mysteries of life that still haunted him. He found satisfaction and a rare peace of mind in this community of

> young and old scientific researchers in all of these buildings pondering over this same mystery and determined, if possible and not unlike myself, to find out some little something about it. The eternal mystery! How did it come to be? We creatures running over the surface of this planet, how did we come to

be? How do we function internally as well as externally? Growth, decay, mind, our emotions, love, hate, our hungers and thirsts, our sensations or lack of them—our so-called knowledge and ignorance—how real or unreal are all of these.[54]

When Dreiser addressed an assembly of the Cold Spring Harbor researchers on August 24, 1937, he praised them with a barrage of religious metaphors that displays the spiritual significance that he connected with scientific research. He referred to them as "the new priesthood—vastly superior to the past priesthood of the churches, the monasteries, the nunneries, their schools and colleges of propaganda." The investigators reminded him of "the early Christian brotherhoods—the monks of the Thebaid," and he found it "comforting and healing to be among them." In his conclusion, he stated that "these men and women seem to be anointed. They are holy, as holiness in life may be. And I am happy and feel absolved to be in their company and hear the truth of nature."[55]

Although Dreiser was emotionally and seemingly spiritually uplifted by the work that he saw taking place inside the laboratories at Cold Spring Harbor, the most important and intense experience of his stay was aroused by a plot of flowers growing along the pathway outside one of the laboratories. The beauty and delicacy of flowers had long inspired Dreiser's thoughts about the designing force behind nature. He often relaxed by wandering through the wildflowers that grew in the fields around his home at Iroki, and several years before his Cold Spring Harbor visit, in a poem called "Interrogation," he had inquired of the "Creative Force":

> Are flowers thoughts of yours, perhaps?
> They are most lovely thoughts,
> The loveliest of all your thoughts
> And ways;
> Of all your forms the best,
> Most beauteous.

One afternoon as he left one of Cold Spring Harbor's research laboratories, Dreiser was attracted to "some small yellow flowers" moments after he had been studiously observing some slides of living cells under the microscope. As he stooped to examine them, he discovered "the same beauty, the same *design*, the same exquisite detail that I had been seeing all day in the tiny organisms under the microscope." At that moment Dreiser seemed to realize that his scientific and philosophic attempts "to interpret this business of life to myself" had actually been a search for spiritual enlightenment. "It was plain to me," he wrote, "that there must be a divine, creative Intelligence behind all this—Not just a blind force, but a great Artist, who made all these things with such love and care." After this experience, Dreiser began to view the universe from a different perspective, seeing "not only the intelligence, but the love and care that goes into all created things."[56]

This moment of intuitive insight left its mark on Dreiser's thought, convincing him that his own emotional responses to nature were just as valuable as intellectual studies of nature. His trust in the authority of his intuitive insights now consciously surpassed the authority of scientific explanation. The power of feeling overcame the power of reason. His thought in the remaining years of his life would grow steadily more mystical, as he immersed himself in the study of transcendentalism, Quakerism, and Hinduism and devoted less energy to the study of science. In one of his final notes made during his visit to Cold Spring Harbor, Dreiser reflected on the merits of the personal, emotional response to nature as opposed to the exact, scientific study of the universe around him, indicating clearly his future inclination toward the former:

> Although a writer, and without practical knowledge of either chemistry or physics, or mathematics, or astronomy, or the instruments, scales, weights, lenses, chemicals, or charts and graphs with which they can be scientifically dealt, still I have, as I imagine, the largest physical and chemical aspects of life itself—its trees, flowers, insects, birds, fish, animals and men—their individual as well as collective actions and reactions, emotions or compulsions to observe and ponder over. And for these of course, I need neither microscope nor retort, nor test tube, nor scale. They are under my eyes.[57]

6. From Mechanism to Mysticism

Dreiser's philosophy of the universe became openly religious in the final years of his life. After his "mystical" experience at Cold Spring Harbor in 1937, his essays, notes, and letters were full of references to "the Deity," "the Creative Being," and "God." Most of the essays, including those for his book of philosophy, which he eventually renamed *Notes on Life*, remained unpublished in his lifetime. Except for a few letters to admiring readers of his work, public announcement of Dreiser's faith in God would be posthumous. He was often reluctant or slow to admit his newly realized religious beliefs even to close friends. It was not until May 1944, for instance, that he confessed to his close friend Marguerite Tjader, "Well, I believe in God, now—a Creative Force," and revealed that he had maintained that belief since the incident at Cold Spring Harbor almost seven years earlier.[1]

The conception of God that Dreiser evolved in his last years was a curious mixture of personal intuition and the scientific and pseudo-scientific philosophy that he had absorbed from his years of reading. His notion of God was that of a creator, immanent in the matter and energy comprising the universe:

> Sometimes I think that when people are thinking or talking about Christ or God or Allah or the Divine Spirit today, they are "thinking" of or, better yet, reaching to the great Creative Force that the scientists—their physicists, chemists, biologists, astronomers, geologists, and what not—refer to so cautiously as Matter-Energy, or the Universe.

In a note called "Religion," Dreiser proclaimed his belief that God was closely connected to the energy contained in the ultimate building block of the universe—the atom. "My conception of God," he wrote, "is that force which controls the cosmos, and as near as I can make out the unit of that force is atomic affinity." In a rather forced metaphor in *Notes on Life*, he once again revealed the spiritual significance that he was projecting on the atom by comparing the Trinity of his childhood Roman Catholicism to a trinity of atomic forces:

The forces of the Universe, binding, repelling and stabilizing appear to be three—Triune (Father, Son, and Holy Ghost of Christianity). They are the positive proton in the atom, the neutron, and then a sub-atomic binding force (no name) which holds the protons together, keeps them—since both are positively charged and as such repel each other—from blowing up. It might be called the stabilizer or Holy Ghost.

In a series of even more strained comparisons, Dreiser suggested that it was the love of the "Creative Force" that expressed itself not only as atomic affinity but as a variety of other forces of attraction:

Love is an invisible, imponderable, attractive force. . . . In chemistry it is called atomic affinity and is the basis or activating force of every chemical action. . . . Thus, because hydrogen loves oxygen, we have water and so on up the scale through the most complicated chemical reactions and the power of reason, love; attraction is the activating principle.

Gravitation is the attraction or the love of matter in mass; magnetism and electricity are manifestations of the primary force. In biology, it is the attraction of the opposite sex, the common or garden variety of which, and very often by some, is considered to be contaminated by passion, yet God or the Creative Force is, as you see, love and/or passion.[2]

This identification of God as a creative force expressing itself through the energy and material particles of the atom might be critically dismissed as the attempt of a lifelong naturalist or mechanist, almost as an afterthought, to make room for a spiritual entity in his materialistic conception of the universe. Such an interpretation, however, would deny the very spiritual motives of Dreiser's quest for understanding and would dismiss the religious underpinnings of his lifelong interest in science. Helen Richardson—with whom he had lived intermittently for the past twenty-five years and whom he finally married in 1944—insisted that although he openly expressed his spiritual interests only in the last few years of his life, Dreiser's quest for spiritual enlightenment had been a driving force for most of his adult life. "Dreiser was a mystic, first, last and always," she contended. "He had a cosmic consciousness—a scientific, searching and direct approach to the study of the natural laws of existence. 'Naturalist?' Yes, but a naturalist with an intuition which had its roots in the cosmic elements of the universe itself."[3] So although Dreiser's deification of atomic affinity may initially seem crude and materialistic, it should be recognized as a conclusion that culminated a prolonged search that was primarily spiritual in nature. It was also a conception of a deity that ultimately shared *some* characteristics of the more traditional Western conception of God. For while Dreiser strongly rejected the orthodox Christian notion of an anthropomorphic and personal deity, his identification of God with the forces inherent in the atom and its energy yielded a deity that not only could create the universe but was also invisible to the ordinary senses, indestructible (recall the conservation of energy), all-pervasive in the universe, and to a great extent still unknowable. These last two characteristics in particular were very emphasized in his philosophy, for Dreiser's conception of the deity was that of a God who is at once both immanent and transcendent in the universe.

In Dreiser's philosophy, nature or creation was synonymous with God or the "Creative Energy." He imagined a deity that was "immanent, that is, indwelling or inherent or intrinsic or incarnated as God in nature—'His works.' 'God is all in all.' " Dreiser rejected the more conventional Christian explanation of Creation, which taught that the universe had been created by God out of nothing and had a subsequent real existence independent of God. He maintained, instead, that the creative energy had embodied itself and continued to embody itself as the matter and energy that comprised the universe. The creative spirit and the material creation were one. "The life process or Creative Energy (the electro-magnetic theory of matter and radiation) or Deity must be considered to be a part of the process or *The Process* rather than an external creator." God was not a distant entity that observed nature from another supernatural realm; God was present in the mechanistic processes that were all-pervasive in nature. "Where is God? Why you're in Him," he insisted. "He is not only in and around you but you—what you call you—are a physical and chemical expression of himself, just as is a whale, a star, a planet, a disease germ, an ant, an emotion, a lust, a fever." Recognizing the similarity between his belief in the immanence of the deity in nature and the pantheism of Eastern thought, Dreiser borrowed the Hindu aphorism that "Brahma is in all things. He is also without." He recognized that this notion was also compatible with the philosophy of Mary Baker Eddy's Christian Science movement. While he could still not accept the Christian Science denial of the existence of evil in the universe, he agreed completely with Mrs. Eddy's assertion that "there is no life, truth, intelligence, nor substance in matter. All is infinite Mind and its infinite manifestation, for God is All-in-All." Dreiser also noted the similarity between his conviction of God's immanence and that of transcendentalist thought; in one passage in *Notes on Life* he defined "the breath of life" as the "energy radiation" contained in and emanating from all material things, and he equated that energy with "what Emerson called the Oversoul." Such comparisons with Hinduism, Christian Science, and transcendentalism reveal Dreiser's awareness that although his philosophy was far removed from that of orthodox Christian dogma, it was consistent with the more mystical conception of an immanent deity that other profound religious thinkers had conceived.[4]

While the authority of the Upanishads of ancient India, Mary Baker Eddy, and Ralph Waldo Emerson were in effect appropriated to sanction his notion of God, Dreiser also wanted to impress his reader that the pantheistic conception of an immanent creator was completely consistent with the findings of science. "Buddha and Mary Baker Eddy affirmed an *over* or *one* universal soul," he wrote, "itself *being* and so *containing* all wisdom and all creative power. Modern science sees no other answer than this, but it is not willing to affirm it." Dreiser's irritation obviously continued to be provoked by those scientists who were spiritually blind to the "creative genius" behind the mechanistic harmony of the universe, but he was now confident that his conception of an immanent God in nature was

> not at all remote from the present scientific attitude toward nature; i.e., the Universe (matter-energy in space-time), its laws and *evolutionary processes*, where these are at all distinguishable in the galaxies of space, as well as (and somewhat more particularly) suggesting a creative process (intelligent in so far as man is capable of defining intelligence) existing in and directing the evolutionary process as this same is known to man on earth.

In this assertion that his pantheistic notion of God was consistent with the universe as revealed by science, Dreiser was echoing the assurance of Ernst Haeckel, whose *The Riddle of the Universe* he had read numerous times. Haeckel had written that "in pantheism God, as an *intramundane* being, is everywhere identical with nature itself, and is operative *within* the world as 'force' or 'energy.' [This] view alone is compatible with our supreme law—the law of substance. It follows necessarily that pantheism is *the world-system of the modern scientist*" (Haeckel's emphasis). In fact, much of Dreiser's conception of God was drawn directly from his understanding and interpretation of Ernst Haeckel's philosophy.[5]

Haeckel intended *The Riddle of the Universe* to be more than a summary of nineteenth-century evolutionary and mechanistic thought. Active in reform movements in his native Germany, he constructed the book as a polemic, attacking the conservatism of German religious, political, and educational institutions and outlining a new philosophy supposedly based on the latest findings of science. Haeckel's monistic philosophy most directly assailed the dualism of the Roman Catholic Church, which divides the universe into the natural and supernatural realms of existence. "Dualism, in the widest sense," Haeckel wrote, "breaks up the universe into two entirely distinct substances—the material world and an immaterial God, who is represented to be its creator, sustainer and ruler."[6] Such dualism, he claimed, did not conform to the current scientific understanding of existence.

Haeckel proclaimed that the greatest scientific insight of the nineteenth century had been the discovery of the "law of substance," which was actually his own combining of "the conservation of matter" with "the conservation of energy." Haeckel defined "matter" as that which fills infinite space, or "infinitely extended substance," and according to the law of the conservation of matter, the total amount of matter in space can never change. "Energy" was that force in the universe that produces motion; Haeckel included heat, sound, light, electricity, and even thought as some of the various forms of energy, and according to the law of the conservation of energy, the total sum of those energies in the universe could not be altered. In a conclusion that rests more on metaphysical speculation than scientific proof, Haeckel combined these two laws into his "law of substance," which proclaimed that both matter and energy were the manifestation of an even more primordial, all-pervasive substance. "For us," he wrote, "matter (space-filling substance) and energy (moving force) are but two attributes of the one underlying substance." Haeckel's monistic philosophy, then, rests on the existence of this mysterious, immanent substance that manifests itself as the universe; not only did Haeckel reduce matter and energy into one fundamental concept, but because he allowed spiritual essence as a property of this fundamental substance, he also eliminated the dualistic notion of separate material and spiritual realms of existence: "Monism . . . recognizes one sole substance in the universe, which is at once 'God and nature'; body and spirit (or matter and energy) it holds to be inseparable. The extra-mundane God of dualism leads necessarily to theism; the intra-mundane God of the monist leads to pantheism."[7]

Dreiser's concept of an immanent "Divine Spirit" located in the "Matter-Energy" of the universe seems too close to Haeckel's monistic vision of a spirit-endowed, primordial substance joining matter and energy to be just coincidental. Dreiser's projection of deity onto the atom seems likewise remarkably reminiscent of Haeckel's endowment of the atom with "soul." "Even the atom," Haeckel had written, "is not without a rudimentary form of sensation and will, or, as it is better expressed, of feeling (aesthesis) and inclination (tropesis)—that is, a universal 'soul' of the simplest character." And Dreiser's curious assertion that the divine love contained in matter-energy caused the attraction of hydrogen and oxygen as well as the attraction of the opposite sexes, appears to have been an interpretation drawn directly from Haeckel. For in *The Riddle of the Universe*, Haeckel had explained that

> the different relation of the various elements towards each other, which chemistry calls "affinity," is one of the most important properties of ponderable matter. . . . The irresistible passion that draws Edward to the sympathetic Ottilia, or Paris to Helen, and leaps over all bounds of reason and morality, is the same powerful "unconscious" attractive force which impels the living spermatozoon to force an entrance into the ovum in the fertilization of the egg of the animal or plant—the same impetuous movement which unites two atoms of hydrogen to one atom of oxygen for the formation of a molecule of water.[8]

The monistic philosophy that Haeckel had advocated in a number of his books was attacked as materialistic or atheistic long before the publication of *The Riddle of the Universe*. Part of Haeckel's purpose in that book, therefore, was to deny this charge; he suggested that monism was an alternative to traditional religion that linked the knowledge of modern science to a compatible modern religion:

> Pure monism is [not] identical . . . with the theological materialism that denies the existence of spirit, and dissolves the world into a heap of dead atoms. . . . On the contrary, we hold, with Goethe, that "matter cannot exist and be operative without spirit, nor spirit without matter." We adhere firmly to the pure, unequivocal monism of Spinoza: Matter, or infinitely extended substance, and spirit (or energy), or sensitive and thinking substance, are two fundamental attributes or principal properties of the all-embracing divine essence of the world, the universal substance.

Haeckel's critics, however, were not moved, because his pantheistic vision was still practically equivalent to atheism. In Haeckel's philosophy, God is *wholly* immanent in the universe, and nothing of God, therefore, exists outside of the universe; God lacks transcendence and can thus be totally understood through the natural laws that science was gradually uncovering. As one critic put it, this type of pantheism is atheism, modified only by "calling the universe 'God' and entertaining a certain emotive attitude towards it." Haeckel practically admitted as much:

> Atheism affirms that there are no gods or goddesses, assuming that god means a personal, extramundane entity. This "godless world-system" substantially agrees with the monism or pantheism of the modern scientist; it is only another expression for it, emphasizing its negative aspect, the non-existence of

any supernatural deity. In this sense, Schopenhauer justly remarks: "Pantheism is only a polite form of atheism. The truth of pantheism lies in its destruction of the dualist antithesis of God and the world, in its recognition that the world exists in virtue of its own inherent forces. The maxim of the pantheist, 'God and the world are one,' is merely a polite way of giving the Lord God his *congé*."9

Haeckel's monism is that variant of pantheism that has been termed "pancomism." It is to be distinguished from another variety of pantheism known as "acomism." Rather than defining the totality of God as synonymous with nature, the acomist sees the totality of nature as an expression of God. While both views posit the immanence of God, acomism allows additionally for God's transcendence. The subtle, but significant distinction between the two views is best clarified by A. E. Garvie:

> If [pantheism] begins with the religious belief or the philosophic faith in God as infinite and eternal reality, then the finite and temporal world is swallowed up in God, and pantheism becomes acomism, i.e. the world is an illusion in comparison with God as reality. If it begins with the scientific conception or the poetic vision of the world as unity, then God is lost in the world, and pantheism becomes pancomism. The first is theistic, and the second atheistic; for in the first, if inconsistently, there still survives as a rule a vague apprehension of God as theism conceives Him, and in the second the θεος becomes but a name for the unity of the world . . . .
> The pantheist of the first type is usually more than a metaphysician, as he is often dominated by a religious rather than speculative interest; e.g. how different are Spinoza and Haeckel! The one clothes an intense piety in an altogether too scanty philosophical argument; the other uses the word "God" only as a fig-leaf to hide the nakedness of his materialistic monism. We may dismiss the second type of pantheism as equivalent to naturalism.10

The relevance to Dreiser's philosophy of this long quotation and the preceding digression into Haeckel's philosophy may now begin to become clear. While Dreiser's conception of God's immanence as a force in matter-energy seems clearly to have been derived from Haeckel's monism, his philosophy was shaped as well by other sources that took him in a different direction from Haeckel's pancomism. For Dreiser's conception of God can more accurately be described as "acomism."

The acomist doctrine that the universe possesses no reality in itself, but is a manifestation of an underlying real being describes perfectly Dreiser's idealist notions of existence in the late period of his life. "Life is literally a tissue of illusions," he wrote in *Notes on Life*:

The nature of God, or the Creative force that appears to operate directly through matter-energy . . . is, in fact, the only reality—universal creative reality—the rest being no more than modes, and these same possibly very limited ones of its immense powers and possibilities of self-expression. . . . In fact all may have been intended as a game, may even be a passing dream of the ultimate substance itself.

This vision of the material universe as a dream or illusory projection of an immaterial, but real creative power harkens back to the Fortean speculations that had so fascinated Dreiser as long ago as 1915, when he had first read Fort's "X." And yet, the notions of the incomprehensibility of our existence and the inscrutability of the reality that created it reach back even further in Dreiser's thought to the Spencerian doctrine of the unknowable. While science had been useful in studying nature to discover the laws of the creator who was immanent in nature, Dreiser now believed that each increase in knowledge resulted only in an increase of ignorance. Echoing Spencer's comments on the limitations of "Ultimate Scientific Ideas," Dreiser wrote:

We deduce laws, limiting the operations of what we see; we give properties to matter, energy, space, time, all infinite things, and their combinations, only to find that in spite of all our efforts to know and put things in order, we become aware not of conquering knowledge, but of increasing ignorance. The anarchy of the infinite and ultimate must, it seems, reject the forms and molds and laws into which we try to put things to make them like us, or our so-called minds.

So it seems that to share this point of view is a kind of defeatism for the struggle for knowledge, as Socrates said when he asserted that he was the wisest man because he knew that he knew nothing.[11]

Dreiser, therefore, departed from Haeckel's more materialistic belief that the immanent God of nature could be comprehended intellectually as the sum of natural laws that science was uncovering. Dreiser's God, unlike Haeckel's, was transcendent, and in order to comprehend something of that God, Dreiser put his faith less on the scientific method in his last years, and more, as I shall soon discuss, on the emotional methods of mystical intuition.

Why the "Creative Force" had chosen to manifest itself as the matter-energy of the universe and to evolve life were questions of utmost importance in Dreiser's philosophy as he speculated on the purpose of existence. He continued to envision a utilitarian relationship between the creative power and life, a vision that continued to bear similarity to Fort's deterministic notion that life was the property or tool of a supernatural creator.

Dreiser wrote in *Notes on Life* that "the machines or bodies called man . . . are useful to it as tools," suggesting a utilitarian or servile purpose for existence, but not specifying the precise use or service that life provides the creator. In metaphors more specific than this "tool" metaphor, Dreiser revealed his conclusion that the purpose of life was to provide pleasure to the creative power. The creator, Dreiser wrote, "makes its own forms, then responds to them [just as] you make your own pie and then eat it." Although this metaphorical comparison of God's act of creation to the baking of a pie is rather crude, it suggests that the "Creative Force" had evolved life for the purpose of drawing pleasure or enjoyment from the result of its work. In another note, Dreiser repeated his "tool" metaphor in stating that "we are of It and Its tool," and then immediately followed with a more specific identification of the tool as "Its mirror. And Narcissus-like, It appears to survey and admire and enjoy Itself through Its self-made mirrors." Life as a mirror, providing a tool for the creator to contemplate and appreciate itself, was a metaphorical image that Dreiser repeated frequently in *Notes on Life*. "Exhibitionism . . . ," he wrote. "All existence is [evolving] toward more and more of that—the universe mirroring itself to itself. As Benjamin DeCasseros once put it 'whatever is, aspires to mirrors'."[12] This image of life as a mirror of the creative power nicely reflects Dreiser's acomist notion of a God that is at once both immanent and transcendent in nature. The creator is immanent in life, since life is a mirror reflection of the creator itself, while at the same time the creator is transcendent from life, standing separate from the mirror and observing itself at a distance.

In another metaphor describing the nature or purpose of existence, Dreiser proposed that "the whole process of living in this unit form as we find it here has the earmarks of a carefully planned game, just like any lesser game devised through this same creative force operating through man." The theory that life is a game is another of the commonly occurring themes running through Dreiser's philosophy:

> Observing the life of which we are a part with the sensory equipment provided us and for all of its appearance at times of extreme cruelty or brutality or the reverse, it still appears to be nothing more than a game, mechanistically or intelligently devised and/or a game intended to be played. The principle of the game is no different to the principle in any minor game played by man, whether it be that of football, baseball, hockey, or any game where antagonists of relative strength, sometimes with the same, sometimes with different equipment, are opposed to each other. In sum, the individual is equipped in a

certain way, that is, with a form, a degree of energy, and five, possibly six, senses. With this equipment, he is faced by other individuals of relatively the same equipment, and the contest is not merely one for survival but for joy out of the contest.

In the last words of this statement Dreiser suggests that seeking pleasure is a higher goal in the game of life than merely surviving the contest. This was not a new development in his thought, for, as we have seen, this hedonistic element in Dreiser's thought had appeared in his writing as far back as *Sister Carrie* and even his *Ev'ry Month* essays. The hedonist in Dreiser had always been instinctively drawn to Spencer's proclamation that pleasure-seeking was the ultimate goal of all human behavior. It was only a short step for Dreiser in his philosophy to elevate pleasure-seeking as the ultimate purpose of all existence. "For if this lifegame is not for pleasure I fail to detect what else it is for," he declared. And because the game of life was a reflection of the creator itself, the reveling of living creatures in the pleasures of life became elevated in Dreiser's thought to a form of worship of the deity:

> They love life—which is to say, they love the outward face or *show* of the forces that bring them here. So that though many or all do suffer much or little, rage at times, cry and die or slay themselves, still it is never because they want less of this *show*, of which they are a part and so often curse, but more. They love it. They rage at being given so small a share of its comforts, pleasures, delights. So that sanely and truly they can be said to love this thing that is as God to them. And so to love God. If this is not so, what else is it or can it be?[13]

Humanity's hedonistic pursuits, in other words, nurtured the narcissistic, self-love of the creator.

Conflict is a necessary element of any game, and the struggle for existence was an obvious aspect of the game of life. Dreiser felt the need to reconcile the existence or necessity of pain, violence, and tragedy in a universe created by a God that he now perceived as loving and caring. The suffering inherent in the struggle for existence, he complained, was too often viewed through a narrow subjectivity that emphasized the violence of life. Instead, struggle must be regarded objectively as a necessary part of the larger process of evolution that brought life itself into existence:

> The old doctrine of tooth and claw is not complete. There seems to be and is a constant struggle—no equilibrium is lasting. But the image is also one of Life constantly flowing into new forms. The forms may wage war or arrange an armistice. But life does not make war against itself. It makes life, builds it, and contest appears to be one of its necessary processes.

From the limited, subjective point of view, for example, bacteria that cause disease are considered evil; from the wider perspective advocated by Dreiser, one must realize that "the bacteria which carry disease through the human body are not trying to kill—they are trying to live." The objective, scientific point of view, then, regards the conflicting interaction of all forms of life as the stimulus causing living creatures to adapt, which in turn causes the further evolution of life. "The enormous revelations of Science in regard to nature," Dreiser wrote, "indicate a necessary balance of forces that at one point of man's limited grasp appear evil and at another point good, but which same, in order to achieve the seeming reality called life, are both necessary." Good and evil are not inherent in the overall process, but are merely subjective descriptions, relative only to individual fates in the game of life. The creator's plan is amoral, Dreiser insisted; "in that *plan*—the totality of its structure and movement—is discernably no *intended* evil."[14]

Sorrow and pain were, nevertheless, experienced at times by all living creatures. Dreiser, however, believed that the creator maintained a balance or "equation" in its plan to prevent suffering from overwhelming life. In an essay called "Equation Inevitable" that appeared in his 1920 collection, *Hey Rub-a-Dub-Dub*, Dreiser had given his first prolonged explanation of this concept. He declared that within the mechanistic processes of the universe, some force maintained an "ancient balance of good and evil, or extremities of one kind balanced against extremities of another." Dreiser derived this peculiar notion of balance or "equation" from the Spencerian doctrine of "rhythm" that he had absorbed from *First Principles*. Evolution of life was caused by the adaptation of living beings to change, and change was caused by a constant ebb and flow of "extremities" of forces seeking what Spencer called "rhythm"; every increase in the strength of a force caused a Newtonian-like counterbalancing increase in an opposite force. While the opposing forces seeking Spencer's "rhythm" were of a physical and chemical nature, in Dreiser's reinterpretation of Spencer, the opposing forces seeking "equation" were positive and negative extremes of an emotional or qualitative nature:

> There is in the mechanistic process a balance and proportion, which seemingly without imbalance or disorder involves and permits of love and hate, mercy and cruelty, sorrow and joy, good and evil, ugliness and beauty, truth and falsehood, justice and injustice, ends and beginnings, strength and weakness, courage and fear, ignorance and wisdom, frankness and secrecy, plus interest and ennui.

In his earlier essay "Equation Inevitable," Dreiser had regarded this tendency toward equation as a mechanistic process inherent in the forces of the universe; during the later period of his life, after having identified all force as a manifestation of the original creative force, Dreiser regarded this balance as a purposeful process, willed by the creator as "a seeming intention on the part of the Creative Force to enforce a degree of equality as between the strong and the weak, the just and the unjust, the merciless and the merciful, wealth and poverty, etc."[15]

The total, combined experience of the aggregate sum of living beings was located by Dreiser at a kind of statistical mean between the extremes of pleasure and suffering; the experience of most individuals, however, fell on one or the other side of the balance point, depending on individual strengths and weaknesses and circumstances of fate:

> The existence of both good and evil are generally admitted. And by some, the first is stressed; by others, the second. Personally, such evidence as has been reviewed by me causes me to feel that the entire living process in general, but not in more than a percentage of individual cases, strikes a balance; that is, all details being accounted for, they would show at least 50% of pleasure and 50% of pain of the same volume and weight, for that mythical being, the average man. In the case of the individual, no such comforting balance could be struck. His ills would be greater or less according to his strength or weakness, luck or ill luck.

In his last years, however, Dreiser shifted his thinking regarding the amount of pleasure that one could expect from this fatalistic balance in life. As his intuitive contemplation of a loving and caring creative being increasingly dominated his thoughts, his balanced equation of good and evil, and pleasure and pain, tipped slightly in humanity's favor. Although in a 1939 interview he asserted that "nobody, rich or poor, can escape sorrow and scratches; it's all about fifty-fifty," one month earlier he had confessed to a correspondent that "on the whole" life appeared "more good than evil, and so desirable." Three years later in a letter to his friend Louise Campbell, he referred to life as "a *thought out Game*" that "seems to yield 50% and perhaps more of pleasure as against an opposite percentage of mixed worry & pain—and not always intense pain by any means."[16]

Dreiser's attempt to interpret the meaning of his own life within the metaphysical system he had constructed is perhaps most obvious in his discussions concerning the nature of the artist. As discussed above, Dreiser regarded all forms of life collectively as a tool or mirror that the creative deity uses to express and reflect itself. "One comes into life a driven mechanism," he asserted, "and in response to life—its endless compulsions—does any of many things. But never of its own free will or genius but solely as a contrivance or implement through which nature, the *creative genius of life*, expresses itself." The individuality that each being senses in itself is actually non-existent, since each individual is merely a mechanistically mass-produced fraction of the total energy of life and has been created or evolved only to serve the purpose of the original creative energy. Even the greatest mind, Dreiser wrote, "is nothing more than a mechanistically directed implement—its 'vanity,' if anything, a chemical energizer, intended to make it go or work." If individuality was an illusion or myth, he believed, then so also must individual creative power be:

> The word creation applied to art is wrong. Art is not *created* by an artist. He is not the original source but a contact instrument with and through which life in many forms expresses itself. And life provides not only the beauty but the artist, admirer and slave of beauty, and the *hunger* of the artist which causes him to react to or seek and then to express the beauty and the drama or arrangement which have, for the above reasons, assailed his internalized sensory equipment and caused that to react—that is to register the beauty or drama or both that is affecting him stimuli-wise.

The "creative genius" of the painter, musician, actor or writer was a myth. The artist, instead, was a passive medium that observed and absorbed the beauty and tragedy of life and then captured in art a sense of that spectacle that the "Creative Force" sought to express. This description of the role of the artist bears great similarity to the declaration of artistic purpose that Dreiser had voiced over forty years earlier in *Sister Carrie*; through his spokesman, Ames, Dreiser had explained that artists are "but mediums, through which something is expressing itself. Now, our duty is to make ourselves ready mediums." Considering himself to be merely a passive medium through which the supreme "creative genius of life" spoke seems to have inspired a genuine humility in Dreiser and to have caused him to shrink away from embarrassing praise in his final years. "Whenever wholly sincere attempts are made to pin flowers on me," he wrote, "I feel like an imposter who is taking what does not rightfully belong to him; rather that which belongs to Life as a whole—the Creative Force—not to any so called self-made individual of which there aren't any." The awkwardness and modesty that he felt in responding to letters from admiring readers in these years were refocused into philosophical professions of his own insignificance. "I never know how to reply to a wholly honest letter of praise," he wrote. "No man makes his talents—however small or great. They are gifts from the various forces which have permitted him to be and to do."[17]

*   *   *

In a comment in *Notes on Life* on the inscrutability of the ultimate nature of the atom, Dreiser speculated on two possible reasons for our ignorance: "Whether the difficulty of probing the atom is because the atom has developed a defense policy of keeping its organization to itself or whether we are just poor at observing and analyzing is a question." The first possible cause suggested here is an innate unknowableness, willed by the creative power in its manifestation and operation in matter-energy. The second possibility that Dreiser suggests is a fault in our procedure of study, that is, an inadequacy of the scientific method (observation and analysis) to discover the ultimate secrets of the universe. While this comment only indirectly suggests his suspicion of the limits of science, elsewhere in his philosophy Dreiser more directly revealed his conversion from the scientific method to more mystical methods of enlightenment. "It was Lao-tsze," Dreiser wrote, "who made clear that the Universe is to be apprehended through feeling not 'thinking'." His increasing anti-intellectual bias is similarly revealed in his acceptance of Kant's realization that "the secret of things lie in the inspiration of the human *conscience* rather than in the cunning decrees of human *intellect*."[18]

After his explosion of insight at Cold Spring Harbor in August 1937, Dreiser's reliance on intuition as a means of apprehending God and the meaning of existence strengthened. After the intense experience of perceiving the "love and care" of the creative force in those small, yellow flowers at the edge of the research building, he could write in his philosophy that "the *Kingdom of God* cometh not by observation. Love can place (reach) the witness for itself, in the hearts of all men."[19] Even acknowledging that for some time he had classified himself as "more of a romanticist than a realist," it is hard to imagine Dreiser making such a startlingly mystical statement before this Cold Spring Harbor epiphany. The trust in instinct and feeling that had always characterized his artistic temperament now blossomed into a faith in mystical revelation that would dominate his thought for his last eight years.

Dreiser, therefore, spent considerably less time studying scientific research in these years than he had in the previous period. He had succeeded in building an intuitive and personally satisfying interpretation of the universe that was consistent with, and in fact constructed upon, a foundation of scientific knowledge that he had absorbed in the previous forty years. He seemed no longer to feel the need to expand his scientific learning in his quest for enlightenment. Instead, Dreiser attempted to develop his ideas further through the study of mystical philosophies that paralleled his own spiritual beliefs. His reading now brought him into the mystical realms of American transcendentalism, the Quaker doctrine of "the inner light," and Eastern philosophy, particularly Hinduism.

Dreiser became interested in transcendentalism in 1938, when he began to edit a collection of Henry David Thoreau's writings. *The Living Thoughts of Thoreau*, which was published in March 1939, was arranged under topic headings that reflected themes central to Dreiser's own philosophy; Thoreau's words were headlined, for example, by such Dreiserian catch phrases as "The Limitations of Knowledge," "Good and Evil," "Mind in Nature," and "Life as Imagination and Illusion." Dreiser's arrangement of the Thoreau quotations into these categories as well as the thirty-page introduction that he wrote for the book reveal his strong conviction that he and Thoreau had much in common philosophically.[20] Dreiser discovered, for example, that Thoreau shared his belief in a creative deity who was immanent in the universe. He felt that through the observation of nature, both had come to recognize that "underlying all is a universal, artistic, constructive genius." Throughout Thoreau's writings, Dreiser encountered "this consciousness of that over-soul or energy genius that he pictures and that knows all, does all, is all." Dreiser's identification with Thoreau's ideas, however, at times amounted to an imposition of his own mechanistic-based philosophy onto the nineteenth-century thinker's observations. Dreiser tried to portray Thoreau as a mechanist by calling attention to Thoreau's references to the "mechanism" or "chemistry" of nature in passages such as "The very sod is replete with mechanism far finer than that of a watch," and "Suppose I see a single green apple, brought to perfection on some thorny shrub. . . . What chemistry has been at work there?"[21]

Dreiser also projected his view of an amoral universe onto Thoreau's transcendentalism. As he read Thoreau's descriptions of a battle between two armies of ants, of vultures feeding on dead animals, and of a muskrat biting off its own leg to escape a trap, he sensed that Thoreau's conception of the universal spirit, like his, was of "something above our comprehension of either good or evil, mercy or cruelty, art or the lack of it—as something other than these things yet out of which all of them take their rise." In the struggle for existence, there were many things that people might call evil. How one creature behaves in order to survive might be considered evil by another form of life that is victimized by that behavior, but the evil was relative only to the victim, not to the survivor. Dreiser believed that Thoreau had also come to the realization that the processes of nature designed by the creative force were amoral and that struggle, pain, disease, and death were only one aspect of the "equation" or balance of nature. Dreiser wrote that "Thoreau, like the prophet Job can cry, as by implication he does: 'Though He slay me, yet I will trust him'."[22]

Dreiser frequently underlined or made marginal comments on the passages of Thoreau's writing that he scrutinized in preparation for *The Living Thoughts of Thoreau*. These marginalia often reveal the similarities that Dreiser perceived in his and Thoreau's philosophies. Both writers, for instance, felt that science dealt inadequately with the underlying spirit of all nature. Dreiser marked portions of a long passage in which Thoreau described a questionnaire sent to him by the American Association for the Advancement of Science and his dilemma in answering one particular question requesting to know the branch of science in which he specialized:

> I felt that it would be to make myself the laughing stock of the scientific community to describe or attempt to describe to them that branch of science which specially interests me, *inasmuch as they do not believe in a science which deals with the higher law. . . . The fact is I am a mystic, a transcendentalist, and a natural philosopher to boot.* (Dreiser's underlining)

In another passage noted by Dreiser, Thoreau wrote that "surely the most important part of an animal is its anima, its vital spirit. . . . Yet most scientific books that treat of animals leave this out altogether." Thoreau went on to decry the shallowness of science for studying only the anatomy or behavior of nature's creatures to the exclusion of the underlying "Universal Intelligence" that expressed itself in them. Beside the passage, Dreiser wrote, "Right! Science is trying to prove that the emotions are chemical. But having done so it remains to show what the chemicals represent." Dreiser, however, did not always agree with Thoreau's more sweeping condemnations of science. When Thoreau declared that "Science is inhuman," Dreiser noted, "Not true." When Thoreau wrote that "things seen with a microscope begin to be insignificant. . . . With our prying instruments we disturb the balance and harmony of nature," Dreiser disagreed, suggesting that "prying instruments also reveal hidden wonders and beauties."[23]

Dreiser, nevertheless, agreed with Thoreau that, for the most part,

science was an incomplete method for discovering the secrets of the supernatural. In his introduction to the Thoreau book, Dreiser wrote that for the
"*how-limited* scientists" of the laboratories and universities, "all talk of any
supreme regulating and hence, legal or directing force or spirit is *out*. There
is no known God or Spirit. He cannot be scientifically described *in toto*, if
even in part." In a passage that reveals how Fortean speculations still
colored his mystical outlook, Dreiser wrote that "as a television station
distributes voices, colors, forms, motions, and ideas or thoughts via sounds
and gestures—so some planetary forces may be broadcasting man and
human life to this planet." At such speculations, he wrote, science only
"starts nervously." In place of scientific observation and analysis, Dreiser
now advocated the intuitive contemplation of nature that he had found in
Thoreau. Through intuition, Dreiser believed that he and Thoreau had
discovered the ultimate supernatural entity that the mechanistic nature of
life and the universe suggested:

> Of all my philosophic and scientific reading of recent years from Democritus
> to Einstein, these scattered notes of Thoreau impress me as being more
> illuminative . . . of the implications of scientific results or cosmology. For
> Thoreau as well as Loeb, and at this hour Einstein, in fact, all up-to-the-hour
> science, look upon man and life, chemical and physical, as directed but in a
> purely mechanical sense. Immutable law binds us all. Only, he was not, as so
> many are, willing to label the process as mechanical and stop there. He
> preferred, or rather, as I should say, he was compelled by his sensory reactions
> to all things, to view them as but dimly conscious mechanisms directed by a
> superior and pervasive something, which has not only evolved them, but . . .
> holds them in place and order.[24]

During the same period that Dreiser was studying the intuitive contemplation of the underlying spirit of nature found in Thoreau's writing, he
discovered similar reflections in his examination of Quaker mysticism. In
1938 Dreiser met Rufus Jones at Haverford College. This eminent Quaker
educator served as Haverford's president and also headed the American
Friends Service Committee, which was then involved in efforts to provide
civilian relief for the victims of the Spanish civil war. Dreiser had come to
Haverford to discuss the Friends' relief efforts with Jones, but much of their
discussion eventually turned to Jones's mystical philosophy.

Jones had been described in 1936 as "the most eminent American
mystic, if, in fact, he is not the American mystic *par excellence* . . . , [who]
more than any of the modern mystics has undertaken to bend the mystical
tradition to meet the demands of modern thought." He had been fascinated

by mysticism since 1884, when under the directorship of Pliny Chase he wrote his graduation thesis at Haverford on "Some Exponents of Mystical Religion." Jones published a series of books in the 1930s and 1940s that attempted to bring the mystical doctrine of the "inner light" back to prominence in Quaker thought. He denied the orthodox Christian conception of God as "a remote, far-away Being, who created the world at a definite time." Instead, Jones proposed a mystical conception of God that was very similar to Dreiser's; his books describe the existence of "a living Spirit, a real Presence, a pervasive Life, an enveloping, environing Reality, in whom we live and from whom we draw our spiritual breath."[25]

Jones also wrote on the crisis that modern science had brought to orthodox religious thought. The revolutionary scientific conception of the universe was "not a series of happy guesses," but "unescapable facts about the universe verified by a multitude of workers and buttressed by unimpeachable testimony." The authority of science had caused thousands of university educated youths to abandon the authority of the Bible and to fall away from the traditional religions in which they had been raised. Jones felt that the viable religions of the future must have a mystical conception of "a living Spirit" that inhabits all of the universe and must be free of anachronistic dogma that contradicts the conclusions of science. In a passage underlined by Dreiser in one of Jones's books, the Quaker mystic predicted hopefully that

> some day ministers of Christ and spiritual guides of little children will perhaps learn the truth that the eternal laws of the universe, made manifest in the facts of nature, and the actual processes of history, as they go forward on their way, are revelations of the will of God and must not be misread or ignored.[26]

Dreiser left his 1938 meeting with Jones, impressed by the latter's "comprehensive way of looking at things" and excited by the similarity of their ideas. Soon after, he read two volumes of Jones's autobiography, *Finding the Trail of Life* and *The Trail of Life in the Middle Years*, as well as Jones's history of *The Later Period of Quakerism*. Dreiser carefully studied these three books, as evidenced by the extensive underlining and marginal comments that he made in his personal copies. He wrote "True" next to a Jones passage that declared that "we must admit the reality of a deeper Self who is the life of our lives, and that every little inlet of human consciousness opens into the total whole of spiritual reality." Dreiser noted Jones's belief that some planning mental force had to be responsible for the universal order that science uncovered. He underlined a passage in which Jones pronounced that "there could be no permanent order, no universal law, no coherence, no evolving process, no goal or purpose, without an undergirding Mind." After reading these works, Dreiser wrote to Jones to express his interest in "the Quaker ideal." "Like yourself," he wrote, "I rather feel that it is the direct road to—not so much a world religion as a world appreciation of the force that provides us all with this amazing experience called life."[27]

In one of Jones's books, Dreiser encountered a reference to John Woolman, the eighteenth-century American Quaker mystic. Jones wrote that "Woolman expresses, in both spirit and in deed, better than any other single individual does, the ideal of Quaker mysticism." Dreiser became curious about Woolman and purchased an 1871 edition of *The Journal of John Woolman* with an introduction by John Greenleaf Whittier. He carefully studied the *Journal*, noting Woolman's intuitive faith in an all-pervasive spirit that expressed itself throughout nature and in the human soul. He also examined the introduction, noting especially Whittier's comparison of Woolman to Thoreau, a comparison that Dreiser employed twice in his introduction to *The Living Thoughts of Thoreau*. After reading the *Journal*, he wrote another enthusiastic letter to Jones:

> I can't tell you how much this interests, and I may say thrills me, because I feel that the Quaker Faith is the only true exposition, and, in so far as it is carried out, realization of Christianity in the modern world. However, when I say Christianity, I mean social ethics and equity introduced into life according to scientific principles as I now, at last, understand those to be.[28]

His recent friendship with Jones and his reading of Woolman's *Journal* renewed Dreiser's interest in a project that he had begun and abandoned over twenty-five years before. As early as 1913, Dreiser had planned to write a novel that he described as an "ironic portrayal" about a "good man who loved God and kept his commandments, and for a time prospered and then went into disaster."[29] He had intended to portray the tragedy of a religious man named Solon Barnes, who clung futilely to a blinding faith that indirectly contributed to a series of personal and financial misfortunes. Although Dreiser intended to portray his protagonist as a rigid Quaker, the original inspiration and motivation behind this proposed novel seems to have been his unresolved feelings about his own father's fanatical Catholicism and financial failures. He began several versions of the novel between 1914 and 1920, but found it difficult to write and abandoned it in the early 1920s to turn to the writing of *An American Tragedy*.

In November 1941, Dreiser wrote to his agent, William C. Lengel, to announce that he had temporarily laid aside the work on his book of philosophy to return to writing his novel of Quaker life, *The Bulwark*. The mysticism that now colored his thoughts and his recently acquired admiration for Quakerism caused him to rethink the religious themes of his novel. While it would still contain the criticism of dogmatic religion that characterized his earlier conception of the novel, his portrayal of Solon Barnes would be more sympathetic in his revised version.[30]

The Bulwark tells the story of Solon Barnes's life from birth to death. Dreiser relied heavily on Jones's autobiography and Woolman's *Journal* as sources for his portrayal of incidents in Solon's youth.[31] As an adult, Solon marries a young woman from a wealthy Quaker family, fathers two sons and two daughters, and becomes a prosperous Philadelphia banker. As he becomes materially successful, Solon maintains the outward aspects of Quakerism (discipline, simplicity, honesty), while losing touch with the "inner light" or the awareness of the presence of God within himself and all other human beings. He becomes conservatively rigid in his relations with friends and in the rearing of his children, relying on the Quaker "Book of Discipline" to reinforce his moral authority.

Solon's life begins to deteriorate when his two youngest children, Etta and Stewart, rebel from him and fall away from Quakerism. At the same time, his increasing awareness of the immoral financial practices of his bank forces him to resign his position. His daughter, Etta, eventually moves to Greenwich Village to "live in sin" with an artist, while his son, Stewart, is responsible for the accidental death of a girlfriend, is arrested, and hangs himself in shame in his jail cell. Shortly after this, Solon's beloved wife dies. Through all these tragedies, Solon gradually recognizes that the rigidity and discipline that characterized his moral outlook had been partly responsible for these tragedies. He believes that had he cultivated the mystical sense of the "inner light" instead of the outward dogmatic moralism of Quakerism, his life would have been better spent.

The final chapters of *The Bulwark* portray the renewal of mystical faith in Solon and in the returned prodigal, Etta. Solon's faith is partly restored by his intuitive contemplation of nature. While walking along a creek one day, he pauses to observe a strikingly colored fly sitting on and eating a beautiful flower. Solon is struck by "the art of the Creative Impulse" that is expressed in the beauty of both the flower and the emerald-green fly. His mood darkens briefly as he reflects upon the tragedy of one of nature's beautiful creatures feeding on another. But he soon reaches an intuitive awareness of the amoral character of nature and the place of tragedy in life:

After bending down and examining a blade of grass here, a climbing vine there, a minute flower, lovely and yet as inexplicable as his green fly, he turned in a kind of religious awe and wonder. Surely there must be a Creative Divinity, and so a purpose, behind all of this variety and beauty and tragedy of life. For see how tragedy had descended upon him, and still he had faith, and would have.[32]

Etta's faith is in turn rekindled by her father's renewed faith, and by her reading of John Woolman's *Journal*. As Etta reads the *Journal* to her father, they discover the mystical core of Quakerism:

Here was no narrow morality, no religion limited by society or creed, but rather, in the words of Woolman, "a principle placed in the human mind, which in different places and ages hath had many different names; it is, however, pure and proceeds from God. It is deep and inward, confined to no form of religion nor excluded from any, when the heart stands in perfect sincerity."

Together, they find the meaning of the "inner light" during Solon's last weeks of life. Solon's final words to his daughter before his death are, "If thee does not turn to the Inner Light where will thee go?" to which Etta replies, "Father, I am not worthy of thee—but I see it, now."[33]

When Rufus Jones read *The Bulwark*, published several months after Dreiser's death, he commented that he thought the novel was a failure as fiction. "The author is interpreting a theory of life and action," he wrote, "rather than creating persons who live and breathe and have authentic being." Jones admitted, however, that he was moved by Solon and Etta's discovery of the "inner light," and he detected Dreiser's own mystical faith in the novel's conclusion. "One feels that this fine ending reveals a new stage in the author's life. Here he reaches a new level of insight and sees at last the deeper significance of life."[34]

Jones was correct in his evaluation that Solon's spiritual awakening to the "inner light" was linked to Dreiser's own recent embrace of mysticism. Near the conclusion of the novel, Dreiser had incorporated a mystical encounter that he himself had experienced while writing the novel. Like his earlier discovery of a "divine, Creative intelligence" in the flowers at Cold Spring Harbor, he interpreted this experience as a proof of the "*oneness* of life." One day Dreiser had shot a snake that he had seen crawling in the high grass near his house in Los Angeles. When someone informed him that the snake was a harmless variety of puff adder, he immediately regretted that he had killed the creature. A few days later, Dreiser found a second snake in his yard and assumed that it was the mate of the creature he had killed. He later told friends that when the snake started to move away from him, he spoke to it. "I said I thought it was beautiful and I was sorry that I had killed its mate." After he assured the snake that he would not harm it, he claimed that "it turned and came toward me, passing right across the toe of my shoe— and disappeared into the grass on the other side." Dreiser was profoundly moved by this "revelation" and included it as one of Solon's final experiences in *The Bulwark*. Solon's words in describing the incident to Etta reveal the mystical significance that the experience held for Dreiser. Solon announces:

> I know now that we are so little of all that infinite something of which we are a part—and that there are more languages spoken than we have any knowledge of. . . . I mean that good intent is of itself a universal language, and if our intention is good, all creatures in their particular way understand, and so it was that this puff adder understood me just as I understood it. . . . And now I thank God for this revelation of His universal presence and His good intent toward all things—all of His created world. For otherwise how would it understand me, and I it, if we were not both a part of Himself.[35]

Dreiser's ability to intuit the presence of a universal creative spirit in his experiences at Cold Spring Harbor and with the snake in his yard had provided him with more immediately satisfying spiritual answers than his years of studying science. His portrayal of Solon Barnes's spiritual awakening was actually a fictional reworking of his own mystical discovery of a "creator." When his niece, Vera Dreiser, asked him shortly after the completion of the novel if he now believed in God, Dreiser "answered that he had scientific proof and invited me into his 'laboratory', his novel of spiritual affirmation, *The Bulwark*."[36]

In the last years of his life, Dreiser also became interested in Eastern religions, and he connected the mysticism he found in Zen, Tao, and Hinduism with the mystical philosophy he studied in transcendentalism and Quakerism. In his introduction to *The Living Thoughts of Thoreau*, for instance, he compared Thoreau's use of intuition to the mysticism of Buddha and Lao-tze. When he read the *Bhagavad-Gita*, he underlined a remark in Aldous Huxley's introduction that declared that "John Woolman, the American Quaker, provides the most enlightening example of the way in which a man may live in the world, while practicing perfect nonattachment and remaining acutely sensitive to the claims of the right livelihood." And when he read Harendranath Maitra's comment in *Hinduism* that "It is only in Hinduism, I think, that we find the conception of God assumed in *all* the human relations of life," Dreiser penciled the marginal objection, "Quakers?"[37]

More than the other Eastern religions, Dreiser became fascinated with Hinduism. His interest was probably stimulated by Helen Richardson, who had studied yoga under Swami Prabhavananda for a number of years. As a result of her encouragement, Dreiser read a number of books about Hinduism and found in them a mystical interpretation of the universe that, like transcendentalism and Quakerism, was compatible with his scientific studies and philosophic conclusions. Maitra's *Hinduism* was the principal source of his understanding of the Indian religion, and he was no doubt attracted to Maitra's claim that there was nothing incompatible between the findings of modern science and the Hindu belief in Brahma. Maitra suggested, in a passage heavily marked by Dreiser, that

> if there are innumerable forms of life lower than man, is it not at least as scientific to conceive of innumerable forms higher than man? If every drop of water is full of invisible life, is it not equally possible that the ether is full of etheral life invisible to our grosser senses?[38]

Dreiser found a clear connection between his intuitive conclusions about an immanent creative force in nature and the Hindu conviction that "there is a one and only life—Brahma—beside which there is no other":

> My own meditations on that timeless energy which is obviously the essence of all life, . . . lead me to the conviction that the ancient Hindu conception remains unrefuted. Time, light, space, energy, the eighty or ninety elements and their combinations, atoms, electrons, protons, neutrons, deutrons, quantums, all of the arbitrarily named phases of energy and matter into which they pass and from which they return again, indicate, if anything, but one thing: The presence of an ultimate energy or substance by terms, either as or not as, as it chooses, matter or energy—the one beside which there is no other and out of which all things take their rise.

Convinced that all living beings contained a portion of this immanent "timeless energy," or the spirit of Brahma, Dreiser discovered himself making an immensely significant spiritual conclusion. The existence of the "soul," he confessed, was now a concept with which "at last, after many years of speculation and meditation, I have come to agree." Once he conceded the existence of the soul, it was only a short step for Dreiser to recognize its immortality. Death, he argued, was only a dissolution of the material form of living beings. As a fractional portion of the total creative energy that was indestructible and eternal, the energy of life, or the soul, that was contained in each material form must also be immortal. This was a conclusion, he argued, based on the wisdom of Hindu thought, as well as on the scientific law of the conservation of energy:

> What is important is whether the creative impulse, primarily responsible for the appearance and temporary existence of that form, ceases or not. And now science as well as Brahminic thought return to assure us that it does not, since, given a one and indestructible [form] behind all forms, it could not. At worst, it would have retired into the ultimate, to be extended in what other form or forms we know not. But to die? No. Not though the idea of such a thing as a man die, or a tree, or flower, or bird or world, still that which could make any or all of these—tree, rock, flower, stream, mountain, sea, world—is, and that which can make a sun or sidereal system is not dead and seemingly need not die.[39]

Dreiser's interest in Hinduism found expression in an unusual mystical section at the close of *The Stoic*, his final novel and the long delayed, concluding installment of the Cowperwood trilogy. Critics of the novel have correctly recognized that the digression into Eastern philosophy in the final pages of *The Stoic* is jarringly incongruous in a novel whose main interest lies with an unscrupulous American businessman. Dreiser evidently intended to end his novel by suggesting, as he did in *The Bulwark*, that the mystical contemplation of the universe could allow one to transcend the greed and tragedies of the material world. He wisely realized, however, that Cowperwood's conversion to mysticism would have been totally out of character and unsupported by the biographical evidence of Cowperwood's real-life model, Charles Yerkes. So after Cowperwood's death, Dreiser refocused the novel's attention on the millionaire's former mistress, Berenice Fleming, and on her spiritual journey to India.

Berenice is introduced to Hinduism through her meditations with the Guru Borodandaj. The guru's words of enlightenment reflect once again the mixture of mysticism and science that characterized Dreiser's philosophy at the end of his life. The guru explains that all the universe is composed of atoms, which bear the energy of the eternal spirit known as Brahman. These atoms combine to form cells, which combine into organisms that manifest their own intelligence. The guru instructs that when death occurs, "the force which held the cells together is withdrawn, and they become free to go their own way and to form new combinations. Death is but an aspect of life, and the destruction of one material form is but a prelude to the building up of another."[40]

In a passage discussing the meaning of beauty in life, Dreiser revealed through his guru spokesman his conviction that the chemical compulsions and tropisms that he had studied in science for so many years were the manifestations of the universal spirit. The numerous love affairs that Dreiser had undertaken and that he previously excused as "chemic" determination, were now elevated and rationalized as the attraction of "Divine Love":

> When you see a man being drawn to a beautiful face, do you think that it is a handful of arranged material molecules which really attracts the man? Not at all! Behind those material particles there must be and is the play of divine influence and divine love. . . . So even the lowest forms of attraction derive their power from God himself.

For Dreiser, the eternal spirit was "the great magnet," to which everyone was drawn "like iron filings." The "face of Brahman" was expressed in all forms and designs, and the worship of beauty was actually the worship of the "Reality behind the scenes."[41] In these sentences, which were among the last that he composed in his life, Dreiser's hedonistic compulsion to seek pleasure continued to express itself. His final explanation, however, was no longer scientific, but mystical in nature.

Through his readings in Thoreau's transcendentalism, in Woolman's and Jones's Quakerism, and in Hindu philosophy, Dreiser reached the conclusion that "the spirit is all." As his reliance on personal intuition and revelation increased, his reliance on the revelation of science correspondingly declined in those last years. Yet, Dreiser continued to insist that there was nothing incompatible between the scientific understanding of the universe and his mystical conception of the universe. "There is no conflict between science and religion," he asserted, "—only between science and theology." Dreiser was able to subscribe to a "religion" that was in harmony with the scientific view of nature and was free from the dogmatic and unsupported "theology" of orthodox faiths. Although he was relying primarily on personal intuition to construct his spiritual outlook, he had complete confidence that his beliefs could be scientifically proven. "I not only believe in God," he asserted, "but I can go into any scientific laboratory and prove His existence."[42]

As his time and energy were increasingly consumed by his study of mystical religions, his devotion to scientific matters dwindled, although for a brief time in the late 1930s he did participate in several short-lived projects aimed at popularizing scientific research. In 1937 he developed plans for a radio show in collaboration with his old Woods Hole friend, L. V. Heilbrunn; the program would have dramatized the work of such notable scientists as Robert Millikan, Alexis Carrel, Arthur Compton, Irving Langmuir, and T. H. Morgan. When Dreiser and Heilbrunn failed to sell their idea to the National Broadcasting Company, they developed a new scheme to produce and promote a series of movies about the wonders of modern science. This venture, however, also failed. Finally, Dreiser briefly considered collaborating with Heilbrunn on a novel about scientific research in American universities, but as we have seen, Dreiser's interest in mystical religion eventually turned his attention to novels in which he could address more supernatural themes.[43]

Dreiser's visits to scientific laboratories and his scientific reading declined in his final years. In December 1938, he moved to southern California, where he remained for the rest of his life. Although advancing age and deteriorating health prevented him from continuing to travel around the country to visit laboratories, his new location in the Los Angeles suburbs gave him access to the California Institute of Technology and the Mount Wilson Observatory. His friend Calvin Bridges, who had been located at Cal Tech since 1928 and had previously introduced him to a number of the Institute's researchers, died suddenly of a heart attack in December, shortly after Dreiser's arrival in Los Angeles. Dreiser continued, nevertheless, to visit Cal Tech to discuss the spiritual implications of modern science with his acquaintances, the physicist Robert Millikan and the aeronautical engineer Theodore von Karman. In addition, he made several visits to the Mount Wilson Observatory, where he met the astronomers Edison Pettit and Gustav Strömberg, and where he was permitted to view the spectacular wonders of the "island universes" of the cosmos through their one-hundred-inch reflecting telescope.[44]

Although he no longer felt the need to seek scientific sanction for his mystical beliefs, Dreiser was encouraged to find several scientists in his last years who were willing to express a similar belief in a creative spirit. In 1940, he read *The Soul of the Universe*, written by his Mount Wilson astronomer acquaintance Gustav Strömberg. Strömberg's book was a review of the latest research in astronomy, physics, and biology combined with a spiritual interpretation of the universe. He believed that the order revealed throughout the cosmos by the research of modern science proved that the universe was "*a non-divisible, rational entity.*" He wrote that "the wisdom we see revealed in the organization of the living world, the harmonious, uniform laws exhibited in the inorganic world, and the wonderful mental faculties we have in some mysterious way inherited, all point to the activities of an *all embracing, intelligent, unitary entity.*" This entity, according to Strömberg, expressed itself in each cell of a living creature as a "living but immaterial" wave or form of energy that he called a "genie." These "genii" were responsible for carrying out the creative plan behind the development and organization of the cells of living creatures from the moment of egg-fertilization, and accounted for such higher mental abilities as consciousness and memory. Strömberg believed that the total complex of "genii" in the human body composed the "soul," the faculty that allowed humans to sense or intuit the existence of God. Upon death, the "genii" abandoned the material, protoplasmic body and traveled freely through space until they became reincarnated in a new living form.[45]

Dreiser was fascinated by Strömberg's speculations. He was pleased that, like himself, Strömberg had sensed the existence of God as a form of energy organizing the protoplasm of living cells. "Your 'living but immaterial genii' and 'wave systems' which, in contact with matter, they evoke, interests me greatly," he wrote to the astronomer. Dreiser, however, was troubled by Strömberg's belief that human beings possessed at least partial free will. Strömberg had written that

> personally I feel that God has delegated some of his power of will or decision to human souls, after they have reached a certain state of development. . . . From this viewpoint events on earth, like accidents, death, war, our attitude toward our fellowmen, are partly due to a Cosmic will and partly to my will and that of my fellowmen.

Dreiser wrote that these were conclusions "which for me need clarification," and he asked to meet with Strömberg to discuss the differences in their interpretations of the universe. He was impressed, nevertheless, by Strömberg's belief in God and by his suggestions of the possibility of the reincarnation of human souls.[46]

Dreiser was further encouraged when he attended a conference on religion in 1945 at U.C.L.A. The morning session was chaired by Dr. Arthur H. Compton, the Nobel prize winning physicist whom Dreiser had met at the University of Chicago in April 1935. Dreiser was amazed to hear Compton and the other scientists on the panel admit their belief in "the theory of a Divine Power, calling It various names from Super-intelligence to an Unknown God, but still a God." In the afternoon session that day, Dreiser reported, Compton and the others were challenged by Hugh Miller, a professor of philosophy, who claimed that the confession of spiritual beliefs by the scientists did not go far enough. In a criticism that reflected Dreiser's own dissatisfaction with the self-imposed limitations of scientific inquiry, Miller demanded that the scientists begin to apply their research to the study of the supernatural, asserting that "science can and must pursue religious truth in order to advance."

Dreiser's imagination was stimulated by the conversations he heard at the conference. When he returned from the conference that evening, he told friends how his own scientific observations had led him to intuit the presence of a Divine Spirit in nature. Dreiser spoke of the "miracle" of the winter rye plant, whose root, he claimed, contained up to 14 billion rootlets on each plant. "You can't tell me there's no meaning in those little roots reaching out toward nourishment that's in the soil," he reportedly insisted. The intricacy of the mechanistic design that he had observed was proof to Dreiser of the existence of a creative designer. "I've studied the thing under a microscope and I tell you it's not just a machine. There's something more than we thought in this process by which these plants grow and add life to themselves."[47]

Through the design that he sensed in the roots of the winter rye, in the flowers at Cold Spring Harbor, and even in the avocado tree that grew in the yard of his Hollywood home, Dreiser felt that he could intuit the presence of an all-pervasive Spirit. "Design," he wrote, " . . . is the great treasure that nature or the Creative Force has to offer man and through which it seems to emphasize its own genius and to offer the knowledge of the same to man. Design! Design! Design!" Inspired by the beauty and design that he found in his avocado tree, Dreiser wrote an essay in November 1943 titled "My Creator," which was to have been his first published confession of his faith in God.[48] Because he had laid aside his huge, unassembled book of philosophy to return to the writing of *The Bulwark* and *The Stoic* and because he feared that he would never complete the philosophy, Dreiser felt that this essay was necessary to announce his spiritual faith publicly.

Dreiser opened "My Creator" with an embarrassed apology for his previous philosophical statements, such as the 1928 "Statement of Belief," in which he had proclaimed that his observations of the tragedies and mysteries of life had left him unable to find any meaning to existence:

> At that time my brash and certainly most unpremeditated reply was that I took no meaning from all that I saw unless it was some planned form of self-entertainment on the part of the Creative Force, which cared little if anything for either the joys or sorrows of its creatures, and that, as for myself, "I would pass as I had come to be, confused and dismayed."

Now, Dreiser no longer felt "confused and dismayed." He sensed a genius in the creator's planned "equation" between good and evil, beauty, and ugliness, and ignorance and wisdom. For without evil, ugliness and ignorance in life, how could one ever appreciate the good, beauty and wisdom that permeated the creator's plan? Contrast was a necessary part of the design of the universe:

> Thus, it is evil and evil alone that you use as a yardstick by which you measure any such *good* as befalls you. In other words, when you think of good in any form, you instantly think of something that is not as good, something by which you measure yours as better or, at least, some better.[49]

Through the mystical contemplation of nature's creatures, Dreiser wrote that now "I am really most awed and, to a very great degree, made reverent." He was amazed by "the mechanical and chemical genius of their construction and operation! Also, the amazing variety and, what is more, the almost invariably esthetic appeal of nearly all of their design!" Flowers remained for Dreiser the most significant "revelation" of the creator's existence, and he confessed that whenever he saw them, he was forced to pause and meditate on the "exquisite beauty or import or meaning of the design itself. Design! Design! Design! Could anything in nature be more significant? Or suggestive of thought?"

And so at the end of his life, Dreiser finally found personally satisfying answers to the spiritual questions that had always plagued him. Science had aided him in his quest for enlightenment about the ultimate purpose and meaning of existence, but in his final years it was his personal vision, his intuitive comtemplation of the beauty and design in nature, that brought him the knowledge of "his Creator." In the closing paragraphs of the essay, he not only confessed his faith in and reverence for God, but even expressed a prayer for his continued existence, that implied his hope for an afterlife:

> And so studying this matter of genius in design and beauty, as well as the wisdom of contrast and interest in this so carefully engineered and regulated universe—this amazing process called living—I am moved not only to awe but to reverence for the Creator of the same, concerning whom—I meditate constantly, even though it be, as I see it, that my import to this, my Creator, can be but as nothing, or less, if that were possible.
>
> Yet awe I have. And at long last, profound reverence for so amazing and esthetic and wondrous a process that may truly have been, and for all that I know, may yet continue to be forever and forever. An esthetic and wondrous process of which I might pray—and do—to remain the infinitesimal part of that same that I am now.[50]

Conclusion

In *The Modern Temper* (1929), Joseph Wood Krutch described what he perceived to be a growing disillusionment with science and its accomplishments. The utilitarian limitations of the scientific laboratory and the philosophical pessimism that scientific knowledge seemed inevitably to spawn were becoming increasingly obvious to thinkers in the 1920s:

> Experience has taught us that the method of the laboratory has its limitation and that the accumulation of scientific fact is not, in the case of all subjects, useful. We have learned how certain truths—intimate revelations concerning the origin and mechanism of our deepest impulses—can stagger our souls, and how a clear perception of our lonely isolation in the midst of a universe which knows nothing of us and our aspirations paralyzes our will. We are aware, too, of the fact that art and ethics have not flowered anew in the light, that we have not won a newer and more joyous acceptance of the universe, and we have come to realize that the more we learn of the laws of that universe—in which we constitute a strange incongruity—the less we shall feel at home in it.

The previous generation's faith that every advance in scientific knowledge would contribute to the progressive advance of society now appeared naive and shallow. Huxley's prophesies of a flowering of humanity in the ever-increasing enlightenment of scientific knowledge seemed unfulfilled in a decade struggling to recover from the horrors of world war and searching to find fulfillment in the unfolding materialism of modern life. The scientific achievements, Krutch conceded, had continued to march from the research laboratories, "and yet, in spite of so much success, we are aware of a certain disappointment and of a hope less eager than [Huxley's], as though our victories were somehow barren and as though the most essential things were eluding us." The Victorian era's optimism regarding the twofold promise of science—"an increase first in our powers, second in our happiness or wisdom"—had been shattered by the twentieth-century realization that "it is the first and less important of the two promises which [science] has kept most abundantly."[1]

Krutch was one of a number of critics in the 1920s who commented that in spite of the accumulation of scientific "truths" about nature that had advanced the physical quality of human life, the laboratory had failed to enhance our understanding of human nature. He declared that "the most important part of our lives—sensations, emotions, desires, and aspirations—take place in a universe of illusions which science can attenuate or destroy, but which it is powerless to enrich." Interpreting human behavior and experience from the cold perspective of chemical reactions and sub-atomic attractions had proven unsatisfactory in illuminating the interior realms of emotional, spiritual, and artistic yearnings. Even the more recent scientific philosophers, Krutch maintained, had recognized the limitations of the mechanistic conception of human life and were seeking alternative paths to circumvent the dead end to which the materialistic interpretation of the universe had led them:

> Certainly no one who has taken the trouble to familiarize himself with the most recent scientific and philosophical writing can have failed to observe that, whatever its results, it seems animated more and more by a desire to escape from those ultimately materialistic conclusions which slightly earlier philosophical and scientific writers were striving to achieve. If the end of the nineteenth century found thinkers doing their best to confine man within the framework of a mechanistically conceived nature, the first quarter of the twentieth found them eagerly seeking some way, either scientific or metaphysical, by which he may escape from it. Seeds of discontent are spreading in that vast spiritual bourgeoisie which the nineteenth century created, and its ranks are breaking. Who reads Haeckel now or who, having read him, fails to find the complacency of his atheism even more antiquated than his facts?[2]

Well, as we have seen, Dreiser, for one, still read Haeckel, and the development of his thought in the 1930s and 1940s continued to be influenced by the mechanistic philosophy that he had absorbed at least partially from Haeckel. Nevertheless, the dawning of Dreiser's awareness in the 1920s of the inability or refusal of scientists to probe the metaphysical questions that fascinated him does seem to coincide with the rising critical awareness of the shallowness of science that Krutch described in that decade. Dreiser's attempts in the 1930s and 1940s to spiritualize the mechanistic universe, and more specifically, his acomist deviation from Haeckel's "atheism"—"pancomism" would be the more accurate term—seem illustrative of Krutch's observation of the wider intellectual movement away from the purely materialistic conception of the universe offered by mechanistic science. *The Modern Temper* was published in the same year as Dreiser's sharply critical "What I Believe" essay, and Krutch's words frequently express the same shattered illusions about science that Dreiser was then experiencing: "We are disillusioned with the laboratory, not because we have lost faith in the truth of its findings but because we have lost faith in the power of those findings to help us as generally as we had once hoped they might help."[3]

Dreiser's shifting attitudes concerning the value of science must therefore be seen within the context of a more general intellectual swing that was occurring in the 1920s. This growing critique of science may not have been the predominant attitude of thinkers during that decade; certainly the futurist movement in art and the utopian declarations of social observers like John Dewey and Herbert Croly testify to the continuing enthusiasm for science and its social and artistic possibilities among creators and thinkers of the twenties. Nevertheless, a counterbalancing disillusionment with science—a retreat from the Victorian optimism of the previous generation—was reflected in much of the discussion of the Jazz Age. The cultural historian Frederick J. Hoffman has identified the novels of Sherwood Anderson and D. H. Lawrence, the poetry of T. S. Eliot, the literary criticism of Van Wyck Brooks and John Crowe Ransom, and the social criticism of Lewis Mumford as examples of this retreat from scientific or mechanistic utopianism. Hoffman sees the fundamentalist-evolutionary controversy of the decade as merely one example of a more widespread suspicion of the dehumanizing effects of scientific "truths," and he even interprets the primitivist movement in art, the growing popularity of jazz, and the increasing interest in African culture and art as social and artistic symptoms of a widely felt desire in the twenties to escape the precision and barrenness of modern culture and to retreat into cultures where myth, legend, and spirit still played valuable social roles. In this quest to revive a pre-industrial, pre-scientific system of values, some critics retreated centuries into the past; John Crowe Ransom, for example, found renewed comfort in the authority and orthodoxy of the medieval Church.[4] Dreiser, of course, found it impossible to resort to that extreme. And yet Dreiser's disillusionment with science and his quest for metaphysical answers did carry him to the comfort and security offered by past systems of belief, particularly, as I shall shortly discuss, the romanticism of the late eighteenth and early nineteenth centuries.

Dreiser's artistic and intellectual career spanned the twilight of the Gilded Age and the dawn of the Nuclear Age. His shifting response toward science uniquely illustrates the shift from utopian optimism to disillusioned frustration that Krutch felt in American intellectual life as the nation moved from the Victorian to the modern era. Dreiser's response to the Victorian popularizers of science who had awakened him intellectually had been determined first of all by his background and temperament. His rural education, family superstitions, and brief year at college did little to prepare him intellectually for a deep critical reading of writers like Huxley, Haeckel, or Spencer. His untrained mind, which throughout his life responded more with feeling than logic, approached these writers with the artist's subjective, emotional passion to know, rather than the scientist's objective, intellectual curiosity to learn. Awed by the rising prestige and authority of scientific explanation in the late nineteenth century, he uncritically embraced all that he read.

Dreiser's response was more importantly shaped by the curious romantic tendency of the Victorian popularizers to ponder more than the narrow facts of their research and to speculate on the larger cosmic scheme of things. The "evolutionary scientists" whom he read were also "evolutionary philosophers," whose works glittered with metaphysical and often spiritual interpretation. From Tyndall's muted mysticism and Wallace's glaring spiritualism to Haeckel's apologetic pantheism and Gates's psychogenetic moralism, Dreiser encountered scientific fact entangled with philosophical speculation. Even in Huxley's agnostic attacks on the Bible and Loeb's mechanistic assaults on vitalism, Dreiser encountered interpretations that in their very challenges to orthodoxy conversely implied alternative metaphysical explanations of reality. And in Herbert Spencer's synthetic philosophy, Dreiser encountered the grandest metaphysical speculation of the Victorian era, intermingled with enough appropriated scientific fact and jargon to dazzle him with its authority.

Much has been written about how Dreiser's exposure to these writers influenced his hostility to Roman Catholicism and orthodox religion in general and stimulated the creation of his naturalistic outlook. These scientists and philosophers, however, also shaped Dreiser's expectations of what the study of science could reveal to him. He was drawn not so much to the scientific facts as to the speculative philosophy that sparkled on their pages. These authors not only explained "process" but attempted to explain "purpose"; they not only asked "how" but also addressed "why." Dreiser's initial encounter with science through these nineteenth-century scientists and philosophers, therefore, led him to assume that science addressed itself routinely to ultimate questions about the nature of the universe, the origin of life and the meaning of human existence, the mysteries of human motivation and behavior, the origin of ethics and the meaning of good and evil, and the existence of forces or spirits that implied a realm of being beyond the material cosmos. Dreiser's introduction to science not only shattered his orthodox religious beliefs but left him convinced that science would replace those beliefs with an alternative, more accurate vision of the cosmos. His subsequent fascination with science in the decades following the 1890s was motivated by a passion for knowledge of the unknown force that created and maintained the material universe and of his relationship with that ultimate power. The study of science became a quest for spiritual enlightenment, in his own words, "a form of prayer."

Dreiser's eventual disillusionment with science was caused by his dawning awareness by the late 1920s that many of the modern research scientists of the twentieth century, unlike the Victorian popularizers, refused to address those ultimate questions that he yearned to have answered. Of the dozens of scientists whom he visited in the twenties and thirties, only Robert Millikan and Arthur Compton were willing to speculate publicly that the order of nature revealed by science suggested the existence of a higher creative being. Only the relatively unknown Gustav Strömberg was willing to take a further metaphysical leap by speculating about the nature of the soul or the possibility of reincarnation in his books. None of Dreiser's acquaintances were willing to pursue the scientific study of mind reading, fortune telling, teleportation, spirit communication or apparition, or any of the other mysteries of the "unknowable" that Dreiser demanded be explained. Instead, the typical modern scientist whom he met insisted, like Calvin Bridges, that such supernatural investigations or even speculations were beyond the scope of the scientist's investigation of the natural universe. Within the generation of Dreiser's adult life, metaphysics had been abandoned by the scientist and surrendered to the philosopher, the theologian, and the artist.

Dreiser's attempt at philosophy in the 1930s, then, was a quest to overcome the frustrating limitations of modern science. He sought knowledge beyond the material, natural universe of scientific investigation, knowledge of a spiritual, supernatural realm that science declared to be "unknowable" to its methods. In "seeking to interpret this business of life to myself," Dreiser evolved a metaphysical vision of the universe and existence that was increasingly derived from intuition and emotion, while continuing to claim verification in the authority of scientific explanation. It was perhaps inevitable and certainly appropriate, then, that his final mystical beliefs brought him to that metaphysical mixture of science and religion that was eighteenth- and early nineteenth-century natural theology.

The argument from design was the quasi-scientific proof of God's existence that was prominent in Western thought for the century and a half before Darwin and that achieved its most celebrated expression in William Paley's *Natural Theology* (1802). As the increasing precision of scientific explanation during the Enlightenment began a slow erosion in the authority of religion, eighteenth-century theologians seized upon the authority of Newtonian science to create an argument that attempted to reinforce belief in God. The order of nature revealed by science was utilized as a proof of "the existence, power, wisdom and benevolence of the Deity." Although it was theologians who originated the argument as a rational proof of a loving creator, scientists generally contributed their support enthusiastically. In the first half of the nineteenth century, such prominent American men of science as Edward Hitchcock, James Dwight Dana, and Louis Agassiz portrayed science as "the handmaiden of theology" and promoted scientific research to the public as a means of studying the attributes of the creator. Natural theology, then, became a ironic alliance between scientists and theologians in which belief in God was rationalized and science became romanticized. Natural theology and the argument from design remained powerful until mid-century, when the works of Charles Lyell and Charles Darwin dealt a devastating blow by illustrating that the order or seeming design of nature in the fields of geology and biology could be explained through natural processes that did not necessarily require a supernatural, designing intelligence. While one might still intuit the deity from the design of nature, the design of nature could no longer provide absolute proof of the deity's existence.[5]

Several final observations can be made about Dreiser's arrival in the realm of natural theology at the conclusion of his metaphysical journey. First of all, there is no evidence that Dreiser knew anything of the vogue of natural theology during the eighteenth or nineteenth centuries. The specific phrases "natural theology" and "argument from design" are absent from his writings, and although his interest in Thoreau and transcendentalism may have pointed him in the direction of natural theology, his arrival at the design proof seems to have been achieved without reading William Paley or any of the other theologians or scientists who promoted the movement. One must wonder whether Dreiser, always hostile to orthodox Christianity, would have resorted to those thinkers whose primary concern was the defense of orthodoxy, even had he been aware of them. Instead, Dreiser, who considered himself "more of a romanticist than a realist," simply evolved independently a personal rationale for belief that paralleled the primary defense of belief of the Romantic Era. Like the thinkers of that earlier age who ironically transformed science from the cause of doubt into the bastion of faith, Dreiser utilized science to escape a hopeless conception of the universe as a godless, self-operating mechanism and to secure a spiritual vision of the cosmos as a divine creation. Both in exploiting the authority of science for spiritual purposes and in interpreting the complex processes and order of nature that science revealed as a proof of the deity's existence, Dreiser's philosophy was a curious twentieth-century reoccurrence, independently evolved, of eighteenth- and early nineteenth-century Romantic thought.

Secondly, one might be tempted to dismiss Dreiser's final philosophical beliefs as intellectually shallow. Perhaps the lack of scholarly attention to Dreiser's philosophical writings lies in his reaching a philosophical conclusion that was in vogue over two centuries earlier and that had been generally dismissed nearly one century earlier. There may be a lack of intellectual sophistication in Dreiser's inability to go beyond his factual knowledge of Darwinian evolution to realize that the philosophical implications of evolutionary theory undercut the use of design as a proof of a supernatural designer's existence. One should recall, however, that Dreiser's responses to life and nature were always more importantly emotional than intellectual, that his philosophy was built more on intuition and faith than on logic and reason, and that he was, after all, an artist and not a philosopher or scientist. The real value of his final philosophy lies not in its originality, its intellectual sophistication, or its contribution to the canon of American philosophy, but in the personally satisfying closure that it gave Dreiser's troubled and confused, lifelong quest to know the unknowable.

Finally, in concluding his metaphysical search for enlightenment with a spiritual faith based on the design argument, the two warring halves of Dreiser's brain that Mencken had identified—his romantic and realist sides—became joined in harmony. The vestigial remnant of his childhood religion and superstitions that fed his lifelong intuitive suspicions of a supernatural realm and a intelligent, directing force behind the material face of the universe was able to become reconciled with the scientific cosmology that he had first encountered as a young adult and whose materialistic interpretation of the universe had left him initially devastated and later disillusioned. The romantic side of Dreiser dominated the outcome, for the reconciliation was achieved only by adapting his realist side to the demands of his intuition and emotion. The resulting philosophy provided Dreiser a peace and satisfaction while achieving a personal reconciliation between science and religion that has been difficult for many thinkers in the twentieth century to achieve.

Notes

Introduction

1. Ellen Moers, *Two Dreisers* (New York: Viking Press, 1969), 133–52, 159–69, 240–70; Ronald E. Martin, *American Literature and the Universe of Force* (Durham, N.C.: Duke University Press, 1981), 215–55.

2. H. Alan Wycherley, "Mechanism and Vitalism in Dreiser's Nonfiction," *Texas Studies in Literature and Language*, 11 (Summer 1969), 1039–49.

3. Robert H. Elias, *Theodore Dreiser: Apostle of Nature*, emended ed. (Ithaca, N.Y.: Cornell University Press, 1970); Charles Child Walcutt, *American Literary Naturalism: A Divided Stream* (Minneapolis: University of Minnesota Press, 1956); Marguerite Tjader, *Theodore Dreiser: A New Dimension* (Norwalk, Conn.: Silvermine Publishers, 1965).

Chapter 1

1. Theodore Dreiser, *A Book About Myself* (New York: Boni & Liveright, 1922), 457, 458.

2. H. L. Mencken, *A Book of Prefaces* (New York: Knopf, 1917), 74, 75.

3. Theodore Dreiser, *Dawn* (New York: Horace Liveright, 1931), 5–6, 25.

4. Dreiser, *Dawn*, 134, 130, 129.

5. Helen Dreiser, *My Life with Dreiser* (New York: World Publishing, 1951), 289.

6. Dreiser, *Dawn*, 60, 61, 63.

7. Dreiser to H. L. Mencken, 13 May 1916, in Thomas P. Riggio, ed., *Dreiser-Mencken Letters: The Correspondence of Theodore Dreiser and H. L. Mencken, 1907–1945*, 2 vols. (Philadelphia: University of Pennsylvania Press, 1986), 1:231; Dreiser, *Dawn*, 198; see also Ellen Moers, *Two Dreisers*, 136–37.

8. Dreiser, *Dawn*, 370.

9. Dreiser, *Dawn*, 393–95.

10. Dreiser, *Dawn*, 453.

11. Dreiser, *A Book About Myself*, 59; *Dawn* MS, ch. cix, [11–12], as quoted in Elias, *Theodore Dreiser: Apostle of Nature*, 39.

12. Theodore Dreiser, "Peter," in *Twelve Men* (New York: Modern Library, 1928), 8, 10, 31.

13. Dreiser, *Dawn*, 518–20.

14. Dreiser, *A Book About Myself*, 196–97; Dreiser, *Dawn*, 553. Dreiser's con-

fession of "faith in a greater benevolent Power" is found in his "Heard in the Corridors" column of the *St. Louis Globe Democrat* of 18 February 1893. The reflection is attributed to Austin D. Brennan, but evidence indicates the greater likelihood that it is Dreiser's own expression of faith. T. D. Nostwich, the editor of *Theodore Dreiser's "Heard in the Corridors" Articles and Related Writings* (Ames: Iowa University Press, 1988), has concluded that Dreiser occasionally "made up" interviews that he "ascribed to friends or family members." Austin D. Brennan was Dreiser's brother-in-law, and there is no evidence that Brennan was in St. Louis in the winter of 1893. See Nostwich, xxii, 72–72. Robert Elias also concluded that the confession was "patently his [Dreiser's] own." See *Theodore Dreiser: Apostle of Nature*, 48–49.

15. Dreiser, *A Book About Myself*, 197.

16. Dreiser, *A Book About Myself*, 458–59.

17. Dreiser, *A Book About Myself*, 459.

18. Dreiser, *A Book About Myself*, 34.

19. Thomas Henry Huxley, *Science and the Christian Tradition* (New York: D. Appleton, 1909), 245–46, xvi.

20. Thomas Henry Huxley, *Science and the Hebrew Tradition* (New York: D. Appleton, 1894), vi–vii, 207–8, x.

21. Huxley, *Science and the Christian Tradition*, 241, 34.

22. Dreiser, *A Book About Myself*, 457.

23. Huxley, *Science and the Christian Tradition*, 228, 22.

24. Theodore Dreiser, "The Descent of the Horse," *Everybody's Magazine*, June 1900, 543–47.

25. A. S. Eve et al., *Life and Work of John Tyndall* (London: Macmillan, 1945), 283–84.

26. Dreiser scholars have previously not identified the specific work by Tyndall that Dreiser read in 1894. My conclusion that he read *Fragments of Science* (New York: D. Appleton, 1897) is based on his reference to material from Tyndall's "Musings on the Matterhorn, July 27, 1868," 89–90, in his "Reflections" column in *Ev'ry Month*, 2 (September 1896), 4–7.

27. Tyndall, *Fragments of Science*, 210, 197.

28. Tyndall, *Fragments of Science*, 2.

29. Tyndall, *Fragments of Science*, 89–90; Dreiser, "Reflections," *Ev'ry Month*, 2 (September 1896), 4–5.

30. Dreiser, *A Book About Myself*, 457–58.

31. Herbert Spencer, *First Principles* (New York: D. Appleton, 1896), 45.

32. Spencer, *First Principles*, 106.

33. Spencer, *First Principles*, 48.

34. Dreiser, "Reflections," *Ev'ry Month*, 2 (August 1896), 7.

35. Frank Harris, *Contemporary Portraits*, 2nd series (New York: by the author, 1919), 91.

36. Dreiser to H. L. Mencken, 13 May 1916, in Riggio, ed., *Dreiser-Mencken Letters*, 1:231.

37. Spencer, *First Principles*, 559.

38. Dreiser, "Reflections," *Ev'ry Month*, 2 (September 1896), 4.

39. Spencer, *First Principles*, 85–86, 223–25.

40. Dreiser, *A Book About Myself*, 458.

41. Herbert Spencer, *The Data of Ethics* (New York: A. L. Burt, n.d.), 14.

42. Spencer, *The Data of Ethics*, 20.

43. Spencer, *The Data of Ethics*, 162.

44. Spencer, *The Data of Ethics*, 52–53. For a discussion of the hedonistic elements of Spencer's philosophy, see Hugh Elliot, *Herbert Spencer* (Westport, Conn.: Greenwood Press, 1970), 183–85.

45. Spencer, *The Data of Ethics*, 334; Dreiser, *Dawn*, 168.

46. Dreiser to Bettina Morris, 29 July 1920, quoted in W. A. Swanberg, *Dreiser* (New York: Charles Scribner's Sons, 1965), 249.

47. Ellen Moers, *Two Dreisers*, 141–42; Charles Darwin, *The Origin of Species by Means of Natural Selection; or, The Preservation of Favored Races in the Struggle for Life*, 6th ed. (New York: A. L. Burt, n.d.), and Charles Darwin, *The Descent of Man and Selection in Relation to Sex* (New York: A. L. Burt, 1874).

48. Morse Peckham, "Introduction to the Variorum Edition of *The Origin of Species*," in Philip Appleman, ed., *Darwin: A Norton Critical Edition* (New York: W. W. Norton, 1970), 99.

49. Among the best discussions of the impact of Darwinism and social Darwinism on American culture is Richard Hofstadter's ground-breaking work *Social Darwinism in American Thought, 1865–1915* (Philadelphia: University of Pennsylvania Press, 1945), as well as Paul F. Boller, *American Thought in Transition: The Impact of Evolutionary Naturalism, 1865–1900* (Chicago: Rand, McNally, 1969), and Cynthia Eagle Russett, *Darwin in America: The Intellectual Response, 1865–1912* (San Francisco: W. H. Freeman, 1976).

50. A complete collection of *Ev'ry Month* unfortunately does not exist. The Theodore Dreiser Papers (hereafter cited as UPa) in the Department of Special Collections of the University of Pennsylvania's Van Pelt Library has twelve of the issues that Dreiser edited. The best published collection of Dreiser's "Reflections" columns is found in Donald Pizer, ed., *Theodore Dreiser: A Selection of Uncollected Prose* (Detroit: Wayne State University Press, 1977), 36–116.

51. Dreiser, "Reflections," *Ev'ry Month*, 2 (September 1896), 4.

52. Dreiser, "Reflections," *Ev'ry Month*, 3 (February 1897), in Pizer, ed., *Theodore Dreiser: A Selection of Uncollected Prose*, 106–8.

53. Dreiser, "Reflections," *Ev'ry Month*, 2 (June 1896), 4.

54. Dreiser, "Reflections," *Ev'ry Month*, 4 (May 1897), 21.

55. Dreiser, "Reflections," *Ev'ry Month*, 2 (June 1896), 4–5.

56. Dreiser, "Reflections," *Ev'ry Month*, 4 (May 1897), 21.

57. Dreiser, "Reflections," *Ev'ry Month*, 2 (August 1896), 6–7.

58. Dreiser, "Reflections," *Ev'ry Month*, 4 (May 1897), 21.

59. "Now Comes Author Theodore Dreiser Who Tells of 100,000 Jennie Gerhardts," *Cleveland Leader*, 12 November 1911, Cosmopolitan Section, 5, reprinted in Pizer, ed., *Theodore Dreiser: A Selection of Uncollected Prose*, 185.

60. Dreiser, *A Book About Myself*, 458.

61. Alan Trachtenberg, *The Incorporation of America: Culture and Society in the Gilded Age* (New York: Hill & Wang, 1982), 112. Trachtenberg's Chapter 4, "Mys-

teries of the Great City," strikes me as an especially useful explanation of the bewilderment of Dreiser and many of his contemporaries in comprehending modern urban life.

62. Trachtenberg, *Incorporation of America*, 121.

63. Trachtenberg, *Incorporation of America*, 122.

64. Henry Steele Commager, *The American Mind* (New York: Bantam Books, 1970), 110–11.

65. Charles Rosenberg, *No Other Gods: On Science and American Social Thought* (Baltimore: Johns Hopkins University Press, 1976), 3.

66. Dreiser to Frank Harris, 14 January 1917, in Robert H. Elias, ed., *Letters of Theodore Dreiser: A Selection*, 3 vols. (Philadelphia: University of Pennsylvania Press, 1959), 1:247.

67. Dreiser to Mencken, 2 November 1909, in Riggio, ed., *Dreiser-Mencken Letters*, 1:37.

Chapter 2

1. Theodore Dreiser, "Fame Found in Quiet Nooks: John Burroughs," *Success*, 1 (September 1898), 5–6; "John Burroughs in His Mountain Hut," *New Voice*, 16 (19 August 1899), 7, 13; "Apples: An Account of the Apple Industry in America," *Pearson's*, 10 (October 1900), 336–40; "Fruit Growing in America," *Harper's Monthly*, 101 (November 1900), 859–68: "Plant Life Underground," *Pearson's*, 11 (June 1901), 860–64; "The New Knowledge of Weeds," *Ainslee's*, 8 (January 1902), 533–38; "The Problem of the Soil," *Era*, 12 (September 1903), 239–49. See Moers, *Two Dreisers*, 142–43 for further comments on these articles. Theodore Dreiser, "The Treasure House of Natural History," *Metropolitan*, 8 (December 1898), 595–601; "Electricity in the Household," *Demorist's*, 35 (January 1899), 38–39; "The Horseless Age," *Demorist's*, 35 (May 1899), 153–55; "Great Problems of Organization III: The Chicago Packing Industry," *Cosmopolitan*, 25 (October 1898), 615–26. A number of these articles can be found in Yoshinobu Hakutani, ed., *Selected Magazine Articles of Theodore Dreiser: Life and Art in the American 1890s*, 2 vols. (Rutherford, N.J.: Fairleigh Dickinson University Press, 1987).

2. Theodore Dreiser, "McEwen of the Shining Slave Makers," in *The Best Short Stories of Theodore Dreiser*, intro. by James T. Farrell (New York: Thomas Y. Crowell, 1974), 99–115.

3. Dreiser, "Reflections," *Ev'ry Month*, 2 (June 1896), 4, 5.

4. Dreiser had first encountered Tolstoy at Indiana University, where he and Ratliff took turns reading *What to Do* aloud to one another. Dreiser, *Dawn*, 395, 397. For the influence of Tolstoy's *What to Do* on Dreiser, see Moers, *Two Dreisers*, 43–56, 175–76, and Donald Pizer, *The Novels of Theodore Dreiser: A Critical Study* (Minneapolis: University of Minnesota Press, 1976), 65.

5. See Moers, *Two Dreisers*, 3–169 and Pizer, *The Novels of Theodore Dreiser*, 31–42 for discussion of the sources of *Sister Carrie*.

6. Riggio, ed., *Dreiser-Mencken Letters*, 1:232. Page references refer to Theodore Dreiser, *Sister Carrie*, Pennsylvania Edition, ed. John C. Berkey, Alice M.

Winters, James L. W. West III, and Neda Westlake (Philadelphia: University of Pennsylvania Press, 1981).

7. T. D. Nostwich suggests in his collection of *Theodore Dreiser's "Heard in the Corridors" Articles and Related Writings*, 155, n. 143, that Ames may be at least outwardly modeled on the renowned Nicola Tesla, whom Dreiser had encountered in St. Louis in 1893. Donald Pizer, however, suggests that Ames's attitudes are a reflection of Dreiser's own ideas at the time that he wrote the novel. Pizer, *The Novels of Theodore Dreiser*, 66.

8. Dreiser's frank portrayal of Carrie's affairs did, in fact, cause great difficulties in the publication of the novel. His first choice for a publisher, Harper and Brothers, rejected the manuscript, complaining that Dreiser's "touch is neither firm enough nor sufficiently delicate to depict without offense to the reader the continued illicit relations of the heroine." His second choice, Doubleday, Page and Company, gave Dreiser a verbal assurance of publication after an enthusiastic reader's report from Frank Norris. Later the company tried to be released from this unwritten contract after the senior partner, Frank Doubleday (or possibly his wife), read the proofs and found the story vulgar. After Dreiser insisted that the agreement be honored, Doubleday published only a modest number of copies and declined to advertise or promote the novel. See "*Sister Carrie*: Manuscript to Print," in *Sister Carrie*, Pennsylvania Edition, 519–30.

9. Donald Edson Gates, *Elmer Gates and the Art of Mind-Using* (New York: Exposition Press, 1971), x; this book is an uncritical and rather unsatisfying biography of Gates written by his son; Dreiser to Arthur Woodward, Spring? 1900, in Elias, ed., *Letters*, 1:49.

10. Elmer Gates, "Extracting Perfume from Flowers by Electricity," *Mail and Express Illustrated Saturday Magazine*, 7 March 1903, 4; "Gates' Double Microscope," *American Monthly Microscopic Journal*, 19 (January 1898), 7; Herman T. Lukens, "Correspondence," *American Journal of Psychology*, 10 (1898), 164. See also Elmer Gates, "A Mega-Microscope," *Popular Science News*, 31 (December 1897), 265–69, and "Electrographs of the Electro-Static Current Made with a Camera," *Scientific American*, 81 (7 October 1899), 288–89.

11. "Society of the Capital," *New York Times*, 18 November 1894, 1; Elmer Gates, "Brain Building and Mind Building with Special Reference to Sense Training of the Eye and Ear, and Teaching Mentally Defective Children," in National Education Association, *Journal of the Proceedings of the 37th Annual Meeting*, Washington, 7–12 July 1898, 1052; Elmer Gates, "The Art of Mind Building," *Metaphysical Magazine*, 4 (1896), 89, 1, 176; Elmer Gates, "The Science of Mentation," *The Monist*, 5 (1895), 594.

12. Gates, "The Science of Mentation," 589.

13. Lukens, "Correspondence," 163.

14. Gates to Dreiser, 11 December 1901 (UPa); see also Gates to Dreiser, 3 March 1900, 17 April 1900, 27 April 1900, and 29 May 1900 (UPa); Elmer Gates, *The Relations and Development of the Mind and Brain* (New York: Philosophic Co., 1903) is a reprint of his 1896 articles that appeared in *Metaphysical Magazine*.

15. Theodore Dreiser, "The Training of the Senses," unpublished TS (UPa).

16. Dreiser to Arthur Henry, 23 June 1900, in Elias, ed., *Letters*, 1:52.

17. Page references in the following discussion are to the following editions: *Jennie Gerhardt*, University of Pennsylvania Dreiser Edition, ed. James L. W. West III (Philadelphia: University of Pennsylvania Press, 1992); *The Financier* (New York: New American Library, 1967); *The Titan* (New York: New American Library, 1965); *The "Genius"* (New York: New American Library, 1984). The actual order of composition varies from the order of publication. About half of *Jennie Gerhardt* was written in 1901, before Dreiser's breakdown. He did not return to the novel until after his removal as Butterick editor in the fall of 1910. His autobiographical novel, *The "Genius"*, was written next, between December 1910 and April 1911. *The Financier* was written between September 1911 and July 1912, and *The Titan* occupied him from February to December 1913. In the spring of 1914, Dreiser returned to *The "Genius"*, rewriting the happy ending of the original to present Witla in his final scene contemplating the mysteries of Herbert Spencer's "unknowable." See Pizer, *The Novels of Theodore Dreiser*, 96–105, 133–35, 160–61, 186.

18. See Pizer, *The Novels of Theodore Dreiser*, 191–93, for a discussion of Cowperwood's women.

19. Dreiser, *Dawn*, 167; Spencer, *The Data of Ethics*, 53.

20. Gary N. Calkins, "Protozoa and Disease," *Century Magazine*, 67 (April 1904), 931–40.

21. Martin, *American Literature and the Universe of Force*, 233; Pizer, *The Novels of Theodore Dreiser*, 11.

22. George Milbry Gould (1848–1922) was a Philadelphia physician and ophthalmologist. Gould's *The Infinite Presence* (1910) was an effort to prove the existence of God in the light of contemporary scientific knowledge.

23. Edgar Lucien Larkin (1847–1924) was a prominent astronomer, not a physicist, as Dreiser misidentifies him. Larkin was a frequent popularizer of the wonders of astronomy and was appointed director of the Mount Lowe observatory in California in 1900.

24. Martin Fichman, *Alfred Russel Wallace* (Boston: Twayne Publishers, 1981), 127. Fichman discusses Wallace's interest in spiritualism in 122–31.

25. Alfred Russel Wallace, *The World of Life: A Manifestation of Creative Power, Directive Mind, and Ultimate Purpose* (New York: Moffat, Yard, 1911), 364.

26. Herbert Spencer, "Ultimate Questions" in *Facts and Comments* (New York: D. Appleton, 1902), 300–304. Dreiser quotes nearly the entire final three paragraphs of this essay.

Chapter 3

1. H. M. Lydenberg to Theodore Dreiser, 15 January 1915 (UPa).

2. Carl Snyder's *The World Machine: The First Phase—The Cosmic Mechanism* (London: Longmans, Green, 1907) is a history of the development of astronomy from pre-Greek conceptions to the nineteenth-century mechanistic conception. While this book was important in introducing Dreiser to the mechanistic interpretation of the universe, Dreiser's mechanistic conception of life was more importantly derived from Jacques Loeb, Ernst Haeckel, and the other thinkers discussed

in this chapter. George W. Crile's *Man—An Adaptive Mechanism* (New York: Macmillan, 1916) was an argument for the thesis that "man is essentially an energy transforming mechanism, obeying the laws of physics, as do other mechanisms" (v). Jacques Loeb, *The Mechanistic Conception of Life*, intro. by Donald Fleming (Cambridge, Mass.: Belknap Press of Harvard University Press, 1964); Dreiser to Edward H. Smith, 10 January 1921, in Elias, ed., *Letters*, 1:336. The mention of Fischer, Carrel, and Ballou apparently refers to the Swiss biochemist Emil Fischer (1852–1919), the French-American surgeon Alexis Carrel (1873–1944), and the American ichthyologist William Hosea Ballou (1857–1937).

3. In 1906, the *New York Times* wrote about Loeb's experiments in artificial parthenogenesis that "a consensus of opinion among biologists would show that he is voted rather a man of lively imagination than an inerrant investigator of natural phenomena," to which Mark Twain replied:

> In the drift of years I by and by found out that a Consensus examines a new thing with its feelings rather than with its mind. Now, as concerns this "creation of life by chemical agencies," reader take my advice: don't you copper it. If you find that you can't control your passions, if you feel that you have to copper something and can't help it, copper the Consensus. It is the safest way—all history confirms it.

From Mark Twain, "Dr. Loeb's Incredible Discovery," in Charles Neider, ed., *The Complete Essays of Mark Twain* (Garden City, N.Y.: Doubleday, 1963), 590.

4. Jacques Loeb to Dreiser, 3 June 1919 and 13 January 1923 (UPa). My research for this chapter was greatly aided by the opportunity to examine the Ellen Moers Collection in the Butler Library Special Collections at Columbia University. Moers's *Two Dreisers* contains an excellent examination of the influence of both Loeb and A. A. Brill on Dreiser (240–85).

5. Jacques Loeb, *Comparative Physiology of the Brain and Comparative Psychology* (New York: G. P. Putnam's Sons, 1900), 12; P. A. Levine, "Jacques Loeb, the Man," *Science*, 59 (1924), 427.

6. See Donald Fleming's introduction to *The Mechanistic Conception of Life* for information regarding the state of mechanistic science in Germany at the time of Loeb's training. For further information about Loeb's life and work, see Philip J. Pauly, *Controlling Life: Jacques Loeb and the Engineering Ideal in Biology* (New York: Oxford University Press, 1987); Paul DeKruif, "Jacques Loeb, The Mechanist," *Harpers*, 146 (1922–23), 182–90; Robert L. Duffas, "Jacques Loeb: Mechanist," *Century Magazine*, 108 (1924), 374–83; W. J. V. Osterhout, "Jacques Loeb," in National Academy of Sciences, *Biographical Memoirs*, XIII (Washington, D.C.: National Academy of Sciences, 1928), 318–401; and T. Brailsford Robertson, "The Life and Work of a Mechanistic Philosopher—Jacques Loeb," *Science Progress*, 21 (1926), 114–29.

7. Loeb, *The Mechanistic Conception of Life*, 16, and *The Organism as a Whole: From a Physicochemical Viewpoint* (New York: G. P. Putnam's Sons, 1916), 123.

8. Loeb, *The Mechanistic Conception of Life*, 16; Duffas, "Jacques Loeb: Mechanist," 379. For further information, see Jacques Loeb, *The Organism as a Whole*, Ch. 14, 349–69.

9. Loeb, *Comparative Physiology*, v, 14.

10. Fleming, intro. to Loeb, *The Mechanistic Conception of Life*, xxiv.

11. Jacques Loeb, *Forced Movements, Tropisms, and Animal Conduct*, Monographs on Experimental Biology, vol. 1 (Philadelphia: J. B. Lippincott, 1918), 161–62.

12. Loeb, *The Mechanistic Conception of Life*, 66, and *Forced Movements, Tropisms, and Animal Conduct*, 49.

13. Jacques Loeb, "Mechanistic Science and Metaphysical Romance," *Yale Review*, 4 (1915), 775, and *The Mechanistic Conception of Life*, 32.

14. Dreiser to James T. Farrell, 10 May 1945, in Elias, ed., *Letters*, 3:1017.

15. Although Ellen Moers states that Loeb's earliest general magazine piece in this period was "Mechanistic Science and Metaphysical Romance," published in July 1915, "Freedom of Will and War," *New Review*, 2 (1914), 631–36, appeared in November 1914, making it his earliest published piece in a non-scientific journal and therefore possibly the first piece Dreiser read. See Moers, *Two Dreisers*, 259.

16. Loeb, "Freedom of Will and War," 631, 632–33.

17. Loeb, "Mechanistic Science and Metaphysical Romance," 772.

18. Loeb, "Mechanistic Science and Metaphysical Romance," 783–85.

19. Dreiser to Loeb, 9 April 1919, Jacques Loeb Papers, Library of Congress, Washington, D.C. The Loeb Papers are hereafter cited as (LC).

20. Loeb, *The Mechanistic Conception of Life*, 28.

21. Loeb, *The Mechanistic Conception of Life*, 5, 33.

22. Theodore Dreiser, *Tragic America* (New York: Horace Liveright, 1931), 7; Theodore Dreiser, *America Is Worth Saving* (New York: Modern Age Books, 1941), 284. Dreiser's progressively more radical critique of American capitalism can be traced in his *Dreiser Looks at Russia* (New York: Horace Liveright, 1928), as well as in the two works cited above. Dreiser joined the Communist Party in July 1945, five months before his death.

23. Ellen Moers has a more complete study of the light imagery of *Sister Carrie* in *Two Dreisers*, 100–11.

24. Theodore Dreiser, "A Lesson from the Aquarium," *Tom Watson's Magazine*, 3 (1906), 308, reprinted in Pizer, ed. *Theodore Dreiser: A Selection of Uncollected Prose*, 159–62; Dreiser, *The Financier*, 7–9, 446–47; Fleming, intro. to Loeb, *The Mechanistic Conception of Life*, xvii–xviii.

25. Louise Campbell, ed., *Letters to Louise: Theodore Dreiser's Letters to Louise Campbell* (Philadelphia: University of Pennsylvania Press, 1959), 12; James T. Farrell, *The League of Frightened Philistines* (New York: Vanguard Press, 1945), 13–14; W. M. Frohock, "Theodore Dreiser," in Charles Child Walcutt, ed., *Seven Novelists in the Naturalist Tradition: An Introduction* (Minneapolis: University of Minnesota Press, 1974), 102.

26. Dreiser himself never dated his original reading of *The Riddle of the Universe*. The earliest reference to Haeckel in Dreiser's writing that I have found is in the revised conclusion to *The "Genius"* that Dreiser wrote in the summer of 1914. This reference is actually contained within the long quotation from Alfred Russel Wallace's *The World of Life* (1911) that I have discussed in Chapter 2. Because Wallace's *The World of Life* argues at length against the passive, pantheistic conception of God that Haeckel proposed in *The Riddle of the Universe*, it seems a good

conclusion that Dreiser's first awareness of Haeckel's book came from his reading of Wallace. I am convinced, however, that his discovery of Haeckel preceded his discovery of Loeb. In 1921, Dreiser confided to Edward H. Smith that he had been reading and rereading Haeckel for years (Dreiser to Smith, 10 January 1921, in Elias, ed., *Letters*, 1:337), and the "chemic" prose of his four novels published between 1911 and 1915, especially *The Financier* and *The Titan*, suggest Haeckel's influence. Ellen Moers also concluded that Dreiser had encountered Haeckel years before he read Loeb (*Two Dreisers*, 244).

27. Ernst Haeckel, *The Riddle of the Universe at the Close of the Nineteenth Century*, trans., John McCabe (New York: Harper & Brothers, 1900), 4, 243–44, 351.

28. I have delayed discussing Haeckel's monistic philosophy and theological speculations until my discussion of Dreiser's *Notes on Life* in Chapter 6.

29. Haeckel, *The Riddle of the Universe*, 222, 91, 140, 64, 136.

30. Dreiser to Edward H. Smith, 10 January 1921, in Elias, ed., *Letters*, 1:337; Thomas P. Riggio, James L. W. West III, and Neda Westlake, eds., *Theodore Dreiser: American Diaries, 1902–1926* (Philadelphia: University of Pennsylvania Press, 1983), 311; Elias, *Theodore Dreiser: Apostle of Nature*, 231.

31. Swanberg, *Dreiser*, 234; Moers, *Two Dreisers*, 262. Dreiser's relationship to Ed and Edith Smith is revealed in a thinly disguised story about the Smiths' marriage titled "Olive Brand," in *A Gallery of Women*, 2 vols. (New York: Horace Liveright, Inc., 1929), 1:61–129.

32. "Brill, Abraham Arden," in Allen G. Debus, ed., *World Who's Who of Science: A Biographical Dictionary of Notable Scientists from Antiquity to the Present* (Chicago: Marquis Who's Who, 1968). Among the works Brill translated were Freud's *Three Contributions to a Theory of Sex* (1910), *The Interpretation of Dreams* (1914), *Wit and Its Relation to the Unconscious* (1916), *The History of the Psychoanalytic Method* (1917), and *Totem and Taboo* (1918). For a further discussion of Village Freudianism, see Frederick J. Hoffman, *Freudianism and the Literary Mind* (Baton Rouge: Louisiana State University Press, 1957), 57–58, 61–64. For a further discussion of Brill's contributions, see Nathan G. Hale, Jr., *Freud and the Americans: The Beginnings of Psychoanalysis in the United States, 1876–1917* (New York: Oxford University Press, 1971), 389–96.

33. Dreiser to Brill, 17 December 1926, and Dreiser to Mrs. Brill, 13 July 1927 (UPa); A. A. Brill, *Psychoanalysis: Its Theories and Practical Application* (Philadelphia: W. B. Saunders, 1913); Dreiser to Brill, 20 January 1919, and Brill to Dreiser, 25 January 1919 (UPa).

34. Theodore Dreiser, "Remarks," *Psychoanalytic Review*, 18 (1931), 250, reprinted in Pizer, ed., *Theodore Dreiser: A Selection of Uncollected Prose*, 263–64. This article is the published text of "Remarks of Mr. Dreiser at the dinner in honor of Professor Sigmund Freud on the occasion of his 75th birthday and in his absence read by Dr. A. A. Brill, New York, May 6, 1931."

35. Theodore Dreiser, "Neurotic America and the Sex Impulse," in *Hey Rub-a-Dub-Dub: A Book of the Mystery and Wonder and Terror of Life* (New York: Boni & Liveright, 1920), 131, 136, 126.

36. For a discussion of the deterministic elements in Freudianism, see Gerald

N. Izenberg, *The Existentialist Critique of Freud* (Princeton, N.J.: Princeton University Press, 1976); Abraham Kaplan, "Freud and Modern Philosophy," in Benjamin Nelson, ed., *Freud and the Twentieth Century* (Gloucester, Mass.: Peter Smith, 1974), 218–22; and Perry Westbrook, *Free Will and Determinism in American Literature* (Rutherford, N.J.: Fairleigh Dickinson University Press, 1979), 112–14.

37. Sigmund Freud, *Three Contributions to a Theory of Sex*, trans., A. A. Brill (New York: E. P. Dutton, 1962), 74. For further information on the influence of Brücke and the other mechanists on Freud, see Frank J. Sulloway, *Freud, Biologist of the Mind: Beyond the Psychoanalytic Legend* (New York: Basic Books, 1979), 13–25.

38. Ellen Moers argued in *Two Dreisers* (256–64) that Dreiser derived the use of the word "chemism" from his reading of Freud.

39. Dreiser, "Olive Brand," 125–26; Max G. Schlapp and Edward H. Smith, *The New Criminology: A Consideration of the Chemical Causation of Abnormal Behavior* (New York: Boni and Liveright, 1928).

40. Dreiser, "Olive Brand," 127.

41. See Charles Rosenberg and Carroll Smith-Rosenberg, "The Female Animal: Medical and Biological Views of Women," in *No Other Gods*, 54–70.

42. Theodore Dreiser, "American Tragedies," review of *The New Criminology* by Max G. Schlapp and Edward H. Smith, *New York Herald Tribune Books*, 10 June 1928, 1–2.

43. Dreiser to Mencken, 9 April 1919, in Riggio, ed., *Dreiser-Mencken Letters*, 2:344; Dreiser to Loeb, 29 May 1919 (LC).

44. Loeb to Dreiser, 3 June 1919 (UPa).

45. Swanberg, *Dreiser*, 240, 263; Dreiser to Loeb, 26 August 1920 (LC).

46. Loeb to Dreiser, 11 September 1920 (UPa).

47. Riggio et al., eds., *Theodore Dreiser: American Diaries*, 396–97.

48. Theodore Dreiser, *The Hand of the Potter* (New York: Boni and Liveright, 1918), 27; Mencken to Dreiser, 16 December 1916, in Riggio, ed., *Dreiser-Mencken Letters*, 1:281–82. A comparison of the 1916 and 1919 versions located in the Dreiser Collection reveals that Dreiser made extensive additions to pages 191–200 of the printed version.

49. Dreiser, *The Hand of the Potter*, 193, 197, 199–200.

50. Theodore Dreiser, "Suggesting the Possible Substructure of Ethics," unpublished TS, 9 (UPa); the essay has been printed in Pizer, ed., *Theodore Dreiser: A Selection of Uncollected Prose*, 206–11; Dreiser to Mr. Bann, 23 September 1920, in Elias, ed., *Letters*, 1:286.

51. Dreiser, *Dawn*, 112.

52. From *Dawn* MS, ch. iv, as quoted in Elias, *Theodore Dreiser: Apostle of Nature*, 181; Dreiser, "Suggesting the Possible Substructure of Ethics," 5 (UPa); Dreiser, "Olive Brand," 126; Dreiser to Esther McCoy, 24 December 1924, in Elias, ed., *Letters*, 2:430.

53. Dreiser, *The Financier*, 145; "Dreiser Says Religion Total Loss in America," *El Paso Evening Post*, 26 April 1930, 8; Hy Kraft told to W. A. Swanberg, 20 April 1963, quoted in Swanberg, *Dreiser*, 375; Dreiser, *Dawn*, 167.

54. Theodore Dreiser, "I Find the Real American Tragedy," *Mystery Magazine*, 11 (February 1935), 9–11, 88–90, reprinted in Pizer, ed., *Theodore Dreiser: A*

Selection of Uncollected Prose, 291–99. The emphasis in this quote (see p. 297 in Pizer) is Dreiser's.

55. Dreiser, "I Find the Real American Tragedy," 291, 292 in Pizer.

56. Dreiser, "I Find the Real American Tragedy," 296, 297, 298–99 in Pizer.

57. Loeb, *The Mechanistic Conception of Life*, 33; Dreiser, "I Find the Real American Tragedy," 297 in Pizer.

58. Dreiser to Ed Smith, 20 February 1927 (UPa); Loeb, *The Mechanistic Conception of Life*, 33; Ed Smith to Dreiser, 21 February 1927 (UPa); Dreiser, "I Find the Real American Tragedy," 299 in Pizer.

59. Moers, *Two Dreisers*, 228; page references are from Theodore Dreiser, *An American Tragedy* (New York: Signet Classics, 1964).

60. Theodore Dreiser, "A Word Concerning Birth Control," *Birth Control Review*, 5 (April 1921), 5.

61. "A Letter from Vienna to Theo. Dreiser—And His Reply," *Tempest*, 1 (2 April 1923), 3.

62. Quoted in Gilbert Cosulich, "Theodore Dreiser Asserts Religion Is Total Loss and Its Dogma Worn Out," *Tucson Daily Citizen*, 30 April 1930, 7.

63. Cosulich, 7; Dreiser, "American Tragedies," 1.

64. Dreiser, "American Tragedies," 2.

Chapter 4

1. Mencken, *A Book of Prefaces*, 93, 12.

2. Dreiser, *Dawn*, 6–7.

3. Dreiser, *Dawn*, 6–8.

4. Mencken, *A Book of Prefaces*, 92–93.

5. Theodore Dreiser, "Free," in *Free and Other Stories* (New York: Boni and Liveright, 1918), 45; H. L. Mencken to Dreiser, 21 August 1918, in Riggio, ed., *Dreiser-Mencken Letters*, 1:315.

6. Robert Yoder, "The Wondrous Box of Dr. Abrams," in Alexander Klein, ed., *Grand Deception: The World's Most Spectacular and Successful Hoaxes, Impostures, Ruses and Frauds* (Philadelphia: J. B. Lippincott, 1955), 113–14; Helen Dreiser, *My Life with Dreiser*, 54–55; Dreiser to Llewelyn Powys, 19 July 1921, in Elias, ed., *Letters*, 1:372–73; H. L. Mencken to Dreiser, in Riggio, ed. *Dreiser-Mencken Letters*, 2:445. See also Riggio et al., eds., *Theodore Dreiser: American Diaries*, 369, 371–72, 375–76, 379–81, 383–84.

7. Dreiser, *A Book About Myself*, 269; Dreiser, *Sister Carrie*, 48; see T. D. Nostwich, ed., *Theodore Dreiser—Journalism, Volume One: Newspaper Writings; 1892–1895*, University of Pennsylvania Dreiser Edition (Philadelphia: University of Pennsylvania Press, 1988), 146–61, 170–74, 188–206.

8. Untitled TS, Box 177, Charles Fort folder #1 (UPa).

9. Ouija board notes, 26 December 1915 and January 1916, as described in Elias, *Theodore Dreiser: Apostle of Nature*, 189.

10. Dreiser to Charles Yost, 17 January 1939 and 27 January 1939, in Elias, ed., *Letters*, 3:835–36.

11. Untitled TS, Box 177, Charles Fort folder #1, 9–10 (UPa).

12. Dreiser to Arthur Henry, 23 July 1900, in Elias, ed., *Letters*, 1:53; Theodore Dreiser, "Giff," in *A Gallery of Women*, 1:274–75. See also Riggio et al., eds., *Theodore Dreiser: American Diaries*, 180, 200, 239.

13. Dreiser, "Giff," 261–62.

14. Mencken to Dreiser, 11 January 1921 and 2 February 1921, in Riggio, ed., *Dreiser-Mencken Letters*, 2:420, 424; unpub. TS titled "Charles Fort," Box 177, Charles Fort folder #4, 3 (UPa).

15. For a biography of Fort, see Damon Knight, *Charles Fort: Prophet of the Unexplained* (Garden City, N.Y.: Doubleday, 1970).

16. Marguerite Tjader, *Theodore Dreiser: A New Dimension*, 20; Dreiser, "Charles Fort," 1 (UPa).

17. Unpublished interview with Dreiser by Reed Harris, March 1932?, 7, Box 177, Charles Fort folder #4 (UPa).

18. Dreiser, "Charles Fort," 8 (UPa).

19. Fort to Dreiser, 8 May 1914 and Dreiser to Fort, 12 May 1914, in Elias, ed., *Letters*, 1:166–67.

20. Dreiser, "Charles Fort," 10–13 (UPa).

21. Reed Harris interview, 15 (UPa).

22. Dreiser, "Charles Fort," 13 (UPa); Theodore Dreiser, "The Dream," in *Hey Rub-a-Dub-Dub*, 60–73.

23. Dreiser to Fort, 10 July 1915, in Elias, ed., *Letters*, 1:193; Waldemar Kaempffaert to Dreiser, 27 October 1915 (UPa); Reed Harris interview, 4 (UPa).

24. Fort to Dreiser, 1 December 19[15?] (UPa); Knight, *Charles Fort*, 55; Americus Vespucius Symmes, *The Symmes Theory of Concentric Spheres, etc.* Compiled by Americus Symmes from the writings of his father, Captain John Cleves Symmes (Louisville, Ky.: Bradley & Gilbert, 1878); Fort to Dreiser, 31 March 1916 (UPa); Dreiser to Fort, 11 October 1915, in Elias, ed., *Letters*, 1:197.

25. When Fort learned that Dreiser had attempted to persuade Liveright to publish his manuscripts, he sent Dreiser the following tribute:

> I have honored you.
> I have invented something. I named it after you.
> It's a meatless cocktail.
> You take a glass of beer, and put a live goldfish in it—instead of a cherry or olive or such things that occur to a commonplace mind.
> You gulp.
> The sensation of enclosing a squirm is delightfully revolting.
> I think it's immoral. I have named it the Dreiser cocktail.

From Fort to Dreiser, 21 January 1918 (UPa); Fort to Dreiser, 3 June 1916 (UPa).

26. Charles Fort, *Wild Talents* (New York: Claude Kendall, 1932), 128.

27. Tiffany Thayer, intro. to Charles Fort, *The Books of Charles Fort* (New York: Henry Holt, 1941), xix; Fort, *Wild Talents*, 128.

28. Charles Fort, *The Book of the Damned* (New York: Boni and Liveright, 1919), 7, 88, 156.

29. Dreiser to Fort, 27 April 1919 (UPa); Reed Harris interview, 16 (UPa). Fort was delighted by Dreiser's success and sent a congratulatory note to him:

As a humbler discoverer to a greater discoverer, I offer you my congratulations.
Charles Fort has discovered Monstrator and Azuria and Melancus and the Upper Sargasso Sea.
But Theodore Dreiser has discovered Charles Fort.

From Fort to Dreiser, 12 April 1919 (UPa). In spite of Liveright's fear that the book would attract no attention, several reviews by major American authors revealed that Fort's theories appealed not only to Dreiser's peculiar tastes. Ben Hecht wrote in the *Chicago Daily News*, "I am the first disciple of Charles Fort. He has made a terrible onslaught on the accumulated lunacy of fifty centuries. The onslaught will survive, entrenching itself behind the derisive laughter of all good citizens" (quoted in Charles Fort obituary, *New York Herald Tribune*, 5 May 1932, 19). Booth Tarkington also revealed his fascination with Fort in *The Bookman*: "Who in the name of frenzy is Charles Fort? . . . I'm just pulling up from influenza and this blamed book kept me up all night when I certainly should have slept. . . . People must turn to look at his head as he walks down the street; I think it's a head that would emit noises and explosions, with copper flames playing out from the ears" (Booth Tarkington, *The Bookman*, as quoted in Knight, *Charles Fort*, 69–70).

30. Fort to Dreiser, 30 April 1919 and ? May 1920 (UPa).

31. Unpublished interview with Anna Fort by Dreiser, 4, Box 177, Charles Fort folder #3 (UPa); Dreiser to David Stern, 22 January 1929 (UPa); Helen Dreiser, *My Life with Dreiser*, 224.

32. Charles Fort, *New Lands* (New York: Boni and Liveright, 1923), 86, 239–40.

33. Louise Campbell, ed., *Letters to Louise*, 53; Helen Dreiser, *My Life with Dreiser*, 223; Swanberg, *Dreiser*, 390; Fort to Dreiser, 26 August 1930 (UPa); Dreiser to Fort, 27 August 1930, in Elias, ed., *Letters*, 2:507.

34. Dreiser to Fort, 18 November 1930 and 14 January 1931 (UPa); Dreiser to Miss Lucienne Southgate, 25 March 1931 (UPa); H. G. Wells to Dreiser, 9 April 1931, in Elias, ed., *Letters*, 2:531–32; Dreiser to Fort, 22 April 1931 (UPa); Dreiser to Wells, 23 May 1931, in Elias, ed., *Letters*, 2:532–33; Dreiser to Margaret Sanger, 9 September 1931 and 10 October 1931 (UPa).

35. Fort, *Wild Talents*, 310; Fort obituary, *New York Herald Tribune*, 5 May 1932, 19.

36. Dreiser to Richard R. Smith, 24 January 1934 (UPa); Dreiser to Aaron Sussman, 12 April 1934 (UPa). Dreiser's difficulty with these articles is reflected by the numerous drafts found in Box 177, Charles Fort folder #1 (UPa).

37. Dreiser, "Charles Fort," 11 (UPa); Dreiser to Edward H. Smith, 1 March 1920 (UPa); Reed Harris interview, 12 (UPa). Even Richard Lingeman's two-volume biography of Dreiser fails to discuss Fort at any length and contains only five very brief references to him. See Lingeman, *Theodore Dreiser: At the Gates of the City, 1871–1907* (New York: G. P. Putnam's Sons, 1986), 401, 405, and *Theodore Dreiser: An American Journey, 1908–1945* (New York: G. P. Putnam's Sons, 1990), 20–21, 104, 115.

38. Dreiser, "Charles Fort," 16–17 (UPa); Reed Harris interview, 9 (UPa).

39. Fort, *New Lands*, 32; Fort, *Wild Talents*, 97.

40. Reed Harris interview, 4–5 (UPa); Dreiser to Wells, 23 May 1931, in Elias, ed., *Letters*, 2:532–33.

41. Harris, *Contemporary Portraits*, 91; Theodore Dreiser, *A Hoosier Holiday* (New York: John Lane, 1916), 153, 343–44.

42. Reed Harris interview, 16 (UPa).

43. Dreiser to John H. Chase, 14 March 1934 (UPa); Theodore Dreiser, "Man and Romance," *Reedy's Mirror*, 28 (28 August 1919), 585; Dreiser, *A Hoosier Holiday*, 27.

44. Dreiser, *A Hoosier Holiday*, 95, 27.

45. Dreiser, *A Hoosier Holiday*, 368.

46. Theodore Dreiser, "The Blue Sphere," in *Plays of the Natural and the Supernatural* (New York: AMS Press, 1969), 55–82.

47. Dreiser, *A Hoosier Holiday*, 347; Dreiser, "Laughing Gas," in *Plays of the Natural and the Supernatural*, 83–118.

48. Dreiser, "In the Dark," in *Plays of the Natural and the Supernatural*, 119–48.

49. Dreiser, "The Spring Recital," in *Plays of the Natural and the Supernatural*, 149–74.

50. Reed Harris interview, 16 (UPa).

51. Dreiser, "The Dream," 61–62.

52. Dreiser, "The Dream," 71.

53. Edward H. Smith to Dreiser, 3 January 1921, in Elias, ed., *Letters*, 1:335–36; the Odin Gregory play mentioned by Smith was *Caius Gracchus*, intro. by Theodore Dreiser (New York: Boni and Liveright, 1920). Smith probably objected to Dreiser's praise of the supernatural sections of the play; e.g., "In the fifth act, the mingling of the real with the unreal, of the supernatural and the phantastic with the commonplace, is so deliciously handled, that the eerie is no longer so" (Introduction, 7).

54. Mencken to Dreiser, 1 December 1920 and 11 December 1920, in Riggio, ed., *Dreiser-Mencken Letters*, 2:411, 416.

55. Dreiser to Smith, 10 January 1921 and 31 January 1921, in Elias, ed., *Letters*, 1:336, 345–46.

56. Mencken to Helen Dreiser, 4 February 1946, and Mencken, "A Eulogy for Dreiser," in Riggio, ed., *Dreiser-Mencken Letters*, 2:729, 805–6.

57. Fort, *Wild Talents*, 107–8.

58. Fort, *Wild Talents*, 249; Dreiser, "Charles Fort," 16 (UPa).

59. Theodore Dreiser, "In the Matter of Spiritualism," *Bohemian Magazine*, 17 (1909), 425; Dreiser, *The "Genius"*, 281; Reed Harris interview, 29, 18–19 (UPa); Dreiser, "Giff," 1:276. Dreiser refers to Fabre's experiments with "The Great Peacock" moth, about which he read in his copy of *The Life of the Caterpillar* (New York: Dodd, Mead, 1906), 246–78.

60. Reed Harris interview, 5–6; Dreiser, *Dawn*, 588–89.

61. Theodore Dreiser, *Moods Philosophical and Emotional—Cadenced and Declaimed* (New York: Simon and Schuster, 1935), 6, 344.

62. Dreiser to Wells, 23 May 1931, in Elias, ed., *Letters*, 2:532–33; Dreiser, *A*

Hoosier Holiday, 153. Sir James Hopwood Jeans, *The Universe Around Us* (New York: Macmillan, 1929) was a popular survey of contemporary astronomy and nuclear physics.

63. Dreiser, *Dawn*, 198; Mencken, *A Book of Prefaces*, 95; Dreiser to George Vaughan, 13 September 1933, in Elias, ed., *Letters*, 2:641.

Chapter 5

1. Theodore Dreiser, "Statement of Belief," *Bookman*, 68 (September 1928), 25.
2. Neil Hitt, "Author and Destiny Reach a Compromise," *San Francisco Chronicle*, 10 February 1939, 7.
3. Hitt, "Author and Destiny," 7; Theodore Dreiser, *Notes on Life*, ed. Marguerite Tjader and John J. McAleer (University: University of Alabama Press, 1974), 14, 10.
4. Fort to Dreiser, 1 May 1915 (UPa).
5. *Collecting Net*, 3 (21 July 1928), 1.
6. Frank R. Lillie's *The Woods Hole Marine Biological Laboratory* (Chicago: University of Chicago Press, 1944) is the best history of the first fifty years of this research facility. Marine Biological Laboratory, Woods Hole, Mass., *Annual Announcement* (Lancaster, Pa.: Lancaster Press, 1928), 10, and Marine Biological Laboratory, Woods Hole, Massachusetts, *Thirty-First Report for the Year 1928—Forty-First Year* (n.p., n.d.) 17, 38.
7. *Collecting Net*, 3 (21 July 1928), 1; Louise Campbell, ed., *Letters to Louise*, 54; Dreiser to Franklin and Beatrice Booth, 7 July 1928, in Elias, ed., *Letters*, 2:470.
8. Dreiser to Franklin and Beatrice Booth, 7 July 1928 and 16 July 1928, in Elias, ed., *Letters*, 2:469, 471; Swanberg, *Dreiser*, 342; Marine Biological Laboratory, *Report for 1928*, 28.
9. See Garland E. Allen, *Thomas Hunt Morgan: The Man and His Science* (Princeton, N.J.: Princeton University Press, 1978) and Garland E. Allen, "The Rise and Spread of the Classical School of Heredity, 1910–1930: Development and Influence of the Mendelian Chromosome Theory," in Nathan Reingold, ed., *The Sciences in the American Context: New Perspectives* (Washington, D.C.: Smithsonian Institution Press, 1979), 220.
10. Allen, *Morgan*, 168–69; Helen Dreiser, *My Life with Dreiser*, 191; Tjader, *Dreiser: A New Dimension*, 32–34.
11. Helen Dreiser, *My Life with Dreiser*, 189–90.
12. Helen Dreiser, *My Life with Dreiser*, 189; *Collecting Net*, 3 (21 July 1928), 12.
13. Dreiser to Franklin and Beatrice Booth, 16 July 1928, in Elias, ed., *Letters*, 2:471; Helen Dreiser, *My Life with Dreiser*, 189; *Collecting Net*, 3 (21 July 1928), 1–2; see also Dreiser to Ruth Kennell, 20 July 1928 (UPa).
14. Dreiser to Dr. John Churchman, 10 October 1928, to Robert Chambers, 2 February 1929, to S. C. Brooks, 20 April 1929, and to L. V. Heilbrunn, 12 June 1929; Churchman to Dreiser, 13 October 1928; Chambers to Dreiser, 31 January 1929 (UPa); Boris Sokoloff, *The Crime of Dr. Garine*, intro. by Theodore Dreiser (New York: Covici Friede, 1928).

15. Heilbrunn to Dreiser, 30 June 1929; Bridges to Dreiser, 19 June 1929 and 23 August 1929; Dreiser to Heilbrunn, 12 June 1929, and to Osterhout, 6 April 1929 (UPa). The conversation between Bridges and Dreiser is reported in Tjader, *Dreiser: A New Dimension*, 32–34.

16. Theodore Dreiser, "What I Believe," *Forum*, 82 (November 1929), 279–81, 317–20.

17. Anderson to Dreiser, 12 January 1936, and Dreiser to George Douglas, 15 December 1934, in Elias, ed., *Letters*, 3:768; 2:710; Campbell, ed., *Letters to Louise*, 12, 104.

18. Dreiser to George Jean Nathan, 11 September 1932, in Elias, ed., *Letters*, 2:598.

19. Dreiser to Bridges, 23 November 1932, to Leonor Michaelis, 14 March 1933, to Robert Chambers, 16 May 1933, 12 June 1933, and 21 June 1933, Chambers to Dreiser, 15 June 1933, and 29 June 1933, Dreiser to Albert Einstein, 11 December 1933 (UPa). Dreiser also sent a series of identical letters to numerous scientists between 13 January and 2 February 1933; each of these letters read: "Along with its varied material, *The Spectator* is always pleased to consider suggestions for the presentation of scientific deductions or discoveries, as yet unrevealed or not widely publicized or known, involving interesting or unusual methods or data, as well as a critical or ironic comment on phases of current scientific life."

20. Dreiser to Nathan and Boyd, 5 December 1932, and to Sherwin F. Kelly, 3 March 1933 (UPa); Dreiser to Nathan, 7 October 1933, in Elias, ed., *Letters*, 2:643.

21. Tjader, *Dreiser: A New Dimension*, 65.

22. Dreiser to Smith, 31 January 1921, in Elias, ed., *Letters*, 1:346.

23. George Douglas to Dreiser, 1 November 1929 (UPa); Dreiser to Douglas, 11 January 1935, in Elias, ed., *Letters*, 2:711–12.

24. Dreiser to Douglas, 11 January 1935, and 7 January 1935, in Elias, ed., *Letters*, 2:712–13, 711.

25. Dreiser to Douglas, 11 January 1935 and 28 January 1936, in Elias, ed., *Letters*, 2:712 and 3:769–70; Helen Dreiser, *My Life with Dreiser*, 249.

26. Dreiser to Douglas, 15 December 1934, in Elias, ed., *Letters*, 2:709–10; Theodore Dreiser, "The Myth of Individuality," *American Mercury*, 31 (March 1934), 337–42; Theodore Dreiser, "You, the Phantom," *Esquire Magazine*, 2 (November 1934), 25–26.

27. Dreiser, "You, the Phantom," 25, 26.

28. Dreiser, "You, the Phantom," 26, and Dreiser, "The Myth of Individuality," 337, 341.

29. Douglas to Dreiser, 7 January 1935, and Dreiser to Douglas, 26 January 1935, in Elias, ed., *Letters*, 2:711, 719–20; Douglas voiced his understanding of Dreiser's philosophy in a short poem that he sent to Dreiser on 1 January 1935 (UPa):

> If Dreiser's argument be true,
> I am not I, you are not you.
> Or, putting it another way:
> They are we and we are they.

30. Dreiser to Douglas, 26 January 1935, in Elias, ed., *Letters*, 2:720.

31. Dreiser to Douglas, 16 March 1935, in Elias, ed., *Letters*, 2:737.

32. Dreiser to Osterhout, 4 April 1935 (UPa), and to Simon Flexner, 1 June 1935, in Elias, ed., *Letters*, 2:745; Osterhout to Dreiser, 11 April 1935, Flexner to Dreiser, 20 March 1935 and 3 April 1935 (UPa); Dreiser, *Notes on Life*, 106.

33. Swanberg, *Dreiser*, 340; Dreiser to Harvey Brace Lemon, 20 June 1935, in Elias, ed., *Letters*, 2:744; Dreiser, *Notes on Life*, 291

34. Dreiser, *Notes on Life*, 8, 102.

35. Dreiser to Brill, 30 May 1935, and to Millikan, 16 March 1935 (UPa); Robert H. Kargon, *The Rise of Robert Millikan: Portrait of a Life in American Science* (Ithaca, N.Y.: Cornell University Press, 1982), 146–48. See also Daniel J. Kelves, *The Physicists: The History of a Scientific Community in Modern America* (New York: Knopf, 1978) for a discussion of Millikan's contributions and controversies; Helen Dreiser, *My Life with Dreiser*, 250.

36. See Lincoln Barrett, *The Universe and Dr. Einstein* (New York: Bantam Books, 1973), 32–34; Fort, *Wild Talents*, 107–8; Millikan's "What I Believe" was republished in *Living Philosophies* (New York: Simon & Schuster, 1931), 37–53, see 45; Dreiser to Bridges, 16 March 1935, and to Millikan, 16 March 1935; Bridges to Dreiser, 23 March 1935 (UPa); Dreiser, *Notes on Life*, 41–42.

37. Helen Dreiser, *My Life with Dreiser*, 250–51; Dreiser to Joel Stebbins, 30 August 1935, in Elias, ed., *Letters*, 2:749; Dreiser, *Notes on Life*, 12–13.

38. Dreiser to the General Electric Company, 25 November 1935, to R. B. Hanna, 16 December 1935, to W. D. Coolidge, 10 January 1936, and to Irving Langmuir, 30 December 1935 and 17 January 1936 (UPa); Dreiser, *Notes on Life*, 317–18, 172. Dreiser's introduction to the principle of the conservation of energy came from Herbert Spencer's *First Principles*, where this principle is discussed under the designation of "the persistence of force." See Ronald E. Martin, *American Literature and the Universe of Force*, xii–xiii and chs. 1 and 2, for a discussion of the role of this principle in nineteenth-century thought and in Spencer's philosophy in particular.

39. Dreiser to Karl Lark-Horowitz, 22 July 1936 (UPa); Dreiser, *Notes on Life*, 30.

40. Dreiser to George W. Crile, 9 April 1936 and 23 April 1936 (UPa); Dreiser to Crile, 7 August 1936, in Elias, ed., *Letters*, 3:776; Dreiser, *Hey Rub-a-Dub-Dub*, 160, 247; George W. Crile, *The Phenomena of Life: A Radio-Electric Interpretation* (New York: W. W. Norton, 1936), 46, 49; Dreiser, *Notes on Life*, 16, 321–22.

41. "Dr. Hull Urges Psychologists to Revolutionize Their Conceptions on the Intellect," *New York Times*, 5 September 1936, 17; Dreiser to Clark L. Hull, 10 September 1936, in Elias, ed., *Letters*, 3:779; Dreiser to Hull, 1 October 1936 and 21 October 1936 (UPa); Dreiser, *Notes on Life*, 64–65, 4.

42. Dreiser to Mencken, 12 January 1937, in Riggio, ed., *Dreiser-Mencken Letters*, 2:620.

43. Dreiser to Mr. H. J. Gardner, Lippincott Co., 25 February 1935, to I. Kerner, General Medical Book Co., 26 February 1935, and to Calvin Bridges, 16 March 1935, Bridges to Dreiser, 23 March 1935 (UPa); Dreiser to H. L. Mencken, 13 February 1935, and Mencken to Dreiser, 15 February 1935, in Riggio, ed., *Dreiser-Mencken Letters*, 2:577–78; Dreiser to Douglas, 3 April 1935, in Elias, ed., *Letters*, 2:742. There is evidence suggesting that Douglas either followed Dreiser's recom-

mendation to read Loeb or knew about Loeb beforehand; in a letter to Dreiser, 14 December 1935 (UPa), Douglas wrote:

> Truth is our tropism.
> As the moth to the flame so is the seeker to the light that never was on land or sea . . . the moth can see the flame and feel its warmth, but man can never see the light of the world.
> He cannot win, but he may not never quit.
> Who makes the search for truth a solemn game.
> Played against Fate compelling him to flit
> A helpless moth about an unseen flame.

44. Dreiser to Flexner, 1 June 1935, in Elias, ed., *Letters*, 2:745.

45. Harvey Brace Lemon, *From Galileo to Cosmic Rays* (Chicago: University of Chicago Press, 1934), viii; Dreiser to Lemon, 20 June 1935, in Elias, ed., *Letters*, 2:744; Dreiser, *Notes on Life*, 9.

46. Alexis Carrel, *Man, the Unknown* (New York: Harper & Brothers, 1939), 7, 108. For details on Carrel's life and the controversy stirred by this book, see Theodore I. Malinin, *Surgery and Life: The Extraordinary Life of Alexis Carrel* (New York: Harcourt Brace Jovanovich, 1979), and Joseph T. Durkin, S.J., *Hope for Our Time: Alexis Carrel on Man and Society* (New York: Harper and Row, 1965); Dreiser to Mencken, 6 October 1935, in Riggio, ed., *Dreiser-Mencken Letters*, 2:594; Dreiser to Crile, 7 August 1936, in Elias, ed., *Letters*, 3:776.

47. Dreiser to Esther McCoy, 26 February 1936, undated, and 3 April 1936 (UPa); Dreiser to Martha Millet, 28 April 1943, in Elias, ed., *Letters*, 3:986.

48. Dreiser to Douglas, 28 January 1936, in Elias, ed., *Letters*, 3:770; Halley Douglas, telegram to Dreiser, 10 February 1936 (UPa).

49. Dreiser to John McCord, 10? February 1936, and Tom Treanor to Dreiser, 17 February 1936 (UPa).

50. Dreiser to Anderson, 2 January 1936 and 28 January 1936, in Elias, *Letters*, 3:761, 769; see also Anderson to Dreiser, 18 December 1935 and 12 January 1936 (UPa).

51. Tjader, *Dreiser: A New Dimension*, 68.

52. Bridges to Dreiser, 19 June 1937 and 8 July 1937 (UPa).

53. Theodore Dreiser, "Cold Spring Harbor," unpublished MS (UPa); Dreiser to Tjader, in Tjader, *Dreiser: A New Dimension*, 75–76.

54. Dreiser, "Cold Spring Harbor."

55. Theodore Dreiser, "Address to the Long Island Biological Laboratory, 24 August 1937," unpublished MS (UPa).

56. Dreiser, *Moods*, 350; Tjader, *Dreiser: A New Dimension*, 127. 57. Dreiser, "Cold Spring Harbor."

Chapter 6

1. Tjader, *Dreiser: A New Dimension*, 127.

2. Dreiser, *Notes on Life*, 280, 158, 80–81; Theodore Dreiser, "Religion," unpublished MS (UPa).

3. Helen Dreiser, *My Life with Dreiser*, 216.

4. Dreiser, *Notes on Life*, 282, 16, 14; Dreiser to Dorothy Payne Davis, 18 July 1940, in Elias, ed., *Letters*, 3:887.

5. Dreiser to Dorothy Payne Davis, 18 July 1940, in Elias, ed., *Letters*, 3:887; Dreiser, *Notes on Life*, 282; Haeckel, *The Riddle of the Universe*, 288–89.

6. Haeckel, *The Riddle of the Universe*, 20. For information on Haeckel and a brief critical discussion of his philosophy, see Ralph Barton Perry, *Present Philosophical Tendencies* (New York: George Braziller, 1955), 72–75, and Frederick Copleston, S.J., *A History of Philosophy*, 9 vols. (Westminister, Md.: Newman Press, 1963), 7:354–57.

7. Haeckel, *The Riddle of the Universe*, 216, 20.

8. Haeckel, *The Riddle of the Universe*, 225, 224.

9. Haeckel, *The Riddle of the Universe*, 20–21, 290–91; Copleston, *A History of Philosophy*, 7:357.

10. A. E. Garvie, "Pantheism," in James Hastings. ed., *The Encyclopedia of Religion and Ethics*, 13 vols. (New York: Charles Scribner's Sons, 1951), 9:609.

11. Dreiser, *Notes on Life*, 143, 283, 216.

12. Dreiser, *Notes on Life*, 71, 26, 72, 16.

13. Dreiser, *Notes on Life*, 187–88, 284–85.

14. Dreiser, *Notes on Life*, 15, 279; Dreiser to Mary Elizabeth Thompson, 18 January 1939, in Elias, ed., *Letters*, 3:833–34.

15. Dreiser, *Hey Rub-a-Dub-Dub*, 167; Dreiser, *Notes on Life*, 279, 203; Spencer's concept of rhythm is presented in pages 259–81 of *First Principles*; a lengthy discussion of Dreiser's concept of "equation" can be found in Rolf Lunden's *The Inevitable Equation: The Antithetic Pattern of Theodore Dreiser's Thought and Art* (Stockholm: Rotobeckman, 1973).

16. Dreiser, *Notes on Life*, 241; Neil Hitt, "Author and Destiny Reach a Compromise," 7; Dreiser to Mary Elizabeth Thompson, 18 January 1939, and Dreiser to Louise Campbell, 31 December 1941, in Elias, ed., *Letters*, 3:834, 946.

17. Dreiser, *Notes on Life*, 109–10; Dreiser, *Sister Carrie*, 485; Dreiser to Douglas Cooke, 7 October 1938, and Dreiser to F. MacConnell, 12 July 1941, in Elias, ed., *Letters*, 3:816, 930.

18. Dreiser, *Notes on Life*, 222, 248, 259.

19. Dreiser, *Notes on Life*, 259.

20. Theodore Dreiser, ed., *The Living Thoughts of Thoreau* (Philadelphia: David McKay, 1939).

21. Dreiser, Intro., *The Living Thoughts of Thoreau*, 15–16, 21.

22. Dreiser, Intro., *The Living Thoughts of Thoreau*, 21.

23. Excerpts from Thoreau with marginalia in Dreiser's handwriting, Box 196 (UPa).

24. Dreiser, Intro., *The Living Thoughts of Thoreau*, 2, 3–4, 9–10.

25. H. N. Wieman and B. E. Meland, *American Philosophies of Religion* (Chicago: Willet, Clark, 1936), 121–29; Rufus Jones, *The Trail of Life in the Middle Years* (New York: Macmillan, 1934), 230. For a further discussion of Jones's mystical beliefs, see David Hinshaw, *Rufus Jones, Quaker Master* (Freeport, N.Y.: Books for Libraries Press, 1970), 210–20, and Elizabeth Gray Vining, *Friend of Life: The Biography of Rufus Jones* (Philadelphia: J. B. Lippincott, 1958), 249–62.

26. Jones, *The Trail of Life in the Middle Years*, 59, 64.

27. Harriet Bissell Hubbard to Gerhard Friedrick, 23 June 1953, quoted in Gerhard Friedrick, "The Dreiser-Jones Correspondence," *Bulletin of the Friends Historical Association*, 46 (Spring 1957), 24; Jones, *The Trail of Life in the Middle Years*, 169, 232; Dreiser to Jones, 1 December 1938, in Friedrick, "Dreiser-Jones Correspondence," 25–26.

28. Jones, *The Trail of Life in the Middle Years*, 201; John Woolman, *The Journal of John Woolman*, intro. by John Greenleaf Whittier (Boston: James R. Osgood, 1873), 92; Dreiser, Intro., *The Living Thoughts of Thoreau*, 5–6; Dreiser to Jones, 27 January 1939, in Friedrick, "Dreiser-Jones Correspondence," 27.

29. Edgar Lee Masters recalled Dreiser's plan for this Quaker novel in *Across Spoon River* (New York: Farrar & Rinehart, 1936), 329–30.

30. Dreiser to Lengel, 3 November 1941, in Elias, ed., *Letters*, 3:943–44. For a comparison of the contrasting themes of the early drafts and the published novel, see Pizer, *The Novels of Theodore Dreiser*, 299–307.

31. Vining, *Friend of Life*, 28–29; Gerhard Friedrick, "Theodore Dreiser's Debt to Woolman's *Journal*," *American Quarterly*, 7 (Winter 1955), 387.

32. Theodore Dreiser, *The Bulwark* (Garden City, N.Y.: Doubleday, 1946), 316–17.

33. Dreiser, *The Bulwark*, 328, 334.

34. Friedrick, "Dreiser-Jones Correspondence," 33.

35. Tjader, *Dreiser: A New Dimension*, 72; Dreiser, *The Bulwark*, 318–19.

36. Vera Dreiser, with Brett Howard, *My Uncle Theodore* (New York: Nash Publishing, 1976), 232.

37. Dreiser, Intro., *The Living Thoughts of Thoreau*, 8–9; *Bhagavad-Gita: The Song of Life*, trans. Swami Prabhavananda and Christopher Isherwood, and intro. by Aldous Huxley (Hollywood, Calif.: Marcel Rodd, 1944), 17; Harendranath Maitra, *Hinduism: The World Ideal*, intro. by G. K. Chesterton (New York: Temple Scott, 1922), 32.

38. Maitra, *Hinduism: The World Ideal*, 29.

39. Dreiser, *Notes on Life*, 322–23.

40. Theodore Dreiser, *The Stoic* (Garden City, N.Y.: Doubleday, 1947), 296.

41. Dreiser, *The Stoic*, 297.

42. Helen Dreiser, *My Life with Dreiser*, 216; Dreiser, "The Myth of Religion," unpublished MS (UPa); Vera Dreiser to W. A. Swanberg, 22 May 1964, quoted in Swanberg, *Dreiser*, 502.

43. Dreiser to L. V. Heilbrunn, 6 September 1937, Heilbrunn to Dreiser, 8 September 1937, 7 April 1938, 31 May 1939, and 11 February 1940 (UPa); Swanberg, *Dreiser*, 462.

44. Allen, *T. H. Morgan*, 380; Helen Dreiser, *My Life with Dreiser*, 277–78; Tjader, *Dreiser: A New Dimension*, 101.

45. Gustav Strömberg, *The Soul of the Universe* (Philadelphia: David McKay, 1940), 183, 185, 146–47, 212–14.

46. Dreiser to Strömberg, 14 May 1940, in Elias, ed., *Letters*, 3:878–79; Strömberg, *The Soul of the Universe*, 229, 231. Dreiser quoted passages of Strömberg's evidence concerning reincarnation in a letter to Dorothy Payne Davis, in Elias, ed., *Letters*, 3:888.

47. Tjader, *Dreiser: A New Dimension*, 175–76.

48. Helen Dreiser, *My Life with Dreiser*, 291. Although "My Creator" remained unpublished in Dreiser's lifetime, the full essay has been included as the last chapter in *Notes on Life*, 327–33; see 332.

49. Dreiser, "My Creator," in *Notes on Life*, 327, 328.

50. Dreiser, "My Creator", in *Notes on Life*, 329, 330, 333.

Conclusion

1. Joseph Wood Krutch, *The Modern Temper: A Study and a Confession* (New York: Harcourt Brace, 1929), 52, 42, 43.

2. Krutch, *The Modern Temper*, 50, 132.

3. Krutch, *The Modern Temper*, 53.

4. See Chapter 4, "Science and the Precious Object," in Frederick J. Hoffman, *The Twenties: American Writing in the Postwar Decade*, rev. ed. (New York: Free Press, 1965), 275–343; John Crowe Ransom, *God Without Thunder: An Unorthodox Defense of Orthodoxy* (Hamden, Conn.: Archon Books, 1965).

5. Scholars have disagreed on whether natural theology was primarily a scientific or theological development in Western thought. George Daniels has written that "all available evidence indicates that the vogue of natural theology was not a case of theologians misusing science for their own ends, but of scientists trying to attach some of the aura of the theologian to their own profession; that is to say, misusing science for *their* own ends." See Daniels, *American Science in the Age of Jackson* (New York: Columbia University Press, 1968), 51–62. More recently, James Turner has argued that natural theology was predominantly a religious response to the rise of unbelief and has noted that "at the same time, ironically, a prime disturber of belief, the new science, provided a rich lode for theologians to mine." See Turner, *Without God, Without Creed: The Origins of Unbelief in America* (Baltimore: Johns Hopkins University Press, 1985), 54–58, 96–98.

Bibliography

Note: Edited collections of Theodore Dreiser's letters, diaries, and newspaper writings are listed under the name of the editor.

Allen, Garland E. "The Rise and Spread of the Classical School of Heredity, 1910–1930: Development and Influence of the Mendelian Chromosome Theory." In Nathan Reingold, ed., *The Sciences in the American Context: New Perspectives.* Washington, D.C.: Smithsonian Institution Press, 1979.
———. *Thomas Hunt Morgan: The Man and His Science.* Princeton, N.J.: Princeton University Press, 1978.
Barrett, Lincoln. *The Universe and Dr. Einstein.* New York: Bantam Books, 1973.
Bhagavad-Gita: The Song of Life. Translated by Swami Prabhavananda and Christopher Isherwood, introduction by Aldous Huxley. Hollywood, Calif. : Marcel Rodd, 1944.
Boller, Paul F. *American Thought in Transition: The Impact of Evolutionary Naturalism, 1865–1900.* Chicago: Rand, McNally, 1969.
Brill, Abraham Arden. *Psychoanalysis: Its Theories and Practical Application.* Philadelphia: W. B. Saunders, 1913.
Calkins, Gary N. "Protozoa and Disease." *Century Magazine,* 67 (April 1904), 931–40.
Campbell, Louise, ed. *Letters to Louise: Theodore Dreiser's Letters to Louise Campbell.* Philadelphia: University of Pennsylvania Press, 1959.
Carrel, Alexis. *Man, the Unknown.* New York: Harper & Brothers, 1939.
Columbia University, Butler Library Special Collections. Ellen Moers Collection.
Commager, Henry Steele. *The American Mind.* New York: Bantam Books, 1970.
Copleston, Frederick, S.J. *A History of Philosophy.* Vol. 7. Westminster, Md.: Newman Press, 1963.
Cosulich, Gilbert. "Theodore Dreiser Asserts Religion Is Total Loss and Its Dogma Worn Out." *Tucson Daily Citizen,* 30 April 1930, 7.
Crile, George W. *Man—An Adaptive Mechanism.* New York: Macmillan, 1916.
———. *The Phenomena of Life: A Radio-Electric Interpretation.* New York: W. W. Norton, 1936.
Daniels, George H. *American Science in the Age of Jackson.* New York: Columbia University Press, 1968.
Darwin, Charles. *The Descent of Man and Selection in Relation to Sex.* New York: A. L. Burt, 1874.
———. *The Origin of Species by Means of Natural Selection; or, The Preservation of Favored Races in the Struggle for Life.* 6th ed. New York: A. L. Burt, n.d.

Debus, Allen G., ed. *World Who's Who of Science: A Biographical Dictionary of Notable Scientists from Antiquity to the Present*. Chicago: Marquis Who's Who, 1968.

DeKruif, Paul. "Jacques Loeb, The Mechanist." *Harpers* 146 (1922–1923), 182–90.

"Dr. Hull Urges Psychologists to Revolutionize Their Conceptions on the Intellect." *New York Times*, 5 September 1936, 17.

Dreiser, Helen. *My Life with Dreiser*. New York: World Publishing, 1951.

Dreiser, Theodore. "Address to the Long Island Biological Laboratory, 24 August 1937." Unpublished MS in Theodore Dreiser Papers, University of Pennsylvania.

———. *America Is Worth Saving*. New York: Modern Age Books, 1941.

———. "American Tragedies." Review of *The New Criminology*, by Max G. Schlapp and Edward H. Smith. *New York Herald Tribune Books*, 10 June 1928, 1–2.

———. *An American Tragedy*. New York: Signet Classics, 1964.

———. "Apples: An Account of the Apple Industry in America." *Pearson's*, 10 (October 1900), 336–40.

———. *The Best Short Stories of Theodore Dreiser*. Introduction by James T. Farrell. New York: Thomas Y. Crowell, 1974.

———. *A Book About Myself*. New York: Boni & Liveright, 1922.

———. *The Bulwark*. Garden City, N.Y.: Doubleday, 1946.

———. "Charles Fort." Unpublished TS in Theodore Dreiser Papers, University of Pennsylvania.

———. "Cold Spring Harbor." Unpublished MS in Theodore Dreiser Papers, University of Pennsylvania.

———. *The Color of a Great City*. London: Constable, 1930.

———. *Dawn*. New York: Horace Liveright, 1931.

———. "The Descent of the Horse." *Everybody's Magazine*, June 1900, 543–47.

———. *Dreiser Looks at Russia*. New York: Horace Liveright, 1928.

———. "Electricity in the Household." *Demorist's*, 35 (January 1899), 38–39.

———. "Fame Found in Quiet Nooks: John Burroughs." *Success*, 1 (September 1898), 5–6.

———. *The Financier*. New York: New American Library, 1967.

———. *Free and Other Stories*. New York: Boni and Liveright, 1918.

———. "Fruit Growing in America." *Harper's Monthly*, 101 (November 1900), 859–68.

———. *A Gallery of Women*. 2 vols. New York: Horace Liveright, 1929.

———. *The "Genius"*. New York: New American Library, 1984.

———. "Great Problems of Organization III: The Chicago Packing Industry." *Cosmopolitan*, 25 (October 1898), 615–26.

———. *The Hand of the Potter*. New York: Boni and Liveright, 1918.

———. *Hey Rub-a-Dub-Dub: A Book of the Mystery and Wonder and Terror of Life*. New York: Boni & Liveright, 1920.

———. *A Hoosier Holiday*. New York: John Lane, 1916.

———. "The Horseless Age." *Demorist's*, 35 (May 1899), 153–55.

———. "I Find the Real American Tragedy." *Mystery Magazine*, 11 (February 1935), 9–11, 88–90.

———. "If Man Is Free, So Is All Matter." *Forum*, 98 (December 1937), 301–4.

————. "In the Matter of Spiritualism." *Bohemian Magazine*, 17 (1909), 425.

————. *Jennie Gerhardt*. University of Pennsylvania Dreiser Edition. Ed. James L. W. West III; Thomas P. Riggio, General ed. Philadelphia: University of Pennsylvania Press, 1992.

————. "John Burroughs in His Mountain Hut." *New Voice*, 16 (19 August 1899), 7, 13.

————. "A Lesson from the Aquarium." *Tom Watson's Magazine*, 3 (1906), 306–8.

————, ed. *The Living Thoughts of Thoreau*. Philadelphia: David McKay, 1939.

————. "Man and Romance." *Reedy's Mirror*, 28 (28 August 1919), 585.

————. *Moods Philosophical and Emotional—Cadenced and Declaimed*. New York: Simon and Schuster, 1935.

————. "The Myth of Individuality." *American Mercury*, 31 (March 1934), 337–42.

————. "The New Knowledge of Weeds." *Ainslee's*, 8 (January 1902), 533–38.

————. *Notes on Life*. Edited by Marguerite Tjader and John J. McAleer. University: University of Alabama Press, 1974.

————. "Plant Life Underground." *Pearson's*, 11 (June 1901), 860–64.

————. *Plays of the Natural and the Supernatural*. New York: AMS Press, 1969.

————. "The Problem of the Soil." *Era*, 12 (September 1903), 239–49.

————. "Remarks." *Psychological Review*, 18 (1931), 250.

————. *Sister Carrie*. Pennsylvania Edition. Edited by John C. Berkey, Alice M. Winters, James L. W. West III, and Neda Westlake. Philadelphia: University of Pennsylvania Press, 1981.

————. "Statement of Belief." *Bookman*, 68 (September 1928), 25.

————. "Suggesting the Possible Substructure of Ethics." Unpublished TS in Theodore Dreiser Papers, University of Pennsylvania.

————. *The Stoic*. Garden City, N.Y.: Doubleday, 1947.

————. *The Titan*. New York: New American Library, 1965.

————. *Tragic America*. New York: Horace Liveright, 1931.

————. "The Training of the Senses." Unpublished TS in Theodore Dreiser Papers, University of Pennsylvania..

————. *A Traveler at Forty*. New York: Century, 1913.

————. "The Treasure House of Natural History." *Metropolitan*, 8 (December 1898), 595–601.

————. *Twelve Men*. New York: Modern Library, 1928.

————. "What I Believe." *Forum*, 82 (November 1929), 279–81, 317–20.

————. "A Word Concerning Birth Control." *Birth Control Review*, 5 (April 1921), 5.

————. "You, the Phantom." *Esquire Magazine*, 2 (November 1934), 25–26.

Dreiser, Vera, with Brett Howard. *My Uncle Theodore*. New York: Nash Publishing, 1976.

"Dreiser Says Religion Total Loss in America." *El Paso Evening Post*, 26 April 1930, 8.

Duffas, Robert L. "Jacques Loeb: Mechanist." *Century Magazine*, 108 (1924): 374–83.

Durkin, Joseph T., S.J. *Hope for Our Time: Alexis Carrel on Man and Society*. New York: Harper and Row, 1965.

Elias, Robert H. *Theodore Dreiser: Apostle of Nature*. Emended ed. Ithaca, N.Y.: Cornell University Press, 1970.

————, ed. *Letters of Theodore Dreiser: A Selection.* 3 vols. Philadelphia: University of Pennsylvania Press, 1959.

Elliot, Hugh. *Herbert Spencer.* Westport, Conn.: Greenwood Press, 1970.

Eve, A. S. et al. *Life and Work of John Tyndall.* London: Macmillan, 1945.

Fabre, Jean Henri. *The Life of the Caterpillar.* New York: Dodd, Mead, 1906.

Farrell, James T. *The League of Frightened Philistines.* New York: Vanguard Press, 1945.

Fichman, Martin. *Alfred Russel Wallace.* Boston: Twayne Publishers, 1981.

Fort, Charles. *The Book of the Damned.* New York: Boni and Liveright, 1919.

————. *Lo!* New York: Claude Kendall, 1931.

————. *New Lands.* New York: Boni and Liveright, 1923.

————. *Wild Talents.* New York: Claude Kendall, 1932.

Freud, Sigmund. *Three Contributions to a Theory of Sex.* Translated by A. A. Brill. New York: E. P. Dutton, 1962.

Friedrick, Gerhard. "The Dreiser-Jones Correspondence." *Bulletin of the Friends Historical Association*, 46 (Spring 1957), 23–34.

————. "Theodore Dreiser's Debt to Woolman's *Journal*." *American Quarterly*, 7 (Winter 1955), 388–92.

Garvie, A. E. "Pantheism." In James Hastings, ed., *The Encyclopedia of Religion and Ethics*, vol. 9. New York: Charles Scribner's Sons, 1951.

Gates, Donald Edson. *Elmer Gates and the Art of Mind-Using.* New York: Exposition Press, 1971.

Gates, Elmer. "The Art of Mind Building." *Metaphysical Magazine*, 4 (1896), 1–6, 88–93, 153–54, 174–78.

————. "Brain Building and Mind Building with Special Reference to Sense-Training of the Eye and Ear, and Teaching Mentally Defective Children." In National Education Association, *Journal of the Proceedings of the 37th Annual Meeting*, Washington, D.C., July 7–12, 1898, 1051–56.

————. "Can Will-Power Be Trained?" *Success* (March 1900), 93.

————. "Electrographs of the Electro-Static Current Made with a Camera." *Scientific American*, 81 (7 October 1899), 288–89.

————. "Extracting Perfume from Flowers by Electricity." *Mail and Express Illustrated Saturday Magazine*, 7 March 1903, 4.

————. "A Mega-Microscope." *Popular Science News*, 31 (December 1897), 265–69.

————. *The Relations and Development of the Mind and Brain.* New York: Philosophic Co., 1903.

————. "The Science of Mentation." *The Monist*, 5 (1895), 574–97.

————. "We Can Increase Our Mental Power." *Success* (May 1900), 180.

"Gates' Double Microscope." *American Monthly Microscopic Journal*, 19 (January 1898), 7–10.

Gregory, Odin. *Caius Gracchus.* Introduction by Theodore Dreiser. New York: Boni and Liveright, 1920.

Haeckel, Ernst. *The Riddle of the Universe at the Close of the Nineteenth Century.* Translated by John McCabe. New York: Harper & Brothers, 1900.

Hakutani, Yoshinobu. *Young Dreiser: A Critical Study.* Rutherford, N.J.: Fairleigh Dickinson University Press, 1980.

———, ed. *Selected Magazine Articles of Theodore Dreiser: Life and Art in the American 1890s*. 2 vols. Rutherford, N.J.: Fairleigh Dickinson University Press, 1987.

Hale, Nathan G., Jr. *Freud and the Americans: The Beginnings of Psychoanalysis in the United States, 1876–1917*. New York: Oxford University Press, 1971.

Harris, Frank. *Contemporary Portraits*. 2nd series. New York: by the author, 1919.

Hinshaw, David. *Rufus Jones, Master Quaker*. Freeport, N.Y.: Books for Libraries Press, 1970.

Hitt, Neil. "Author and Destiny Reach a Compromise." *San Francisco Chronicle*, 10 February 1939, 7.

Hoffman, Frederick J. *Freudianism and the Literary Mind*. Baton Rouge: Louisiana State University Press, 1957.

———. *The Twenties: American Writing in the Postwar Decade*. Revised edition. New York: Free Press, 1965.

Hofstadter, Richard. *Social Darwinism in American Thought, 1865–1915*. Philadelphia: University of Pennsylvania Press, 1945.

Huxley, Thomas Henry. *Science and the Christian Tradition*. New York: D. Appleton, 1909.

———. *Science and the Hebrew Tradition*. New York: D. Appleton, 1894.

Izenberg, Gerald N. *The Existentialist Critique of Freud*. Princeton, N.J.: Princeton University Press, 1976.

Jeans, Sir James Hopwood. *The Universe Around Us*. New York: Macmillan, 1929.

Jones, Rufus. *Finding the Trail of Life*. New York: Macmillan, 1927.

———. *The Later Periods of Quakerism*. London: Macmillan, 1921.

———. *The Trail of Life in the Middle Years*. New York: Macmillan, 1934.

Kaplan, Abraham. "Freud and Modern Philosophy." In Benjamin Nelson, ed., *Freud and the Twentieth Century*. Gloucestor, Mass.: Peter Smith, 1974.

Kargon, Robert H. *The Rise of Robert Millikan: Portrait of a Life in American Science*. Ithaca, N.Y.: Cornell University Press, 1982.

Kelves, Daniel J. *The Physicists: The History of a Scientific Community in Modern America*. New York: Knopf, 1978.

Knight, Damon. *Charles Fort: Prophet of the Unexplained*. Garden City, N.Y.: Doubleday, 1970.

Krutch, Joseph Wood. *The Modern Temper: A Study and a Confession*. New York: Harcourt Brace, 1929.

Lemon, Harvey Brace. *From Galileo to Cosmic Rays*. Chicago: University of Chicago Press, 1934.

"A Letter from Vienna to Theo. Dreiser—And His Reply." *Tempest*, 1 (2 April 1923), 3.

Levine, P. A. "Jacques Loeb, the Man." *Science*, 59 (1924), 427–28.

Library of Congress, Washington, D.C. The Jacques Loeb Papers.

Lillie, Frank R. *The Woods Hole Marine Biological Laboratory*. Chicago: University of Chicago Press, 1944.

Lingeman, Richard. *Theodore Dreiser: An American Journey, 1908–1945*. New York: G. P. Putnam's Sons, 1990.

———. *Theodore Dreiser: At the Gates of the City, 1871–1907*. New York: G. P. Putnam's Sons, 1986.

Loeb, Jacques. *Comparative Physiology of the Brain and Comparative Psychology*. New York: G. P. Putnam's Sons, 1900.

———. *Forced Movements, Tropisms, and Animal Conduct*. Monographs on Experimental Biology, vol. 1. Philadelphia: J. B. Lippincott, 1918.

———. "Freedom of Will and War." *New Review*, 2 (1914), 631–36.

———. *The Mechanistic Conception of Life*. Introduction by Donald Fleming. Cambridge, Mass.: Belknap Press of Harvard University, 1964.

———. "Mechanistic Science and Metaphysical Romance." *Yale Review*, 4 (1915), 766–85.

———. *The Organism as a Whole: From a Physicochemical Viewpoint*. New York: G. P. Putnam's Sons, 1916.

Long Island Biological Association. *Annual Report of the Biological Laboratory, 1937*. Cold Spring Harbor, N.Y.: Long Island Biological Association, 1937.

Lubbock, John (Lord Avebury). *Ants, Bees and Wasps*. New York: D. Appleton, 1896.

Lukens, Herman T. "Correspondence." *American Journal of Psychology*, 10 (1898), 163–64.

Lunden, Rolf. *The Inevitable Equation: The Antithetic Pattern of Theodore Dreiser's Thought and Art*. Stockholm: Rotobeckman, 1973.

Maitra, Harendranath. *Hinduism: The World Ideal*. Introduction by G. K. Chesterton. New York: Temple Scott, 1922.

Malinin, Theodore I. *Surgery and Life: The Extraordinary Career of Alexis Carrel*. New York: Harcourt Brace Jovanovich, 1979.

Marine Biological Laboratory, Woods Hole, Massachusetts. *Annual Announcement*. Lancaster, Pa.: Lancaster Press, 1928.

———. *Thirty-First Report for the Year 1928—Forty-First Year*. n.p., n.d.

Martin, Ronald E. *American Literature and the Universe of Force*. Durham, N.C.: Duke University Press, 1981.

Masters, Edgar Lee. *Across Spoon River*. New York: Farrar & Rinehart, 1936.

Mencken, H. L. *A Book of Prefaces*. New York: Knopf, 1917.

Millikan, Robert A. "What I Believe." In *Living Philosophies*. New York: Simon and Schuster, 1931.

Moers, Ellen. *Two Dreisers*. New York: Viking Press, 1969.

Mookerjee, R. N. *Theodore Dreiser: His Thought and Social Criticism*. Delhi: National Publishing House, 1974.

Neider, Charles, ed. *The Complete Essays of Mark Twain*. Garden City, N.Y.: Doubleday, 1963.

New York Public Library, Special Manuscripts. H. L. Mencken Collection.

Nostwich, T. D., ed. *Theodore Dreiser's "Heard in the Corridors" Articles and Related Writings*. Ames: Iowa University Press, 1988.

———, ed. *Theodore Dreiser—Journalism. Vol. I: Newspaper Writings, 1892–1895*. University of Pennsylvania Dreiser Edition, Philadelphia: University of Pennsylvania Press, 1988.

"Now Comes Author Theodore Dreiser Who Tells of 100,000 Jennie Gerhardts." *Cleveland Leader*, 12 November 1911, Cosmopolitan Section, 5.

Osterhout, W. J. V. "Jacques Loeb." In National Academy of Sciences, *Biographical*

Memoirs XIII, 318–401. Washington, D.C.: National Academy of Sciences, 1928.

Ostwalt, Conrad Eugene, Jr. *After Eden: The Secularization of American Space in the Fiction of Willa Cather and Theodore Dreiser*. Lewisburg, Pa.: Bucknell University Press, 1990.

Pauly, Philip J. *Controlling Life: Jacques Loeb and the Engineering Ideal in Biology*. New York: Oxford University Press, 1987.

Peckham, Morse. "Introduction to the Variorum Edition of *The Origin of Species*." In *Darwin: A Norton Critical Edition*. Edited by Philip Appleman. New York: W. W. Norton, 1970.

Perry, Ralph Barton. *Present Philosophical Tendencies*. New York: George Braziller, 1955.

Pizer, Donald. *The Novels of Theodore Dreiser: A Critical Study*. Minneapolis: University of Minnesota Press, 1976.

———, ed. *Theodore Dreiser: A Selection of Uncollected Prose*. Detroit: Wayne State University Press, 1977.

Ransom, John Crowe. *God Without Thunder: An Unorthodox Defense of Orthodoxy*. Hamden, Conn.: Archon Books, 1965.

Riggio, Thomas P., ed., *Dreiser-Mencken Letters: The Correspondence of Theodore Dreiser and H. L. Mencken, 1907–1945*. 2 vols. Philadelphia: University of Pennsylvania Press, 1986.

Riggio, Thomas P., James L. W. West III, and Neda Westlake, eds. *Theodore Dreiser: American Diaries, 1900–1926*. Philadelphia: University of Pennsylvania Press, 1982.

Robertson, T. Brailsford. "The Life and Work of a Mechanistic Philosopher—Jacques Loeb." *Science Progress*, 21 (1926), 114–29.

Rosenberg, Charles. *No Other Gods: On Science and American Social Thought*. Baltimore: Johns Hopkins University Press, 1976.

Russett, Cynthia Eagle. *Darwin in America: The Intellectual Response, 1865–1912*. San Francisco: W. H. Freeman, 1976.

Schlapp, Max G., and Edward H. Smith. *The New Criminology: A Consideration of the Chemical Causation of Abnormal Behavior*. New York: Boni and Liveright, 1928.

Snyder, Carl. *The World Machine: The First Phase—The Cosmic Mechanism*. London: Longmans, Green, 1907.

"Society of the Capital." *New York Times*, 18 November 1894, 1.

Sokoloff, Boris. *The Crime of Dr. Garine*. Introduction by Theodore Dreiser. New York: Covici Friede, 1928.

Spencer, Herbert. *The Data of Ethics*. New York: A. L. Burt, n.d.

———. *Facts and Comments*. New York: D. Appleton, 1902.

———. *First Principles*. New York: D. Appleton, 1896.

Strömberg, Gustav. *The Soul of the Universe*. Philadelphia: David McKay, 1940.

Sulloway, Frank J. *Freud, Biologist of the Mind: Beyond the Psychoanalytic Legend*. New York: Basic Books, 1979.

Swanberg, W. A. *Dreiser*. New York: Charles Scribner's Sons, 1965.

Symmes, Americus Vespucius. *The Symmes Theory of Concentric Spheres, etc.* Compiled by Americus Symmes from the writings of his father, Captain John Cleves Symmes. Louisville, Ky.: Bradley & Gilbert, 1878.

Thayer, Tiffany. "Introduction" to Charles Fort, *The Books of Charles Fort*. New York: Henry Holt, 1941.

Tjader, Marguerite. *Theodore Dreiser: A New Dimension*. Norwalk, Conn.: Silvermine Publishers, 1965.

Trachtenberg, Alan. *The Incorporation of America: Culture and Society in the Gilded Age*. New York: Hill and Wang, 1982.

Turner, James. *Without God, Without Creed: The Origins of Unbelief in America*. Baltimore: Johns Hopkins University Press, 1985.

Tyndall, John. *Fragments of Science*. New York: D. Appleton, 1897.

University of Pennsylvania, Special Collections, Van Pelt Library, Theodore Dreiser Papers.

Vining, Elizabeth Gray. *Friend of Life: The Biography of Rufus Jones*. Philadelphia: J. B. Lippincott, 1958.

Walcutt, Charles Child. *American Literary Naturalism: A Divided Stream*. Minneapolis: University of Minnesota Press, 1956.

——, ed. *Seven Novelists in the Naturalist Tradition: An Introduction*. Minneapolis: University of Minnesota Press, 1974.

Wallace, Alfred Russel. *The World of Life: A Manifestation of Creative Power, Directive Mind, and Untimate Purpose*. New York: Moffat, Yard, 1911.

Westbrook, Perry D. *Free Will and Determinism in American Literature*. Rutherford, N.J.: Fairleigh Dickinson University Press, 1979.

Wieman, H. N., and B. E. Meland. *American Philosophies of Religion*. Chicago: Willet, Clark, 1936.

Woolman, John. *The Journal of John Woolman*. Introduction by John Greenleaf Whittier. Boston: James R. Osgood, 1873.

Wycherley, H. Alan. "Mechanism and Vitalism in Dreiser's Nonfiction." *Texas Studies in Literature and Language*, 11 (Summer 1969), 1039–49.

Yoder, Robert. "The Wondrous Box of Dr. Abrams." In Alexander Klein, ed., *Grand Deception: The World's Most Spectacular and Successful Hoaxes, Impostures, Ruses and Frauds*. Philadelphia: J. B. Lippincott, 1955.

Index

This book has been set in Linotron Galliard. Galliard was designed for Mergenthaler in 1978 by Matthew Carter. Galliard retains many of the features of a sixteenth-century typeface cut by Robert Granjon but has some modifications that give it a more contemporary look.

Printed on acid-free paper.